ASKING SMARTER QUESTIONS

Insight is the superpower that drives innovation and enables us to understand the world from other peoples' points of view, be they customers or colleagues, advocates or competitors. This new book from data storyteller Sam Knowles explains how to ask smarter questions – questions that, by design, stimulate more useful answers. This is the shortcut to better productivity, fast-tracked innovation, and organisational success – for businesses, universities, charities, and governments.

For too long, the simple act of asking questions has been overlooked as almost too trivial to contemplate. *Asking Smarter Questions* seeks to champion the art of curiosity by setting out a framework to make every question count. The fundamental building blocks of insight are data and information, joined together in new and often unpredictable ways. The way we surface new data and information and make meaningful connections between data points is by asking smarter questions. By taking this approach, you can make your organisation a less confrontational, more collaborative, and more productive environment in which to work – particularly in the more distributed and remote settings that will characterise the 2020s.

Managers, directors, and leaders will find the universal principles, expert interviews, and data-driven recommendations a source of inspiration to share with their teams. *Asking Smarter Questions* is aimed at professionals in businesses and organisations across all sectors, and will help those working in many functions, including market research, intelligence, insight, analytics, strategy, marketing, communications, planning, product development, and innovation.

Sam Knowles is a data storyteller with more than 30 years' experience enabling organisations to use data smarter and communicate with impact. A classicist with a psychology doctorate, he helps organisations to talk "Human". *Asking Smarter Questions* is the third in Sam's *Using Data Better* trilogy of books, which also includes *Narrative by Numbers* (2018) and *How To Be Insightful* (2020).

"As a qualitative researcher, I love that Sam's book focuses on two underrated, but highly valuable skills: the ability to listen and the ability to ask better questions. Improving skills in these areas will help anyone unlock deeper insight."

Sean Adams, *Global Insights Director, Brand Metrics*

"Few people master the art of the question, yet how can you get to the answers you need when the question isn't right? Erudite, vital, and engaging, Sam Knowles is the expert with the answers to the questions you should be asking."

Steve Bustin, *President (2019–2021), Professional Speaking Association*

"Sam is an expert and thought leader in the world of insight and innovation. In an age when we all need to 'be more human', Sam helps the reader to ask smarter questions and become more impactful in their work."

Sam Chuter, *Innovation Advisor, Sussex Innovation*

"Asking the right questions is a crucial part of building understanding and key to achieving insight. Sam's ability to make you think intelligently about these questions, and then how to narrate what is found, is brilliant."

John Eggleton, *Head of Commercial, Emerald Publishing*

"Sam Knowles is a true innovator in the field of insight. His works take you on a voyage of discovery and never leave you feeling lost or overwhelmed. You'll leave invigorated, challenging ideas in ways you never thought possible. But don't just take my word for it, take a read of this book, you won't regret it."

Simon Frazier, *Head of Marketing & Data Innovation, Institute for Practitioners in Advertising*

"As a business leader who spends every day encouraging people to be more curious about data, I cannot recommend *Asking Smarter Questions* highly enough. Yet again, Sam Knowles has created a warm, engaging, and accessible toolkit for any professional navigating the 21st century."

Richard Freeman, *CEO, Always Possible*

"A fascinating, insightful, and practical read for anyone needing to unleash the superpower of curiosity, to have better conversations, and to drive progress in whatever form – especially innovation. Read it to reawaken your natural curiosity and put it to work."

Belinda Gannaway, *Author, Employee Experience by Design*

"In an age of information overload and data misinterpretation, Sam has the ability to cut through the noise and get to the gist of the matter to enable people to make rational and better decisions."

Dave Henson, *The Slide Presentation Man*

"Sam Knowles has written a must-read primer for all of us who are looking to drive change for the better, in the world of work in general and in the healthcare industry in particular. It's not only a good read, it's also a tool that enables you to turn your curiosity into action that matters."

Beyza Klein, *Patient Engagement Director, Novartis*

"We live in a post-truth world where falsehoods and misinformation appear to carry as much weight as facts and observable truths. The solution is to let the truth shine through using critical analysis, and the key to this is asking the right questions of the right people and being able to evaluate their responses. Sam's book is an excellent guide on how to use smart questioning to establish the truth and evaluate it."

Nick Manning, *Founder, Encyclomedia International*

"Too many consultants think they are doing their best work for their clients when they are in problem-solving mode, whereas they can help their clients even more when they go into the problem-framing space first. Asking incisive, revelatory questions is a critical skill to ensure that the right problem frame is built. Sam Knowles continues his pragmatic pilgrimage with this third book, giving away the usually 'secret' knowledge on how to ask good questions to all who care to read his work. I predict it'll be a well-thumbed book."

Kenneth McKenzie, *Research Lead, Human Insights Lab,*
Accenture

"As we continue to move from too little information to much too much, Sam Knowles is an excellent guide for those seeking to increase the clarity, depth, and ultimately the insights within their data."

Antonio Ortolani, *Partner, Global Head of Knowledge, Insights, Research, and Analytics, Kekst CNC*

"The world is being redefined by two major forces: infinitely abundant data and a blurring of truth and fiction. Critical thinking is essential for navigating this new order, and mastering this starts with asking the right questions."

Christian Polman, *UK Managing Director, Looping Group*

"The power of a brilliant question has been lost in our search engine world. Overwhelmed by data, too often we accept the paid ad version and over time we lose perspective as well as truth. This book reminds you of the power of curiosity, truth, silence, and insight. It might just change the world."

Lucy Paine, *Connector & Communicator, TechSpark*

"I've known and worked with Sam for 10 years. If we need a considered opinion, he's the ideal person to help walk you through the thought process. It's only when you look back that, as in this book, that you realise his first step was to subtly reframe the original question and make it better. He does that because it produces better answers."

Martin Radford, *Business Director, Ebiquity*

"The ability to ask great questions is one of the most important tools available to leaders. It's the key to encouraging thinking which itself is the key to unlocking engagement, productivity, and innovation. This is a very welcome and natural completion of Sam's excellent trilogy of books."

Peter Russian, *Director, Intent Based Leadership International*

"Asking reflective and sometimes uncomfortable questions has been at the centre of my role advising organisations on Equity, Diversity, and Inclusion. Finding ways of asking smarter questions is a continuous goal and area of development in my practice. Who better to explore this topic than Sam Knowles, who taught me so much about being insightful from his previous book, How To Be Insightful."

Sabrina Shadie, *Ethics & Equity Change Maker, D'Rose Development Consultancy*

"Sam has built a reputation for looking at insight in innovative ways. In *Asking Smarter Questions*, he helps us cut out the clutter and get to the heart of the data. A must read for any data-user."

Karsten Shaw, *Director of Analytics, Yonder Consulting*

"I love Sam's previous books and so it was no surprise that this too was a must-read for me. Sam's research and presentation warms your heart. For anyone running a business or an organisation, or who is responsible for people and customers, this book is not just an interesting and enjoyable read. It will give you an invaluable skill that just keeps giving. Asking smarter questions is important, and this book tells you why and how."

Sarah Springford, *CEO, Brighton Chamber*

"I have turned to Sam time and time again to help me make the complex simple - to craft compelling narratives from data and insights. He is a truly masterful storyteller who understands how to tell stories that resonate profoundly."

Martin Vinter, *SVP of Consultancy, Brainlabs*

"Sam Knowles is one of the smartest people I know and one of the most insightful. His new book focuses on what has been an increasingly under-appreciated skill, namely the ability to ask the right questions, rather than making statements dressed up as fact. Not only does this approach lead to better answers, it also leads to better organisations and greater collaboration. Read this book and start asking the right questions."

Ian Whittaker, *MD & Owner, Liberty Sky Advisors*

Using Data Better
A Trilogy

Many organisations and individuals are overwhelmed by data, but it doesn't have to be this way. *Using Data Better* is a practical, entertaining, inspiring trilogy of books that shows how to ask the right questions that surface the right insights and so craft the right stories. The books in the trilogy are: *Asking Smarter Questions*, the critically acclaimed *How To Be Insightful*, and the bestseller *Narrative by Numbers*.

Narrative by Numbers
How to Tell Powerful and Purposeful Stories with Data
Sam Knowles

How To Be Insightful
Unlocking the Superpower that Drives Innovation
Sam Knowles

Asking Smarter Questions
How To Be an Agent of Insight
Sam Knowles

For more information about this series, please visit: https://www.routledge.com/Using-Data-Better/book-series/UDB

ASKING SMARTER QUESTIONS

How To Be an Agent of Insight

SAM KNOWLES

Routledge
Taylor & Francis Group

LONDON AND NEW YORK

Cover image: Ian Murray

First published 2023
by Routledge
4 Park Square, Milton Park, Abingdon, Oxon OX14 4RN

and by Routledge
605 Third Avenue, New York, NY 10158

Routledge is an imprint of the Taylor & Francis Group, an informa business

British Library Cataloguing-in-Publication Data
A catalogue record for this book is available from the British Library

Library of Congress Cataloging-in-Publication Data
Names: Knowles, Sam, author.
Title: Asking smarter questions : how to be an agent of insight / Sam Knowles.
Description: Abingdon, Oxon ; New York, NY : Routledge, 2023. |
Series: Using data better | Includes bibliographical references. |
Identifiers: LCCN 2022006588 (print) | LCCN 2022006589 (ebook) |
ISBN 9781032111155 (hardback) | ISBN 9781032111162 (paperback) |
ISBN 9781003218470 (ebook)
Subjects: LCSH: Insight. | Questioning. | Thought and thinking.
Classification: LCC BF449.5 .K589 2023 (print) | LCC BF449.5 (ebook) |
DDC 153.4—dc23/eng/20220224
LC record available at https://lccn.loc.gov/2022006588
LC ebook record available at https://lccn.loc.gov/2022006589

ISBN: 978-1-032-11115-5 (hbk)
ISBN: 978-1-032-11116-2 (pbk)
ISBN: 978-1-003-21847-0 (ebk)

DOI: 10.4324/9781003218470

Typeset in Joanna Sans
by codeMantra

CONTENTS

ACKNOWLEDGEMENTS AND INSPIRATIONS

In early 2021, I was asked to run a workshop for dozens of insights and analytics professionals in the pharmaceutical sector on how to ask better questions. It seemed like an innocent enough request – and a relevant one, too, for a data storyteller like me, who spends so much of his time knee-deep in data, trying to tease stories from statistics. As I prepared my material for our 90-minute session, I felt unusually excited, though I couldn't fathom quite why this was.

At the same time, I was turning over in the back of my mind what topic might be big enough to be the subject of the third book in my trilogy on using data smarter, to follow 2018's *Narrative by Numbers* and my pandemic baby or 2020's *How To Be Insightful*. It was only when I'd delivered my talk and run the exercises to even better feedback than usual that I realised that the workshop contained within it the seeds of the book that you hold in your hands today.

For that reason, I owe a huge debt of gratitude to my excellent client, **Carin du Toit**, for asking me to run that workshop. We clearly couldn't have fitted even a sliver of the content in this book into a 90-minute workshop over the often-unpredictable medium of Microsoft Teams. But without your specific request, Carin, *Asking Smarter Questions* would undoubtedly have taken longer to create – as an idea, a theme, and now a book. Thanks so much for asking me to run the session. It set me off on the ride that's led to these pages and the growing body of assets, training courses, and materials associated with it. You will always be the fairy godmother to this project.

Dedications in my books often go beyond the human and stray to the feline. It was the insightful **Tony the Cat** last time, and this time I had wanted to dedicate this book to our COVID-era kitten, **Millie**. Born in April 2020 under lockdown 1.0, she arrived with us when restrictions eased, and the fluffiest, cutest, and most adventurous of creatures she most certainly was. I'd wanted to dedicate this book to Millie because of her insatiable curiosity. From her first night with us when we thought she'd escaped from our totally sealed kitchen (she crawled behind the skirting board and made her new home bed on top of a casserole in a drawer under the stove) ... to her spidercat escapades, climbing vertical walls with ease ... to her David and Goliath spats with next door's matriarch, Pearl ... to all the birds and voles and squirrels she introduced us to, some of them alive ... to going out at crepuscular dusk and returning at rosy-fingered dawn. Millie was not only beautiful, she was the personification – the felinification – of curiosity. And you know what curiosity did, now don't you?

On the morning of a memorial service in September 2021, I went out for a run around dawn. I came back to find my phone ringing and ten missed calls from half-a-dozen unknown numbers. Just 454 days after blinking and mewling and mewing into the world, our gorgeous racoon-tailed apricot tabby had been found, knocked down next to the Brighton Road, the other side of the 12-foot fence at the top of our garden. We had no way of knowing whether it was her first or 101st curious foray over the road, but it was most decidedly and agonisingly her last. I recovered and hugged the still-warm body of our gorgeous Mrs Cat, and we wailed as a family at this untimely agony. We've had plenty of death over the years, human and feline, and I've been an orphan longer than I've been a published author. But – save an experience in my tweens, when my best friend "Scribbler" and his brother died in a plane crash – I've never known such raw and untimely a demise of such an instant and important part of the family as the gut-wrenching demise of Millie.

For your curiosity, Millie, which was your undoing, you are forever memorialised in these pages. I champion and encourage curiosity – to ask the smart questions that surface the right data to articulate the right insights and tell the right data-driven, insight-rich stories. But unlike our fluffball – named after Liverpool FC's James Milner (because all of the boy kittens, who would have been called Virgil or Jürgen, had gone) – do make sure you look both ways in your own quest for answers. We cast Millie's ashes into the sea in sight of the Seven Sisters, the sun-kissed January morning of my birthday in 2022, and now she's chasing seagulls.

To my closest of close family – my wife, life, and business partner **Saskia**, to my splendid son **Max**, now a man and headed towards university, I owe everything. The space and Lebensraum, physical and emotional, to carve out the time required to research and shape and craft this book. Now that I know how to write books – with thanks again, and always, to brilliant book whisperer and coach **Beth Miller** – I've realised I don't need to disappear for months to get this done. If I'm disciplined with consultancy work and get the "air traffic control" right (thanks, clients), book writing can fit around life. I'm not a weekends and late nights kinda guy. In fact, as anyone who knows me will tell you, I can't write (or be trusted to write) after 5pm, unless it's old men's cricket match reports. But Saskia and Max provide the emotional bedrock – as well as endless encouragement, squeezes, and hugs – real and virtual – to make the process feel just a normal part of life. For this, much thanks.

Thanks to my publishers at Routledge, particularly my editor, **Rebecca Marsh**. Your faith in me once, twice, three times an author means the world to me, and I'm proud my business books boast your R on the spine and covers. It's a military-industrial exercise with flowcharts and processes to move from manuscript to final copies, and you and your teams make life simple and straightforward.

And finally, thanks to **Kenneth** and **Bay** – 33 years apart, but thrown together in the wake of a tragedy of truly Greek proportions. Although wandering eyes and recidivist, errant natures meant you weren't together long, thanks for seeing past the embers of agony, eyeing one another up, and asking – for me – the smartest question of all: "Shall we give it a go?" I couldn't have wanted better parents.

PREFACE

RUNNING ON EMPTY?

I started writing this book at a canter during the end of October 2021, just before the COP 26 climate conference in Glasgow. While our son was eking out the last of the summer's rays on a much COVID-postponed holiday in Greece with his girlfriend and her family, my wife and I spent a week in a holiday let in Uplyme, just above Lyme Regis on England's Jurassic Coast. She was reading, walking, and meditating – sometimes one or more of those at the same time – while I was writing.

As world leaders prepared to thrash out a decarbonised future, we zipped along from our Sussex base to Uplyme, 100% electric, untroubled by the remnants of the recent fuel distribution crisis that dogged the Johnson government post-Brexit. Our smugness didn't last long. For although there's been life and energy fizzing around Dorset for aeons – the Lyme Regis museum boasts "185 million years of history", sandblasted into its sea-facing, plate glass windows – in some ways the county is just in the foothills of the green energy revolution. The meagre handful of charging points we sought out to top up had all been bagsied by local eco-taxis. At that point, it was more than two years that we'd been petrol-free, and we'd come to quell that "range anxiety" that afflicts electric car newbies. But that all came rushing back when it looked like we might not be able to charge with ease in Lyme.

Eventually we found a big car park towards the top of town with four charging spots, three already taken. We quickly backed in, tethered up, and downloaded yet another new app to allow us to drain this corner of the national grid. Within minutes, range anxiety was quashed in a pub courtyard overlooking the French Lieutenant's Cobb, secure in the knowledge that we'd have a full charge to visit friends in neighbouring Somerset the next day. Long after darkness had fallen, we climbed back up the oh-so-steep hill, slightly warm around the edges from local ale and gin and waved goodbye to Iris[1], our silent steed. I planned to come and collect her the next morning with a run into town.

With the sky dark and mottled anthracite grey, I pulled my hi-vis singlet and head torch and headed down the hill and back into Lyme. I came out onto the seafront and ran the kilometre or more of built-up pathway that runs past the edge of town. The wind lashing at my back, I was pushed along at what I thought was a cracking pace. And then one, then two, three, four other runners swept past me. In short order, they reached the end of the hard and turned, buffeted and hair billowing behind them as they came back into the teeth of the gale. "It's harder on the way back!" more than one of them shouted at me, broad grins.

Had I accidentally stumbled into a Sunday tradition of Lyme Regis, a Dorset version of my home town Lewes' Twitten Run,[2] a lope up and down a dozen lanes that arc like ribs from the High Street?

On a mission to combine picking up our charged car with some bonus exercise, was I taking part in a one-off charity fun run? A Park Run on a Sunday?

Was the constant trail of runners – some of whom lapped me, some of whom I flew past, many of whom were neck and neck – organised, sponsored, or some kind of flash mob?

Was my rosy-eyed ignorance and assumption of the best in others – particularly runners when I'm on an away-run – well placed or misjudged?

Or was what I was part of just another random collection of dinosaurs, flopping up and down the Jurassic Coast?

As I reached 5K and stopped running, most of the way up the hill, I had the chance to find out. For in the car park where Iris had drunk deep of charge overnight, four or five of my fellow runners were chatting, having a coffee, and getting into cars. But I didn't. And for a usually curious fellow like me – one usually who acts on the guidance given Housman's chorus in his *Fragment of a Greek Tragedy*, below – I simply got into the car and drove back to Uplyme.

> My object in inquiring is to know.
> But if you happen to be deaf and dumb
> And do not understand a word I say,
> Then wave your hand, to signify as much.
>
> *Fragment of a Greek Tragedy*, A.E. Housman

As so often, the failure to ask leaves an itch unscratched; an opportunity for learning – for more context and less subjective conjecture – had gone begging. I determined to mend the error of my ways. Surely there has to be a framework for making sense of the world by asking questions, asking better questions, asking smarter questions?

WHAT DO PEOPLE DO ALL DAY?

Later that day – and before I started the hard yards of a week's sifting through two years' notes and planning to get this book formally on the road – we took a road trip to our friends Lucie and Lucas in the heart of the Somerset Levels. We've known them for more than 35 years, originally college mates, and when we lived in London for more than a decade after graduation, often a week and rarely a month wouldn't go by without our seeing one another. Life and locations change, and – not least because of that pesky pandemic – it was three or more years since our paths had last crossed.

As we drove to see our friends who ... do what? Cook? Give cookery masterclasses for foraged food? Ran a pasta kitchen for NHS staff in the ugly, locked-down months? ... I reflected that we often don't really know what the lives of our closest friends actually entail. Perhaps particularly the interesting and creative ones like Lucie and Lucas. Lucas had edited the non-fashion half of *Sunday Times Style* magazine for 20 years, edited – more like co-created – A.A. Gill's restaurant reviews for a decade, and written one of my favourite cookbooks, *Good Things To Eat*. Together, Lucie and Lucas had moved to Somerset and set out to do ... what? Something to do with food? Lots of things to do with food? I determined I'd find out properly over lunch with them that day.

I remembered that Lucas had once written an article for *Style* in a pre-Christmas issue on how to cook the perfect goose. In the 20 weeks running up to early December, he'd cooked one goose each week. As Christmas was coming (and the geese were getting fatter), his timings changed and developed. But 20 times? Just to get it right? Surely that was overkill. And for another piece on creating macarons, he'd taken a three-month sabbatical and tutelage in Paris, just to get the hard shell and chewy middle of those multicoloured, meringue-based confections just so.

Now I'm greedy. I love food, am curious to try new things, and so have a rich and deep motivation to know more about what it is that my foodie friends do all day. Yet my ignorance of their lives is embarrassingly deep. My curiosity for discovering more about the lives my nearest and dearest was first piqued by a favourite childhood book published the year I was born. Richard Scarry's *What Do People Do All Day?* was a present I received for my first birthday from the American side of my family. From Farmer Alfalfa the goat to Blacksmith Fox, from Stitches the Tailor Rabbit to the Grocer Cat family, this paean to the world of finding purpose through work boldly declared that "Everyone is a worker". It was a book ahead of its time and truly asked a smart question.

It's not like friends who work in the city or the law. I've long found those professions to be mystifying, bewildering, confusing. In the early years beyond college, I often gnawed long into the night with fledgling financiers and baby legal eagles. But those Q&As were usually a vain attempt to understand the new and esoteric worlds into which those I knew so well had plunged. Growing up and into the world, through school and university, I'd known so much about the day-to-day lives of my cohort that it felt like failure not to be able to wrap my head around their lives as we made our way as adults. But I found it harder and harder, particularly for those working in finance and law.

THE CURSE OF KNOWLEDGE

Harvard psychologist Steven Pinker has written a broad sweep of popular science bestsellers over the past quarter of a century, moving from his academic heartland of linguistics to how we think, from human nature to rationality. His most meta[3] of books is *The Sense of Style: The Thinking Person's Guide to Writing in the 21st Century*, perhaps the least-read, most elegant, and most widely applicable of his output. In the book, Pinker goes to impressive lengths to describe, detail, and discourage a presentational and expository faux pas called the Curse of Knowledge. His elegant definition of the phenomenon is: "the difficulty in imagining what it's like for someone else not to know something that you know". It's the cause and the consequence of information asymmetry, a fundamental failure of empathy on the part of the person talking. Those guilty of it haven't stopped to ask: *Who's in the audience and what are they likely to know of my area of expertise already?*

The Curse of Knowledge made its first appearance in the *Journal of Political Economy* in 1989. Here, Colin Camerer and his co-authors violated the principles of the Curse – in a delightfully meta way – when they wrote:

> *In economic analyses of asymmetric information, better-informed agents are assumed capable of reproducing the judgments of less-informed agents. We discuss a systematic violation of this assumption that we call the 'curse of knowledge'. Better-informed agents are unable to ignore private information even when it is in their interest to do so; more information is not always better.*

Despite – or perhaps because of? – being afflicted with the very phenomenon it had identified, the paper was an influential line in the sand. At the time of writing this book, it has almost 400 citations in other academic papers, catapulting into the top 1% of all peer-reviewed articles for reach and influence. The year after Camerer et al. pinpointed the curse, Stanford psychologist Elizabeth Newton made it rather more tangible and real. In her 1990 PhD thesis, she described a series of experiments in which participants were separated into two groups: Tappers and Listeners.[4] Tappers were told they would be tapping out the rhythm of a well-known tune, while Listeners were charged with identifying the tune from taps or claps alone. This is a tricky task for Listeners because, without the cues of pitch, tone, and frequency, melodies are so much harder to identify.

Before the experiment, Tappers said that they thought Listeners would correctly identify the tunes they were tapping 50% of the time. In fact, Listeners only recognised 2.5% of the tunes tapped out. Tappers wildly overestimated Listeners' ability by a factor of 20 because of the Curse of Knowledge. As Tappers tap out the rhythm of the tune, they can "hear" it in their heads. Because they know the tune whose syncopated beats they're tapping out, they can't not know it and they assume that others will, too. They're afflicted by the cognitive shortcut, Hindsight Bias. But they're very much mistaken. As Pinker concludes in his admonitory guidance to authors: "The Curse of Knowledge means that we're more likely to overestimate the average reader's familiarity with our little world than to underestimate it" (2014, p.69).

Pinker identifies those categories of knowledge economy workers who are the most likely to suffer from the Curse: academics, researchers, and analysts (familiar territory), Government officials,[5] scientists, lawyers, and those working in finance. Indeed, he goes so far as to suggest that the entire legal and financial services professions are predicated on the Curse of Knowledge. Those working in these areas make their money by using jargon and buzzwords, acronyms and initialisms deliberately designed to keep outsiders outside, confused.

Whenever I've tried to ask those working in law or finance what it is they do all day, I feel like a journalist in a U.K. government press conference on COVID. It's always seemed as if I didn't have a quiver full of smart questions I could use to work out even the rudiments of their worlds. And it's one of the motivations underpinning my decision to make "Beware the Curse of Knowledge" one of my six Golden Rules of data storytelling in my first book, *Narrative by Numbers*.

CLOSER TOGETHER BUT FURTHER APART

The most intense and sustained academic period of my life was when I took a master's and then a doctorate in experimental psychology at the University of Sussex in the first five years of the new Millennium. This period of my life, education, and research was foundational in my journey to becoming a data storyteller, too. And not because I was routinely observing best practice.

I was in a research group led by the excellent Professor Theodora Duka. In our half-dozen-strong team, there were PhD students and postdoctoral researchers, all working in the really quite narrow discipline of human psychopharmacology. We all had research questions that sought to understand why people drank or smoked or popped pills – often despite clear, negative consequences – and what our understanding of behavioural psychology could do to help minimise risk and harm.

I naively went into my doctoral studies. I was aware that there are different ways in which different drugs have their impact on the brain, mind, and body. Yet I was optimistic that being part of a research community, studying in related but different psychopharmacological niches, would lead to reliable and meaningful shortcuts and cross-fertilisation. And while we often had interesting conversations underpinned by common undergraduate learning, I was disappointed that specialisation into alcohol vs nicotine vs MDMA meant there was remarkably little overlap. Specialisation soon generates jargon and unique ways of thinking, its own Curses of Knowledge. Pretty soon I found I'd run out of smart questions that didn't demand a whole lot of new learning.

THE POWER AND POTENTIAL OF DATA

The Big Data world in which we all live provides enormous potential for unlocking solutions to problems that seem, on the surface, to be increasingly difficult to find. Proper needle in a haystack time. The challenge we face in using Big Data sets – or, more correctly, the corner of little big data we need to address the specific problems we're dealing with today – exists on three levels:

- We need to harness and deploy the right data to tell the right stories that move others to action.
- We need to base those stories on meaningful, data-rich insights – profound and useful understandings of people, issues, topics, or things.

- And to get to those insights, we need to ask smarter questions. Smarter questions that bring groups together through a common language, not division. Smarter questions that not only steer clear of the Curse of Knowledge, but avoid it like the plague, bringing Tappers and Listeners closer together in their understanding of the world. Smarter questions that enable mutual understanding – of close friends who do very different things (yes, even lawyers and accountants), from colleagues in the same department to people we've never met on the other side of the world. Smarter questions that empower us to make the most of chance encounters, from holiday runs to where to charge your car in Dorset seaside towns.

My experience of dumb questions and dumb use of data to dumb ends has inspired me for the past nine years in the work I lead through my data storytelling consultancy, Insight Agents. I used to say my purpose was to help companies communicate more effectively; to make judicious use of data in their storytelling but still sound like human beings; and to talk that most unusual and refined of corporate dialects: Human.

Those are all important consequences of what I and my team do for our clients. But now it's even clearer and simpler than that. We help all different sorts of organisations make smarter use of data. Smarter use of data demands that we ask smarter questions. Smarter questions enable us to gather the data we need to surface and articulate genuine insights into the lives of those we seek to influence. And armed with those insights – and obeying the Golden Rules of data storytelling – we can tell more powerful, purposeful, and persuasive stories, underpinned with relevant data.

Turns out, I wrote the books in the wrong order. I started with data storytelling in *Narrative by Numbers* in 2018, followed it up with my model of insightful thinking – the STEP Prism of Insight™ – two years later in *How To Be Insightful*, born under the pandemic. It's only now that we get to step one with *Asking Smarter Questions* in 2022. But I'm hoping that history will be kind and that you, dear reader, will see the links and crossovers between the three titles in this "using data smarter" trilogy as a whole, and overlook the asynchronous chronology and disorder in which these books first appeared. Think of it like starting a meal with dessert, then the main course, and finally the starter. That's actually quite a fun thing to do and tells you something about the restaurant you're in if they will – and particularly if they will not – accommodate such a vice versa request.

In seeking to identify the smartest questions, we can ask to make sense of the world – from the petty daily fripperies to the world's biggest problems, from minimising the impact of COVID-23 to mitigating the damage of man-made climate change – I've dug a long way down. I've followed the principles of the Sweat or curiosity phase of my own model of insight. Indeed – spoiler alert – it turns out that curiosity is one of the most important principles underpinning our ability to ask smarter questions.

So, in addition to broad and deep reading on, around, and nowhere near the subject, I've also been privileged to speak to a wide spectrum of people whose professional and personal success depends on their ability to frame, ask, and analyse the answers to smarter questions. From scientists to police officers, journalists to doctors, Zen Buddhists to coaches, market researchers to those in conflict resolution, lawyers to top-drawer salespeople – thanks so much, one and all, for your time, patience, and insights. You'll meet all of these characters and many more as I seek to establish and codify best-practice, the universal principles of ASQ – Asking Smarter Questions – and how to use questions and questioning as the basis for navigating our noisy world better, using data smarter.

I don't pretend to have spoken to a representative sample of experts in each of the fields I've touched. You may well know a journalist who doesn't use the techniques favoured by Jane Fryer at the *Daily Mail;* you could be a physician who deploys different interrogative strategies from those favoured by Dr James Lewis. But what I've found striking in my journey is not only the range and diversity of different types of smart questions, but also what happens when the planets align. For the on-deadline features writer and the under-pressure GP – with just ten minutes to prepare for, run, conclude, and write-up a patient appointment – it's the innocent, faux-naïve Columbo Question that matters most. Asking *Anything else bothering you?* as a patient stands up and puts their hand on the door to leave is just as likely to reveal a serious, hidden health concern just as *Anything else going on?* can be to encourage a celebrity to reveal a front-page foursome. Columbo Questions ask: *Just one more thing … is there anything that I haven't asked you that I should have asked you?*

I trust you find the smarter questions identified in this book will be helpful in getting the information you need to make sense of the world – to build better insights and understanding, to tell more persuasive stories that are based on genuine, data-driven insights. In your professional life. In your personal life. In your emotional life. Understanding depends on empathy because it's only by putting yourself into the shoes, the mind, the mindset of others that you can truly understand what it's like to be them. This uniquely human ability all depends on evidence, information, or – as we say in the 2020s – data. And getting the right data starts with asking smarter questions.

Thank you, as ever, for your consideration.

NOTES

1 I'm not a sentimental type or someone who tends to imbue inanimate objects with human personalities, and I'd never named a car I'd owned before Iris came into our lives. But when we went fully electric in 2019, I couldn't resist. In early Edwardian England, my great uncle Guy had started one of the country's first car companies, Iris Cars Ltd., in partnership with the son of the artist Alphonse Lergos and in a showroom off Oxford Street. The company was named after the Greek messenger goddess Iris. The company's advertising slogan used the name as an acronym to stand for "It Runs In Silence". None of the company's cars ever ran in silence – quite the opposite, and a common complaint among grumpy owners – so when we took ownership of a car that really did, well, there was no other name we could have called it. There's more at https://www.wikiwand.com/en/Iris_(car)

2 https://twitter.com/twittenrun

3 For a short history of how the humble Ancient Greek preposition *metá* – meaning, simply, "after" – became a stand-alone word for literary and cultural commentary thanks to the writer Douglas Hofstadter, see the footnote on pp.52–53 of *How To Be Insightful*. Regrettably, while I was writing this book, Facebook founder Mark Zuckerberg decided to tarnish the word "meta" for the rest of recorded and mediated time. In late October 2021, the company renamed its parent business Meta as corporate brand as it looks to create, exploit, and monetise the so-called metaverse, defined as "a virtual-reality space in which users can interact with a computer-generated environment and other users". Kind of like Second Life meets World of Warcraft but for

everything, all delivered over Facebook's – sorry Meta's – Oculus Rift virtual reality headsets. Zuckerberg described himself as "always a fan of the Classics" and had chosen the name because it means "beyond" in Greek. That is a meaning of *metá*, but "after" is much more common, hence Aristotle's *Metaphysics* was the philosophical treatise he wrote after he wrote *The Physics*.

4 Stanford PhD candidate Newton's experiments were first exposed to a broad, lay audience beyond the experimental psychological literature by Chip and Dan Heath in their 2007 book *Made to Stick: Why Some Ideas Survive and Others Die*. Chip was professor of "organizational behavior" (sic) in the Stanford Business School when he and his brother wrote *Made to Stick*. There's an excellent summary of Newton's experiments in the Heaths's short 2006 *Harvard Business Review* article on the Curse of Knowledge at https://hbr.org/2006/12/the-curse-of-knowledge

5 The COVID-19 pandemic showcased both villains and heroes in the field of the Curse of Knowledge, a topic we cover regularly in the podcast I co-founded in 2016 and co-host, the Small Data Forum – https://www.smalldataforum.com. Tragically, often in the U.K. and U.S. at least, some government officials responsible for presenting the ever-shifting science as the basis for justifying restrictions and lockdowns were unable to imagine what it was like for the general public not to know what they knew. At a time when we'd never needed experts more – whatever Government ministers, including Michael Gove, had said during the 2016 EU Referendum – we had not had enough of experts. What we dearly needed was experts who could present the science simply and clearly. Too often we got the opposite.

In the U.K., the most egregious example was the horror show set of "SPI-M" charts used at the hastily arranged Hallowe'en 2020 press conference to justify the second lockdown. I picked these apart in my article https://insightagents.co.uk/a-nightmare-on-downing-street/ That event was "organised" by one of the most regular and most arrogant offenders of the Curse of Knowledge, Prime Minister Johnson's now-disgraced chief adviser, Dominic Cummings. Cummings's blog roll is a case study in how to display the Curse at every turn, and the Hallowe'en press conference and slides were the most brilliant example of how not to do things. The worst slide – which even Chief Scientific Officer Sir Patrick Vallance had the self-awareness and good grace to admit was "quite a complicated slide" – is ridiculed and recreated, Curse-free, by the Slide Presentation Man Dave Henson, author of a great book titled *Your Slides Suck!*, in a short film on LinkedIn, here: https://bit.ly/3GcVEit.

Among the ever-present heroes who avoided the Curse of Knowledge in presenting data during the pandemic were Sir David Spiegelhalter, Chairman of the Winton Centre for Risk and Evidence Communication in the Statistical Laboratory at the University of Cambridge, together with Tim Harford and his team on BBC Radio's *More or Less*. Spiegelhalter created the programme in the mid-2000s together with Michael Blastland.

1

WHAT'S ALL THE FUSS ABOUT?

Abstract

Asking smarter questions matters because smarter questions drive smarter, more useful answers. In our world of increasing polarisation and fractured discourse, we need every hack we can muster to bridge our differences of opinion. The in-built inequalities of mature global capitalism have driven a wedge between the haves and the have-nots, a wedge ripped into a gaping chasm, first by the global recession of the late 2000s and then by state-enforced austerity. This led to the rise of the far right and the shockwaves of votes for both Brexit and Trump.

Polarisation and discord have been exacerbated and amplified by both social media platforms and Big Tech's advertiser-funded model that cares little for the well-being of its users. COVID has done nothing to slow this down, despite the green shoots of pro-social behaviour under the first lockdown. Opposing sides shout and escape censure or opprobrium by lurking like trolls in the shadows, failing to ask smarter questions or listen to answers. In this toxic atmosphere of "loudest voice wins", we can only bring ourselves back from the abyss through constructive conversation and a properly Stoic mindset, one that accepts that we can only control our response to events not events themselves.

DOI: 10.4324/9781003218470-1

THE BEST EXAM QUESTION EVER?

In the 30-odd years since I ended my first run of formal education, I've worked with half-a-dozen people who use the phrase "exam question" when taking briefs from colleagues, clients, or collaborators. *What's the exam question?* they'll ask, somewhere between the overeager class swot, keen to revise everything and so prepare themselves for every possible eventuality, and the class slacker who wants to focus on the bare minimum of information they need to secure a pass.

I like that question and have always enjoyed working with others who ask it. I'm more of a swot than a slacker and someone who thrived on exams rather than continual assessment. To be fair, exams were all that was on offer to me through school and university. So, whenever I hear someone use the phrase, it puts me on a war footing. I'm prepared for a serious engagement, one that demands: (i) starting from a point of relative ignorance; (ii) sourcing evidence and data about a topic or issue by asking progressively better-informed questions; (iii) sifting, sorting, and selecting information, into observations, then insights, as things start to fall into place; and (iv) repackaging and reordering inputs into easily understood, creative solutions that address the exam question we've been set.

Perhaps the best actual exam question ever set[1] may, in truth, be apocryphal. But like a lot of apocryphal stories, it serves to make a good point. In the late 1950s, my late father Kenneth ran the Institute of Economics and Statistics at Oxford University. Though he never told any of his many wives or children, he had in fact modelled the Institute and its culture of intellectual curiosity on Bletchley Park, the secretive home of code breakers. It was at Bletchley that Alan Turing and others cracked the code used by the German Enigma machines to send military intelligence before and during World War II. Kenneth was only outed as having had worked at Bletchley by a former Oxford colleague, Asa Briggs, more than 20 years after my father had died.[2]

As well as writing the world's first book on industrial disharmony called *Strikes*, Kenneth was active in advising politicians – usually Labour politicians – and their civil servants on how to work better with trade unions. As part of a progressive (if one-way) exchange scheme, my father also welcomed senior researchers in mathematics from Peking (now Beijing) University. After his retirement in the early 1970s, I remember him telling three stories about a couple of visiting mathematicians.

First, after a month's silent observation, one academic declared loudly and confidently one morning that the world would make more sense if calculations were made not in base ten but base six, the so-called senary numeral system. Her justification? "Because that is the number of petals on a lotus flower". This was beyond my father's mathematical ken, and, taken aback by her enthusiasm and somewhat whimsical justification, he asked the Institute's highest-ranked computer, David Champernowne, what he thought. Champernowne had studied for his PhD alongside Turing at King's College, Cambridge, in the early 1930s. He had his first paper published – on Champernowne's constant, the number 0.1234567891011 – while still an undergraduate. He, too, worked at Bletchley. And to my father's great surprise, Champernowne declared: "She's quite right, you know! Life would be so much easier in senary".

Second, he was foxed by the Chinese rules of reciprocity and safe return home. After dinner in his North Oxford home, my father walked another exchange professor home. The Chinese academic – who spoke very good English – immediately told my father that he now had to walk my father home in gratitude for my father having walked him home. This happened for another round or two, and eventually – with dawn threatening to break – my father eventually gave in and said goodbye to his guest on his own doorstep, exhausted but hoping he hadn't committed an unforgivable faux pas. Apparently not.

And third, during exam season, my father asked the lotus flower/base six advocate what was the hardest and best question she'd ever seen in a Chinese university final paper in statistics. "Ah! That's easy to answer!" she said. "But it's not just statistics. At the end of every undergraduate's four years of study – and whatever they have studied – they must all answer one question, which is phrased as a command: write down everything you know". Candidates were allowed nine hours to complete the exam question, she said, including two breaks to visit the toilet and two for meals.

At first my father thought this nine-hour marathon was some sort of torture, an early contender for the pilot of *Endurance* or *Squid Game*, perhaps, though this was long before reality TV was A Thing or a twinkle in A Thing's Eye. But the more he talked about the question with the Peking academic and other colleagues at the Institute, the more he realised quite what a brilliant exam question it was. Candidates who did well in answering this question-cum-command were not those who listed page after page of facts. The examiners and university authorities weren't remotely interested in what the students knew about their degree course topics – that would be interrogated by the subject-specific papers they had already sat.

Write down everything you know was designed to test students' epistemology – their own theory of knowledge and how they structured the knowledge they had acquired in various different domains: technical subjects, interpersonal skills, emotions, nature, society, The Party (of course), civic duty, and so on. Better marks will almost certainly have been given for answers loyal to Chairman Mao Zedong and his vision for Communist China. But the lotus flower academic indicated that there was remarkable freedom available to students who understood the real impact and import of the question and why it was being asked, not those who misinterpreted it as a call to show off all the facts and data they'd crammed during finals' revision.

When I was growing up and taking tests and then exams at school, Kenneth was retired – at least from his academic day jobs at Oxford. The last 20 years or so of his life he dedicated to monumental glass engraving, often of church windows, and creating more and more arcane typefaces.[3] He did this from a studio built in our back garden where he worked for six or more hours each day, so was very present in my life and very available to gently guide and nudge me with my education. His zeal for learning and unquelled curiosity did put me off reading until after he died in 1988. "You must read this!", "Haven't you read that?", "Surely you've read the other?" were constant refrains around the dinner table. They paralysed me, like an ignorant rabbit in the headlights, to read nothing at all. That aside, his impact on my own spirit of enquiry and curiosity was net positive. Net extremely positive.

Whenever an exam loomed, he was generally pretty laissez-faire and laid back. I was the last of his six (seven? But that's another story) children by four (or five) wives, born between 1933 and 1967, so he'd seen it all before. As a successful student himself, as a parent of many successful students, and as a retired academic through whose hands many successful students had passed, he had a simple but reliable formula for exam success. It all boiled down to three simple initialisms, RTQ, RTFQ, RTFQA: Read The Question. Read The Flipping Question. Read The Flipping Question Again. And though, with time, the "F" took on a fruitier, expletive-deleted tone, RTFQA has become a firm family mantra and shortcut that – to this day – I share with my son when he heads off to the exam hall, real or virtual.

When Kenneth learned that I was intrinsically motivated, when he observed that I was a signed-up member of the RTFQA club, when he saw that I could construct a revision timetable and started to do well in exams, he knew he could lay off the pressure. Although there was one exception.

OF MICE, GHOSTS, AND PAC-MAN

In the run up to my first public exams – O-levels, taken in year 11 at age 16 – it became clear to my father that I was often staying up long into the night. But I wasn't cramming for exams. I was coding, or programming as we called it in the early 1980s. Having scrimped and saved and begged and borrowed, I'd acquired Sir Clive Sinclair's ZX Spectrum a year earlier. Already a budding linguist, I soon learned BASIC and machine code, and revelled in the joys of problem-solving through programming. I even began to make a little money by having print-outs of my programs published in the teen-geek journal of the times, *Popular Computing Weekly*.

I became ambitious – perhaps grandiloquently so, given my O-levels were coming up – and started out on a version of Pac-Man. I don't know if you've ever programmed (or coded) or have had members of your family who do the same. The thing is that programming or coding time – like gaming time – is able to chomp through hours and days and weeks with ease, like Pac-Man through a maze of dots. Both are the quickest route to Mihaly Csikszentmihalyi's optimal experience of "flow" that I know – or at least knew until I discovered running over the Sussex Downs.

With gaming, you "just" have to get to the next level – answer the successively smarter questions set by the game and level designers, by narrative and performance scriptwriters. Kill the spiders, eat the coins, and level up. With programming, you "just" have to convince the computer to do what you want it to do through the frequently inadequate syntax and incomplete language, designed by humans to control hardware also designed by humans. Computer-brain analogies are as unhelpful as computer language-human language comparisons: the human brain is the most powerful supercomputer on earth and human language the most flexible, nested, recombinatorial system, yet devised. Both brains and human language are orders of magnitude more complex than computers and computer languages – particularly ZX Spectrums and Sinclair BASIC – but you take my point.

A few nights before my first O-level, my father came up to bed sometime after midnight. He saw light from the Anglepoise desk lamp flooding under my bedroom door and onto the landing. He knocked gently and asked what I was up to. I tried to turn off the portable TV tethered to my Spectrum and open a large textbook at a plausible page and over the keyboard, but I'd been rumbled. After some grunts and complaints that we really should both be going to bed, I fessed up.

My version of Pac-Man was almost complete, with one – key – exception. In order to make the game challenging, I needed to make the four ghosts – Inky, Clyde, Pinky, and Blinky in the U.S. version; Fickle, Chaser, Ambusher, and Stupid in the Namco original in Japan – follow the chomping yellow mouth as it guzzled dots and cherries. The trouble was that the subroutine I'd written to control the movement of the ghosts was too good. Much more Chaser and Ambusher and very little Fickle or Stupid. Indeed, it was so good that the legend GAME OVER appeared within seconds. My ghosts, you see, could drift through walls.

My father filled the frame of my bedroom door with his Henry VIII heft, musing. Over the course of a couple of minutes, a smile broke on his face, first at the corners of his mouth and then broad and generous and warm. He didn't speak a word of Sinclair BASIC, but he knew a bit about artificial intelligence and a lot about logic, and asked me this question: "Accepting that you don't actually believe in them, what are the essential qualities of a ghost?" A fine time to get philosophical on me, I thought. The last thing I needed was this former classicist to embrace his inner Socrates and quiz me about the Platonic form of a ghost. Tetchy, tired, and with a week's frustration pent-up from failing to bend the Spectrum to my will, I started my list: "Transparent, you can see through them, give you a chill if they pass through you, love Hallowe'en, goo 'Wooooo-oooooo' ... how is this helping?"

"Go on", urged my father.

"Oh, I dunno ... glide effortlessly through walls?"

"BINGO! That version of Pac-man you bought doesn't let the ghosts go through walls, but YOURS does. Yours is far more authentic. Just add a bit of randomness into how the ghosts move – build an algorithm that makes them chase the player but then suddenly wander off, in a very floaty, ghost-like way – and your version will be much more realistic. Or at least much more like the world that you're trying to create. Oh, and one more thing. Why don't you leave it until after your exams?"

I felt like Archimedes in his bath with the King of Syracuse's silver-not-gold crown. I had found it! In the end, I stayed up another couple of hours in defiance of my father's advice, rewrote the subroutine with added jitter, printed the code off on the stinky silver paper of the ZX Printer, saved a copy onto a screechy cassette tape, and parcelled up a package – all before 3am. I slept a little, but woke with a bound in my step. After breakfast with my Kenneth, I left ten minutes early to post the package to *Popular Computing Weekly*. And early in the summer holidays, exams safely out of the way, I was rewarded with "Game of the Week" by the magazine and £40 for my troubles. All because the distance Kenneth had had from the problem I was trying to address – my earliest experience of the perspective of the external consultant – enabled him to ask a smarter question. Thanks, dad.

SMARTER QUESTIONS IN THE AGE OF FRACTURED DISCOURSE

The seminal documentary – hey, rockumentary – *This is Spinal Tap* features the best graveside scene in movie history.[4] Tap are on a make-or-break tour of the U.S., facing setback after setback. Concerts are cancelled or downsized, their new album *Smell the Glove* is banned for sexist imagery, and a stage set of a Stonehenge trilithon is built 12 times too small – 18 inches rather than 18 feet high – thanks to a simple typo on its napkin design (18" not 18'). Manager Ian Faith tries to mutter bad news under his breath in throwaway lines, such as: "The Boston gig has been cancelled. But I wouldn't worry about it though. It's not a big college town."

In a bid to raise flagging morale, Faith arranges for the band to visit Elvis Presley's mansion-turned-mausoleum, Graceland. After a fractious and inharmonious acapella rendition of Presley's *Heartbreak Hotel*, lead guitarist Nigel Tufnell observes: "This is depressing. It really puts a perspective on things, though, doesn't it." Lead singer David St Hubbins retorts: "Too much. There's too much fucking perspective".

Smart is not an adjective much used to describe either Tufnell or St Hubbins, but their observation could easily have been made about the fractured state of public discourse that hangs like a smog over politics, business, and public life in much of the world as we limp through the early 2020s. The inequalities made evident by the global financial crisis and world recession in the four years either side of 2010 were inadequately addressed and then exacerbated by short-term policies of austerity, particularly either side of the Atlantic but also in much of Europe and elsewhere. The spirit of diversity, globalisation, and free movement of individuals that dominated the two decades either side of the Millennium have been swept away by narrow-minded nationalism and a rampaging return to in-groups and out-groups so favoured and openly fostered by right-wing politicians. All topped off with a dollop of the worst global pandemic for a century.

FIRST BREXIT ...

With no evidence of any kind of levelling up – a pernicious phrase in the hands of many a politico, including at the time of writing – divisive, right-wing policies that were previously just dog whistle calls-to-arms to core supporters have gone mainstream. In the U.K. in particular, the political parties founded and run by Nigel Farage – the U.K. Independence Party (UKIP) and then the Brexit Party – played on generations-out-of-date racial and racist stereotypes with extraordinary impact. "Coming over here, taking our jobs, using our health service, stealing our women …".

Thanks to the smug complacency of Tory Prime Minister David "Dave" Cameron and his chancellor Gideon Osbourne, the Remain side in the EU Referendum debate was easily outflanked. This came from a combination of: (a) inadequate leadership and desire from the Government; (b) the effective abstention from engagement by the disastrous opposition Labour leader, Jeremy Corbyn; and, (c) the weaselly worded, targeted Facebook book ads and Three Word Slogans from Vote Leave's evil genius Dominic Cummings. A couple of the worst, most mendacious examples suggested that Turkey – and its 76 million population – was about to join the EU (a lie). With average wages in the U.K. £26,000 but less than £7,500 in Turkey, the Facebook ad asked stoked-up voters to respond to the rhetorical question "GOOD NEWS???" by clicking YES or NO buttons. A second ad suggested imminent mass migration via Turkey from "Britain's new border with Syria and Iraq". Voters were invited to "Click to save our NHS" (National Health Service). Fortunately, these lies masquerading as ads have largely vanished from the internet.

Much to their surprise, Cummings and Vote Leave won the EU Referendum, with 51.8% of those voting choosing to leave the EU. Facebook and Cambridge Analytica proved more than helpful. The result was also a great surprise to two prominent Leave supports on the Tory front benches – former hack and then Foreign Secretary, Alexander Boris de Pfeffel Johnson, and Secretary of State for Justice, Graeme Andrew Logan, the birth name of Michael Gove before he was adopted at four months. Johnson and Gove were the most prominent U.K. cabinet ministers to collude with Cummings and Vote Leave and, though it's made them since, neither believed they would win the Referendum. It also took them a while to get their hands on the levers of power, with Gove stabbing Johnson in the front during the post-Cameron leadership election campaign, though at least that allowed them both to let Teresa May tear herself, her party, and much of the country apart not on their watch.

Johnson, indeed, had written an article for *The Daily Telegraph* – a publication which he refers to as his "real boss"[5] – in full support of the EU, had the Referendum vote gone the other way. In the article, he said that Britain's continued membership of the EU would be "a boon for the world and Europe", arguing:

> This is a market on our doorstep, ready for further exploitation by British firms. The membership fee seems rather small for all that access. Why are we so determined to turn our back on it?

At time of writing, Johnson is now the hard Brexit Prime Minister who – with Cummings's help and the illegal prorogation of Parliament – "Got Brexit Done". With and without Cummings pulling the strings and writing another three-word or three-phrase campaigning slogan, Johnson's premiership has been characterised by a lack of engagement in debate, serried name-calling, and bluff and bluster. He has made a virtue of ignoring facts and data over his version of the truth. Smart questions are swatted away like irritating gadflies and debate has been replaced by cloth-eared monologue.

... THEN TRUMP

Across the Atlantic, maverick outsider and serial corporate bankrupt, Donald Trump, saw the success of Vote Leave as a springboard to enhance his chances of election to the presidency. Trump invited Farage and his strategists to speak at rallies and advise behind the scenes. An incredulous world – particularly the out-of-touch liberal elite – sneered at Trump's predictions that his battle with "Crooked Hillary" would be "Brexit plus, plus, plus". His hate-filled, fact-light, evidence-free sloganeering – from "Lock her up!" to "Build the wall!" – ensured he did, indeed, become POTUS 45.

From almost any perspective – including from that of many inside and outside the Republican Party who voted for him in 2016 and again in 2020 – Trump's presidency was calamitous, toxic, and divisive. For the sake of balance, I should probably say "first term" rather than "presidency", as Biden looks unlikely to stand in 2024 and Trump has been raising funds for re-election since the day he left office. But the role of facts and evidence and answering smart questions were always low on Trump's to-do list. Before Trump (and Johnson, not to mention

Jair Bolsinaro and Viktor Orbán) heads of state were routinely held to account by the fourth estate: the press and now more broadly the news media, increasingly online.

Yet, whenever Trump was challenged by a media outlet who hadn't supported him – or asked a smart question he didn't want to answer or couldn't without compromising the image he'd created for himself – he'd knee-jerk back with the parroted line, "Fake news!" The same is increasingly true of Trump's peers and opposite numbers in the U.K., Brazil, Hungary, and elsewhere. It's not just the first among equals; it's their cabinet ministers and spokespeople, too. And then some.

Throughout the Trump presidency, many traditional – what The Donald would knee-jerk-label "Fake News" – and modern media platforms and outlets kept score on the President's mendaciousness. The *New York Times* was particularly assiduous; the more he lied, the more resource they put into fact checking. PolitiFact is one of the best, run by the Poynter Institute for Media Studies. Inconveniently enough for Trump, the Institute is based in St Petersburg, Florida. It is a not-for-profit journalism school and research organisation which declares its purpose proudly on its digital masthead thus: "Our only agenda is to publish the truth so you can be an informed participant in democracy. We need your help". There's more at https://www.politifact.com

PolitiFact has a six-point scale into which it categorises the verity and veracity of information politicians present as fact. This ranges from True on the left to Mostly True, Half-True, Mostly False, False, and – most delightfully of all – Pants on Fire. At the time of writing (October 2021), six of the ten most recent Trump facts checked had been rated as Pants on Fire, with the other four declared False. Fifty-three per cent of the 942 facts checked by the service fall into those last two, far-right categories. Just 3% were found to be True, 8% Mostly True, and 12% Half-True. The smarter question posed by such sites and services is this: "Is [THIS STATEMENT] from former President Trump true and how might we corroborate his claims?"

The spirit, imagination, and crowd-sourced inventiveness of services such as PolitiFact drive an important wedge between the demagogues and the people. It's a spirit captured in the excellent U.K.-based organisation,

Tortoise Media, which for the past three years has been in the vanguard of what it calls the "slow news movement". It describes itself as being a response to two problems, the daily noise and the power gap, defined on its about us page in this way:

The daily noise: we are overwhelmed by information. The problem isn't just fake news or junk news, because there's a lot that's good – it's just that there's so much of it, and so much of it is the same. In a hurry, partial, and confusing. Too many newsrooms chasing the news, but missing the story.

The power gap: the divide between the powerful and the powerless is widening. We feel locked out. Alarmed by the lack of vision, hungry for leadership in business, technology, and society. We believe in responsibility; we care about dignity.

Tortoise was founded by former *Times* editor, James Harding, whose job immediately prior to setting up Tortoise was director of BBC News. One of his enduring actions in that role was to establish a permanent Reality Check team to "check and debunk deliberately misleading and false stories masquerading as real news", particularly false stories and facts being shared widely on social media. When launching Reality Check, Harding said: "The BBC can't edit the internet, but we can't stand aside either". www.credibilitycoalition.org lists more than 250 organisations around the world that do something similar to Reality Check, from AFP Factuel to ZimFact.

But despite the well-intentioned, impactful actions taken by these organisations, the way modern media is architected means the reach and behaviour of demagogues gets louder and amplified. Politicians don't just call "fake news" on the old, established TV channels and press outlets. They do it online, from cnn.com to *The Wall Street Journal* online. Much more importantly and with direct reach into their followers' echo chambers, they do it on and through social media channels and platforms. These are better-termed owned media channels, where the politicians are the medium and – to mangle Marshall McLuhan – they have total control over the message. And when the general voting public observe their leaders behaving like this – dodging debate and evading smart questions by bluster and cat-calling – they do the same. In spades.

Amid the tragedy of COVID-19 – more than a quarter of a billion cases and more than five million deaths worldwide at the time of writing – there have been very few silver linings. For those opposed to the multifarious ways in which Trump brought politics and political office into disrepute, there was a fatal flaw that led to his undoing and saw him well beaten by Biden in November 2020. This was the roughshod, data-light, fact-free way in which he misled the U.S. Government's response to what he repeatedly – and with racist malice aforethought – spat through gritted teeth as "the China Virus".

At turns he denied it would be serious, suggested it would disappear by Spring Break 2020, recommended injecting bleach as a cure, displayed a laughable inability for even rudimentary statistics – most notably in his interview with Jonathan Swann from Axios HBO[6] – failed to show leadership on social distancing or mask wearing or vaccination, conflated freedom to do as we please with freedom to infect the vulnerable ... the list goes on and on. Without COVID, political pundits believe, Biden and Harris couldn't have held off Trump and Pence. Thanks to his cataclysmically poor mishandling of the U.S. Government's response – including sideling and ridiculing the brilliant Anthony Fauci, who had been so instrumental in tackling the HIV/AIDS epidemic for 40 years – Trump lost.

Throughout his business career, Trump has shown himself to have a very thin carapace and be a man who readily takes offence to the slightest of sleights. More than this, he has a reputation of being a very bad loser. For months ahead of the November 2020 vote, Trump stoked his supporters – both rabid and more modern – to prepare them for defeat by not accepting it. Every state where the vote was close, Trump pressurised Governors to hold recounts. When recounts showed a given state had, indeed, voted for Biden-Harris, Trump demanded a revote. He refused to accept the original results, the recounts, or the will of the people.

In the chill early days of January 2021, Trump did nothing to discourage – and everything to encourage – his "Stop the Steal" foot soldiers from attacking the U.S. Capitol in an attempt to overturn the results of the election by force. Speaking in Washington before the attack, he said at a highly mediated rally: "If you don't fight like hell, you're not going to have a country anymore". Trump incited his supporters to attack the literal and symbolic home of global democracy. Five people died in the attacks. Almost 150 police officers were injured, four of whom committed suicide within six months of the attack. All thanks to a bad loser rejecting the truth and using social media to foment civil unrest in an attempt to subvert democracy. Though that's not quite how he put it.

THE TOXIC ROLE OF SOCIAL MEDIA IN THE DEMISE OF DEBATE

Candidly, discourse and dialogue are the wrong words to describe what passes for debate in the modern, hypermediated world. People don't stop to ask smarter questions. They don't wait for answers. They shout as loud and as intimidatingly as they can in an attempt to browbeat, bully, or coerce others into submission. Or else they lurk in the digital undergrowth and launch savage, personal attacks on those they disagree with, often dripping with racist, sexist, genderist, orientationist abuse ladled on thick. Hiding in anonymity in plain sight behind a fake or misleading profile, unmoderated by platform operators, they get away with it again and again and again.

It didn't have to be this way – abuse and incitement to violence – and it doesn't have to stay as the new and the next normal. And while you might take some convincing from here that asking smarter questions can play an important role in leading the fightback, I'd encourage you to bear a few things in mind. Asking smarter questions isn't just about turning the tide on social media vitriol and demagoguery, though I believe it can have a role there and explain how and why shortly. Asking smarter questions can help you to achieve a whole lot more than equilibrium, and I'll come to that throughout this book, too. That said, I can easily understand how – after the last few pages in which I've set the context for one, very important role that asking smarter questions can play – you might think that my prescription for change through smarter questions was little more than pissing in the wind. Or, as the French say, *enculer les mouches*.

Before we get there, let's consider the role and responsibilities of Big Tech in how we got to where we are today. The promise of digital technology and social media platforms was supposed to be all about democratisation, sharing the means of production and commentary with the masses. Those whose opinions and content resonated strongly would surely float the surface. The role of Twitter in the Green movement in Iran in 2009 (and more recently Telegram), the role of Facebook in unleashing democracy in Egypt and Tunisia during the Arab Spring in 2011. Anyone with a smartphone and a decent connection – and good enough ideas – appeared to have the power to change the status quo and usher in positive change.

The *New Yorker*'s resident book writer, Malcolm Gladwell, got very excited by the potential of social media platforms to propel and accelerate revolutions, but soon got cold feet and rowed back some overambitious, under-researched claims. As often, he saw both the potential upsides and downsides of the innovative power of technology before others. Seems like we in the West – with our so-called stable and mature democracies – got a little bit too starry-eyed too soon.

As in social change through social media, so an end to consumer rip-offs in social commerce. The wisdom of digital savvy shoppers – finding the best bargains for flights, crowdfunding the production of new products, and the rise and rise of disintermediated direct-to-consumer (D2C) brands seemed to offer greater commercial freedoms and democratic rights to consumers the world over. From mattresses to bamboo socks, pizza ovens to monthly razors with just two blades, cutting out the middle man became the new mass distribution. Until, of course, the very consumer goods companies that had been outflanked bought the D2C upstarts for billions and changed things back.

The inventor of the World Wide Web (www), Tim Berners-Lee, is often to be heard lamenting the fact that his baby has become a place were bad, base, and primarily commercial things happen. "It wasn't meant to be this way" is the message that underpins his annual complaint, often to mark the March birthday[7] of the Web. It's like when the playwright Tom Stoppard once confronted the theatre critic of a heavyweight British newspaper saying he'd never intended his play to be understood as the critic described, to which the critic is said to have replied: "Yes, but you only wrote it!" As the sculptor and calligrapher Eric Gill observed: "The artist does the work. The critic has the inspiration."

Berners-Lee has a point in his annual lament for the lost soul of the worldwide web. What's more, you wait all chapter for a quote from Tom Stoppard and then get two in two paragraphs. For Stoppard also lamented how, under commercial pressure, journalism swapped its purpose from education, information, and (moral) elevation to simply diversion, distraction, and entertainment. Some years ago, he observed:

> The whole notion of journalism being an institution whose fundamental purpose is to educate and inform and even – one might say – elevate, has altered under commercial pressure, perhaps, into a different kind of purpose, which is to divert and distract and entertain.

Though composed in the predigital age, the same words could be used of the 30-plus years' downward slide of the Web, while intensified commercial pressures with more to win (and lose) have pulled online media platforms into blacker, more malevolent Stygian depths.

Here are five reasons which explain why and how the information carried over the www has been so toxic and threatening to discourse, and why a renaissance in asking smarter questions can help to turn the tide.

1. **The Web and the digital and social media platforms that sit on top of it are a septic tank**. As well as the best, the worst of all life is there. Biased, blinkered, and bigoted thinking has always existed, muttered in the corners of pubs or organised meetings. Now it has a home – a permanent repository – where it and its regurgitators can meet and coalesce and form echo chambers of poison and hate, from terrorists to QAnon, incels to the AfD. The loudest, most coercive, most aggressive – usually male, often white – voice wins. There's no debate or discussion, no genuine questions asked that really seek answers, and no answers listened to. For a medium technically capable of presenting, sharing, and preserving multiple points of view, the internet is doing a spectacularly bad job.

2. **Volunteering an opinion, urging action – including action that causes mental and physical harm to others – can all be done behind the cloak of anonymity**. Facebook and other social media platforms claim that only genuine, authenticated accounts tied to real,

single individuals are table stakes for participation in their platforms. Independent observers such as Bob Hoffman, the self-proclaimed AdContrarian,[8] have observed that Facebook deleted seven billion fake or duplicate or dormant accounts in 2020, questioning (a) the claimed audience reach behind their closely guarded walled garden and (b) how serious they are about rooting out toxic or anonymous players.

3. **Bad actors can be and sometimes are removed, but often long after the event**. Trump may be serving an indefinite ban on Twitter and Facebook. When those bans were imposed after the storming of the Capitol in January 2021, he and his followers moved to Parler. Google Play and the Apple took the app down from its App stores until Parler banned Trump and his followers – and Amazon web services took the app down from its servers. One step ahead of the bans, Trump et al. moved to his own website, the dark web, and are now talking about creating their own, walled garden, alt.right platform to create a new echo chamber. Created by a company called RightForge, the platform is laughably called Truth Social.

    But often, the action of freezing accounts and barring membership is too late. In her 2021 whistle-blowing testimony to first the U.S. Congress and then to a Select Committee in the U.K.'s House of Commons, former Facebooker Frances Haugen has shown how the culture of her former employers prioritised profitability over public good. Great respect is due to the 2018 whistle-blower Christopher Wylie and Carole Cadwalladr – his amanuensis at the British newspapers *The Guardian* and *The Observer* – whose reporting led to the collapse of sneaky consultancy Cambridge Analytica. But Haugen's repeated testimony takes whistle-blowing against Facebook to a whole new level. Indeed, it threatens the very existence of the platform and makes an anti-trust break-up of the company more and more likely. At least, that's how the media – old news and competitive Big Tech – are reporting it.

4. **Big Tech exists to make money from advertising**. This is true of Alphabet (the parent company of Google and YouTube), Meta (the new corporate entity for Facebook, Instagram, and WhatsApp since

October 2021), and Twitter, as well as many other, bit-part players in the panoply of social media platforms. This may not have been evidenced in their noble, founding statements of purpose – Google's, you may recall, was "Don't be evil" in the early days. Yet, 90% of jobs in Big Tech and glorified ad sales roles. Actually, many of them aren't all that glorified, although they're usually paid well above market rates. Most platforms pay little or no corporation tax in their ex-U.S. operations and employees are incentivised to maximise revenue.

The platforms are free to use. Because they are free to users – as Netflix documentaries from *The Great Hack* to *The Social Dilemma* show time and again – then the users are the product. We are things – eyeballs, brains, people – to be sold to. Social platforms are funded by serving targeted advertising, based on your search history (though this will become more complex – for advertisers at least – after the demise of third-party cookies on Google Chrome from some time in 2022 or 2023 onwards).

5. **The tech giants don't take content moderation of the threat of regulation and fines remotely seriously**. If you record a video of a child doing something cooky on a sunny beach and upload it to a social platform and choose to include a snippet of The Beatles' *Sunny Afternoon* as the soundtrack, your clip will be downloaded immediately from said platform. You'll be sent a snotty message which might see you temporarily or permanently banned from using the platform. Like the fictional Office of Scientific Intelligence from the 1970s series *The Six Million Dollar Man* and *The Bionic Woman*, Big Tech clearly "has the technology" – and the people – to monitor and remove content it deems inappropriate. In the case of the *Sunny Afternoon* video, it is content that could see a platform lose money for breach of copyright from the music rights owners, Sony/ATV.

In 2017, the 14-year-old British teenager Molly Russell killed herself after looking at graphic images of self-harm and suicide on Facebook's photo-sharing app, Instagram. In the understandable outcry over Molly's death and the laudable campaigning started and still ongoing by her father, Facebook wheeled out its big guns to reassure the world it took the issue seriously. I can still recall watching interviews with Facebook executives Steve Hatch and the former Deputy Prime Minister Nick Clegg – the Vice President (VP) of Global Affairs, no less – about the tragedy and the company's response to it. As they spoke and reassured their interviewers – who were asking them very smart questions – they both claimed there was by then "virtually no" self-harm content findable on Instagram. On both occasions, I performed a simple search using the term "self-harm". This brought back a torrent of images I can't unsee and led to my decision to withdraw from the platform. Yet had *Sunny Afternoon* being playing underneath the videos, well, I can't imagine I'd have found anything.

Lastly, Big Tech isn't remotely intimidated by the ability than national and transnational government bodies, including the EU, have to fine them. Big Tech's pockets are so deep that they can readily absorb fines of tens or hundreds of millions or even billions of pounds, euros, or dollars. Indeed, only Big Tech can withstand and absorb the threat and the reality of such fines almost without blinking. Facebook serves advertising to almost half the planet, and Alphabet isn't far behind.

WHERE DO WE GO FROM HERE?

A couple of dozen pages in and – perhaps contrary to your expectations on buying this book – we appear to be in the middle of a dystopian nightmare. That wasn't what the blurb promised. This is a book about asking smarter questions, but in an age of demagoguery, shouting not listening, and Big Tech platforms apparently engineered to make the worst of an already very bad job, how can asking smarter questions even begin to patch up this world of fractured discourse? (ASIDE: That's a good question, Sam.) Where's all that fun stuff gone – about Chinese exams and Pac-Man being chased by ghosts that go through walls? I suggest we turn to a modern take on Stoic philosophy to set us back on track.

I've already listed the timely demise of Trump – at least for now – as one of the enduring positives coming out of the pandemic. I had two others. One was a regular, fortnightly walk on the Sussex Downs with my friend Tim, even in the depths of the deepest lockdowns. We talked and drank coffee and ate almond croissants, rambling and chatting all at the same time. We've walked every style and byway of paths in and around Lewes, and we now know the sheep on first-name terms.

The other was making regular time for more and more varied reading, and for more than a year, I was part of a vibrant business book club, run over Zoom (how else?). Towards the fag end of the grimmest three months I can recall – lockdown 3.0, January to March 2021 – we read Ryan Holiday's *Ego Is The Enemy*. I could tell from the title alone that it wouldn't be like many other business books – particularly autobiographies (which I usually find pompous and tedious in equal measure), or "Netflix: My Role In Its Success"-type books. From the title of Holiday's book and the cover boasting the bust of a Roman noble whose head had been knocked off, this was clearly going to be different. But I wasn't prepared for this latter-day Marcus Aurelius, a man who was born when I was in the second year of university, has already been the marketing director of American Apparel, and writes such brilliant, engaging, and life-altering books.

Ego Is The Enemy is infused with Stoic thinking – ancient Stoic thinking, from Marcus Aurelius, Seneca, Epictetus. Authors whom – as a classicist through school and university – I'd read very little of, not least because I'm much more of a Hellenist than a Romanist. But the way Holiday brings this much misunderstood philosophy to life – in *Ego Is The Enemy* and particularly in *The Daily Stoic*; one quote a day from one of Holiday's philosopher heroes, applied to the modern knowledge economy and business environment – is transformational.

There's a lot more to Stoicism than I could hope to cover or do justice to here – and in any case, that's Ryan's job and he does it brilliantly. It's also almost nothing to do with bearing up, having a stiff upper lip, and other elements of the caricatures of Stoicism that have been prevalent since ancient times onwards. But it's everything about mindset[9] and accepting that there are many things you can't control in the world around you – in your close, personal, and business relationships; in your community and country; in society and the world – but what you can control is your reaction to them. Faced with the toxic sludge and the tsunami of shouty illogic and bile-rich irrationality in politics, business, and public life, you could feel depressed. Or you could use your own wit and experience and creativity to navigate your here and now and respond with more perspective and distance. That demands asking smarter questions, and it most definitely demands better listening.

OPPOSITES ATTRACT

What do you do when someone sends you a link to a video or a blog that they've liked and suggests you watch or read it? If you're like me, you bookmark it in a growing list of "must watch" or "read when I get time" folders and then feel oppressed a year later when you find those folders have 30 bookmarks in them and you haven't watched or read any of them. Or, as happened to me recently, you sit down in earnest to plan your next book and are hugely grateful to whichever member of your circle sent you all these links and plough through them with glee. Initial glee which can quickly flip to boredom and gloom, as none of them seem to offer the key to unlock what you thought it might. And then you hit gold.

Julia Dhar's TED Salon: DWEN talk is called "How to have constructive conversations". It sounded promising when I first stumbled across it and – bonus! – it's only 10'31" long. I watched it slack-jawed. Then I watched it again, taking notes. And then I watched it a third time, just to make sure my slacked-jawédness and scribbled notes were justified. They were.

Dhar is a three-time school debating champion, well versed in the *ars rhetorica*. Her schtick is all about having constructive conversations; her subtitle – and subtext – is all about having such dialogue "when it feels like the divide is unbridgeable". In her scant ten minutes, Dhar tells us about her father, who toured the U.S. with a camera in 2016 – in the pre- and peri-Trump times. It's clear that she and her father are not supporters of the man who went on to become the 45th U.S. President. But what he wanted to do was find a way to find out why otherwise rational, wise, good people should be attracted to a man so divisive and bigoted and unprepared to brook dissent or differences of opinion. It truly was a case of a bleeding heart liberal throwing himself into the lion's den.

Dhar's father is a gentle, non-confrontational soul, but it's clear he's no mouse. As he started every conversation for which he had the aspiration to be constructive, he said of this interlocutor's point of view: "I never really thought about it exactly that way before. What can you share that would help me see what you see?" The impact, she reveals was galvanic. Her father got to understand why it was they thought what they thought. But more than that, they came to understand why it was he disagreed with what they thought, and both parties ceded ground and moderated their views. The results weren't a homogenous mush of bland nothingness. There wasn't universal agreement or switching of sides. But there was understanding, the understanding that can only come from a constructive conversation, driven by a smart set up and an even smarter question.

As I've explored above, the twenty teens has been a period of very few and very poor questions, dogmatic shouting, and a failure to listen. Dhar's pa's experiment acknowledges that, accepts it's not his role to change that, and controls what he can: his emotions and his reaction to the situation rather than the situation itself. How very Stoic. Ryan Holiday would be proud.

Dhar draws out three principles from the experiment.

1. **At least one party in a heated debate needs to be willing to choose curiosity over clash** if you're looking for a constructive conversation and understand the other party's point of view. This is the approach that was taken consistently by the EU's Chief Negotiator with the U.K. over Brexit, Michel Barnier, though not – always – his U.K. opposite number, David Frost.

2. As in improvisational theatre and comedy, if you want to have a constructive conversation, you need to **treat a discussion like a climbing wall, not a cage fight**. This means looking for handholds to grab on to and pull yourself up, not no-holds-barred Greco-Roman wrestling with just verbal eye gouges and toe breaking prohibited.

3. **The discussion needs to be anchored in purpose**, the purpose of mutual understanding, if not agreement. This invites people to inhabit a future possibility. It's like virtual time travel. By removing tension, it takes us to a future possibility here and now.

So this is one of our first, smarter questions, one of the best questions in the world that we'll come back to in the final chapter. Try it out in a hostile corporate meeting. Try it out when a teenager is stewing in fury at an apparent sleight or clipping of wings or liberty at the dinner table. Try it out at a post-COVID family reunion when it turns out that your maiden aunts – think Marge Simpson's sisters, Patricia Maleficent and Selma Bouvier – are rabid anti-vaxxers and you're not:

> *I never really thought about it exactly that way before.*
> *What can you share that would help me see what you see?*

IT'S NOT JUST ABOUT SAVING THE WORLD; IT'S MUCH MORE IMPORTANT THAN THAT

During lockdown 1.0, I attended a webinar run by the *Financial Times* and the consultancy McKinsey. Together, these organisations run an annual business book of the year competition. The webinar was hosted by Andrew Hill, the pink newspaper's management editor. He had an august panel of the great and the good in business writing and publishing, featuring well-known writers, editors, and publishers. Towards the end of the webinar, Hill asked his panel to travel a year forward in time and consider what topics they'd be looking to see covered in business books published in 2021. More interesting was his smarter, second question: what topics would they not want to see? What issues had received quite enough exposure, thanks very much?

On the plus side, there was a lot of talk about "the new normal", "hybrid working", "agile working", and "leadership in post-office cultures". Not bad for May 2020, barely six weeks into the pandemic. Some aspects of some of those have become clichéd and outdated since the webinar, but remember, this was a time at which it was still perfectly acceptable for news articles and corporate blogs to use the word "unprecedented". How quickly that changed.

When it came to topics on which we needed no more books, the panel was of one mind and one voice. The most over-discussed, over-mediated topic on which no more ink should be spilled was purpose. For much of the past ten years, many corporations have spent a vast amount of time navel-gazing and a vast amount of money on consultants gazing at their navels with them on the *why* of business in general and their business in particular. A whole purpose industry has sprung up, helping companies and brands to find and articulate the reasons why they do what they do beyond the functional outcome or consequence of making money and delivering a return on investment. In the unanimous and strongly held view of every member of the *FT*-McKinsey panel, we'd had enough time spent, money invested, and ink spilt on purpose.

At first I found this troubling. With my second book *How To Be Insightful* just published, I was beginning to work on ideas for a third in my trilogy on using data smarter. In helping companies to make smarter use of data, I often work with them to develop a clearer articulation of their purpose. My consultancy, Insight Agents, had just finished a very successful project with the global logistics business Crown Worldwide, and we'd helped them land on a powerful and authentic purpose statement: "Making it simpler to live, work, and do business anywhere in the world". A humble set of words which, over the following year, the company embedded within its operations and went to win armfuls of industry awards.

This wasn't the first successful purpose project I'd been involved in and it wouldn't be the last. I'd surveyed the business books on purpose and thought I'd found a niche – a practical, actionable how-to guide on creating and landing purpose within a business. Many of the other books in the space are light on practicalities, and it's become my trademark to write practical business books. The other challenge is that many in the purpose business have got carried away by the "doing good" side of purpose – about the environmental, social, and government (ESG) impact they can have – while forgetting that the principal consequence of a well-run business is cash. Cash for investors. Cash for shareholders. Cash for employees. And cash for economies in the form of income and corporation taxes – at least if you're not part of the Big Tech cartel.

Hell, I even had a title in my working notes for this book, poking one in the eye of the woke-washing purpose mongers: "It's not about saving the world: It's much more important than that". I wanted to set out a roadmap and a manifesto for purpose that would help others succeed as Crown had, that put ESG in its proper place in the hierarchy of corporate needs. And here was Andrew Hill and his esteemed panel, raining on my parade. So, I shelved the purpose book, kept it as a consultancy offer, and also kept the title in my quiver as a guiding principle for the next book.

It was some months later that my client Carin du Toit gave me the clarity to see I could more meaningfully conclude my "using data smarter" trilogy of books with this book. When I realised that I should focus on how asking smarter questions can help us to achieve that goal, I started to set out the situations in life when asking smarter questions can be helpful. I knew that I'd want to cover the context of our personal and professional lives in the 2020s – the tremors and aftershocks of Brexit, Trump, and COVID; the divisions between us and them, in-groups and out-groups, so successfully and toxically amplified by Big Tech's amoral digital and social media cash machines. But doing no more than asking smarter questions to change all that is a vain aspiration – and as the title of the book on purpose I never wrote said, it's not about changing the world. It's much more important than that.

So, let's start our journey to asking smarter questions by addressing two, erm, questions. First, a *why?* question and then a *when?*. The *why?* question is *What's the purpose of asking questions?* – see, Mr Hill, you can't shake purpose out of me that easily. And the *when?* question is *When might it be helpful to ask smarter questions?* These sections will be short and punchy, more like lists than a narrative, and for each answer to the overarching *why?* questions, I'll give a sample question by way of illustration. At this stage, we don't need more than that. We'll cover the essential qualities of both good and bad questions in later chapters.

For now, then, we'll focus on the *why*s and *when*s of asking smarter questions, illustrated with examples. Some of these might be familiar and trigger further questions in your mind. Most of them will feature again, in the theme and topic chapters in the book and in the exercises designed to help you develop and ask smarter questions. I've listed them like this at the end of this chapter to trigger your subconscious mind to start thinking how you use questions currently and how you might ask even smarter questions.

WHAT'S THE PURPOSE OF ASKING QUESTIONS?

To understand others – their points of view, opinions, and motivations for action.

Why have you stopped wearing a mask in enclosed public spaces?

To make sense of the world.

Is it nobler in the mind to suffer the slings and arrows of outrageous fortune or take arms against a sea of troubles and, by opposing, end them?

To understand our place in the world.

Why are we here? What's life all about? Is God really real, or is there some doubt?

To seek and obtain clarification.

I only called you 15 minutes ago. How did you get here so quickly, Mr Wolf?

Because we're nosy.

Why did Epiphanie and John stay in the same hotel during that conference in Venice?

To satisfy our curiosity.

Who was that who came to visit Stefan after midnight? (Chapter 4 is all about the power and role of curiosity.)

To challenge something you don't think is right.

Would you mind wearing a mask while you work inside my house?

To reveal and make sense of causal relationships.

Did A cause B, B cause A, or were both A and B a result of a hidden third cause C?

To determine whether there are patterns in the data the support or reject our hypotheses.

Has the vaccination programme successfully severed the link between infection, severe illness, and death?

To gain or share perspective.

What are the essential qualities of a ghost and do the ghosts in your version of Pac-Man exhibit these qualities?

To understand what others think about a topic or issue.

I voted Leave, wear a Make America Great Again baseball cap, and will never have a COVID jab – how about you?

To clarify what we think about a topic or issue.

Should I trust a social media platform company with my personal data? After all, they do very generously provide me with free access to their services.

To gather specific information.

Can you tell me where you were and what you were doing between the 9.45pm and 10.15pm last Thursday evening?

To build on the specific information you've obtained and start to set it in context.

Can you describe what the atmosphere was like in the Dog and Duck around ten o'clock last Thursday evening? Anything strike you as unusual?

To piece together a story and test its coherence.

Was that the only thing you did to Mr Bacon – nudge his arm and spill a few drops of his pint? Nothing else before he pulled a baseball bat from his bag and started hitting you over the head with it?

To reveal agendas that could otherwise remain hidden.

Was there any other reason you went to the pub apart from having a drink?

To get beneath the surface.

How are you, really? (The "really" is what's essential here.)

To understand the root cause of an issue or event.

Why? Why? Why? Why? Why? (We'll come back to root cause analysis, the Five "Whys"? and the power – and limitations – of "Why?" as a question in Chapters 3, 4, and 5.)

To surface and articulate genuine insights into the lives of those we're looking to influence.

What it's really like to be a general practitioner working in today's National Health Service?

To surface and articulate genuine insights into the lives of those we're looking to help.

Can you describe what your life is like today compared to the time before you were diagnosed with heart disease?

To demonstrate empathy.

Can you tell about what it's like to work with teenagers who've been excluded from school?

To demonstrate antipathy.

How can you be so stupid?

To assert control in a conversation.

Leaving the sudden appearance of the unidentified flying object (UFO) on one side for the moment, can we focus on what it was you said to Mr Bacon after you'd spilled his pint?

To cede control in a conversation.

What do you think is most important about the incident?

When we don't know but we need to know.

Well, what happened here then?

To help inform our decision-making.

What's the range of this model on a full charge, and how much does that cost compared with a tank of petrol?

To challenge our assumptions.

Will it really make a difference to my grandchildren's futures if I don't fly to that meeting in Jakarta?

To choose between options.

To be or not to be? THAT is the question.

To discover options we never even knew were possible.

You mean it doesn't have to be boom or bust and there really is a middle way? Can you tell me more, Mr Brown?

To confirm our biases and justify a decision.

How many polar bears lives am I saving by not flying to Jakarta for that conference?

To take a brief.

What do you want to achieve, by when, and with what outcome?

To start a conversation with a stranger.

How do you spend your time? (This is the mentalist, illusionist, and author Derren Brown's favourite question. So much better than What do you do?)

To start a conversation with a friend.

How have you been spending your time since I saw you last?

To understand someone's passions.

What lights you up?

To avoid making mistakes.

How do I share my screen so you can see my slides but not my email?

To minimise trouble.

What can I do to make you feel less angry that I've turned up at our daughter's wedding?

To avoid guessing or making assumptions, projecting what we imagine the answer might be.

I imagine it must be difficult getting around the house after suddenly losing your sight. But why don't you explain what it's like for you?

To learn from history or experience.

How did people stop the transmission of Spanish flu in 1918? Although the world is very different today, is there anything our ancestors did that we should do today? (See *The Premonition* by Michael "Moneyball" Lewis)

To flush out useful information that you suspect someone else is holding onto.

Just one more thing … is there anything that I haven't asked you that I should have asked you? (There's a lot more on this, the Columbo Question, in Chapters 8 and 9)

WHEN MIGHT IT BE HELPFUL TO ASK SMARTER QUESTIONS?

When meeting someone new for the first time.

When meeting someone you know very well for the nth time.

On a date.

In an interview – for a job, for a university, for a promotion.

In an interview for a blog or vlog, podcast, news or features article, or as part of a book.

During a negotiation of any sort, particularly one in which there is information asymmetry, specifically when you know less than the party with whom you are negotiating.

When comparing the offers made by different suppliers tendering for your business.

When assessing whether a bid for funding deserves it, has the potential to generate meaningful return on investment, will have impact.

When taking a brief from a client or prospect, colleague or collaborator.

When building/shaping/conducting market research.

When looking to make a breakthrough discovery in academic research.

When seeking to unearth the truly relevant data that can support and substantiate a story, making it more powerful and purposeful (see how in *Narrative by Numbers*).

When seeking genuine insight – a profound and useful understanding of a story, issue, topic, or thing (see how in *How To Be Insightful*).

When you're looking to develop a genuine innovation, from social policies to products, from services to drug design.

When you want to disrupt an old, established market that has always played by the same rules.

When trying to determine what actually happened – in a personal or industrial accident, after a crime, or in the wake of a political calamity.

When buying something – anything – particularly a big-ticket item such as a property or a vehicle.

When you don't know the answer – and you accept that you don't know it – and you realise that you have an opportunity to learn from others.

When you think you've hit a dead end and explored all possible avenues of discovery.

When "the dogs bark" and suggest something there's something fishy going on.

When "the dogs don't bark" and everything seems normal and in its proper place. (Angela Gallop, the forensic scientist of her generation, used this notion in the title of her 2019 book, *When the Dogs Don't Bark: A Forensic Scientist's Search for the Truth*. There's an interview with Angela in *How To Be Insightful*.)

When you're looking to find the real or authentic culture that you're visiting.

When negotiating red tape – for instance, understanding the latest, ever-changing regulations for travelling under COVID restrictions.

When your curiosity is piqued.

SUMMING UP

I trust you read the more portentous passages of this chapter in James Earl-Jones's voice, part Darth Vader, part every thrilling movie trailer you've ever seen. I'm not naïve enough to suggest that a Stoic mind-set combined with the simple act of asking smarter questions will bring balance to the Force and eradicate the polarisation that inequality and austerity, Big Tech and COVID have wreaked on public discourse. But I do passionately believe that both of these strategies have an important and till now understated role to play in helping to foster more constructive conversations.

Before we turn to the power of "Why?" – as well as its Achilles' heel – to the critical importance of curiosity and open-mindedness in asking smarter questions, and to the essential qualities of both good and bad questions, we need to go on a journey through space and time. We need to travel back to a time way, way back many centuries ago, not long after the Athenian empire began.

QUESTIONS ABOUT QUESTIONS – INTERVIEW 1 OF 14

NAME	Venki Ramakrishnan
ORGANISATION	Cambridge University Laboratory of Molecular Biology
ROLE	Nobel Laureate

Venki Ramakrishnan is a pre-eminent structural biologist. Today, he runs the Ramakrishnan Lab at the Medical Research Council (MRC) Laboratory of Molecular Biology on Cambridge University's Biomedical Campus. Born in India in 1952, his illustrious research and academic career on both sides of the Atlantic was garlanded with the Nobel for Chemistry in 2009, shared with Thomas Steitz and Ada Yonath. He was knighted in 2012 for services to molecular biology. Venki served as the 62nd President of the Royal Society from 2015 to 2020. As well as leading the MRC lab in his name at Cambridge, he also works in venture capital in the field of molecular biology. We spoke about the importance of asking smarter questions in both scientific enquiry and VC:

> *Questions play a critical role in science. They determine what you actually go after, what the problem is you're looking to solve. And once you've established that, you use questions to work out how you go about it. There's a whole series of choices to make, each phrased as a question, building up into a question tree. But the most fundamental question is: what do we really want to know?*

For Ramakrishnan, a truly smart question is one that is interesting enough not to have an obvious answer, but not so remote or infeasible that you can't think of how you might make use of it. "There's a delicate balance to be struck", he notes, "between research questions that are trivial, merely incremental, and so boring on the one hand, and questions that are beyond our reach right now as science isn't quite ready for them on the other. The best discoveries are just over the horizon. That's the best place to attack".

In the early 2010s I worked for one of the U.K.'s most successful ever "madmen", Michael Greenlees. The godfather of modern British advertising, Mike was one of the founders of the 1980s and 1990s powerhouse agency, Gold Greenlees Trott. He is of one mind with Venki when it comes to innovation in consultancy services, all served up with an ice hockey analogy: "Pitch them not where you know the puck will land, but where you anticipate it's going to land in 18 to 24 months' time."

The ability to keep an open mind – and ask open questions – is a motif and best practice recommendation that will recur time and again in this book. Shunryu Suzuki, the monk perhaps most responsible for introducing Zen Buddhism to the West – particularly the U.S. – via his teachings and best-selling book *Zen Mind, Beginner's Mind*, observed: "In the West, they only respect experts. But the expert mind is the closed mind". This is the very opposite of the expert approach espoused by both Mike and Venki.

Someone who asks smart questions is, in Ramakrishnan's eyes, open and either able or courageous enough to leave their comfort zone. Most people will ask the next obvious question, building on the previous discovery. But harder questions are not *What's next?* but *What do I actually want to know?* That could be several steps on from where we are today, and the path to that point in the future isn't necessarily clear. Something that isn't clear makes you feel, by its very nature, uncomfortable, like you're plunging into the unknown. As the journalist Dean Nelson says in *Talk to Me*, his book on asking better questions and getting better answers from interviews: "Asking obvious questions is like using clichés in your writing ... never use the first simile or metaphor that comes to mind" (p.115).

To get out of the rut of just asking the next, obvious question – in fundamental science and in life more broadly – Venki recommends constant self-monitoring and self-surveillance. "We're lucky if we ask a handful of really important questions in our lifetime," he observes. In science, a breakthrough leads to a number of clear next steps for which we don't need specific, smart questions. In that phase, researchers are effectively capitalising on the breakthrough. Then, there's a plateau or impasse where the global community is focused on the area in question and publishes data that corroborates the breakthrough or shows some interesting nuances, but nothing new. That's the point at which we need to step back and ask what the next really big thing we want to learn is.

Ramakrishnan was one of three scientists to win the Nobel Prize for Chemistry in 2009. Nobel is a big deal; the biggest of big deals, candidly. From the outside, it seems like it would only be awarded to those who can ask (and answer) the smartest of questions. When we spoke, I was interested to know whether there's anything different about how you ask (and answer) questions that satisfy the Nobel Committee:

> To be honest, the Nobel is a by-product, not an aim; think of it like that. If you can get into the discipline of asking yourself really important questions such as 'What is it that I really want to understand? What is my field waiting for?' and successfully pursue that, then, Nobel or not, you'll have done something really significant. But as I say, the Nobel is a very occasional by-product – not to mention a very great honour.

With another hat, Venki advises venture capital funds on which promising businesses in his field deserve investment. Some of the considerations he uses for framing smart questions for academic enquiry are echoed in VC:

> You want to support companies that are doing something to greatly advance an area and not be one of hundreds of players all doing the same thing. So smart money – guided by smart questions – follows truly original ideas or approaches that have the potential to carve out a niche thanks to breakthroughs in intellectual property. That's just like academia.

What differs in the consideration mindset and questioning approach in VC is that you have to take account of the market and assess whether there is, indeed, a market for the breakthrough under development. There also needs to be a way for the products the science delivers to stand out and differentiate themselves from competitors or other, less effective answers to the same question:

> This just doesn't apply to academia. Academics don't worry about a market. A significant academic breakthrough will be valued for its own sake, for its ability to create a new field or significantly develop an existing one. A field is a market for academics. Pure research is a reward in itself. Also, academic and VC timelines vary wildly. At the short end, they're similar; at the long end, they're completely different. Return on investment means very different things to a biotech grant-making body and a biotech VC fund.

In the next chapter, titled "What did the bloody Greeks ever do for us?", we'll consider the legacy of the Classical period Greek philosophers – Plato, Aristotle, and Plato's teacher and inspiration, Socrates. As we'll explore in detail there and beyond, the Socratic method starts from a position of ignorance and asks questions in order to build up knowledge. "All I know is that I know nothing", Socrates is said to have said – many times over. He believed that accepting ignorance and starting from there was fundamental to acquiring wisdom. And it's a thought that occurs in the Eastern as well as Western philosophical traditions. Laozi, the reputed author of the *Tao Te Ching* is said to have said: "The wise man knows he doesn't know. The fool doesn't know he doesn't know".

Starting from that position of ignorance, the Socratic method progressively tests and rejects hypotheses when arguments show that hypotheses lead to contradictions. I was interested to know if this approach – and one of its scientific great-grandchildren, Popperian null hypothesis significance testing – reflects Venki's own approach to asking smarter questions in fundamental science in general, molecular biology in particular:

> It can do, but I don't like to be dogmatic about how science works. Hypothesis testing – test and prove or disprove – is how philosophers view science in theory. But philosophers don't really know much about how to do science in practice. Real science sometimes works that way, but sometimes it follows instincts or hunches – we spot something interesting in an unexpected place, and we'll do experiments as explorations. Science is multi-faceted, and you can't reduce it all to the Socratic style of thinking.

When it comes to creating questions for a subject matter area where not much is known, Ramakrishnan encourages researchers to embrace the explorer's mindset. Three questions should guide exploratory research:

1.   Why am I exploring in this area?
2.   What do I hope – expect – to find? What is the range of my expectations?
3.   If I find something interesting and it doesn't fit into a preconceived, well-established framework, how would I recognise it as interesting?

This is very definitely non-Socratic and takes most scientists well beyond their comfort zone – as we've already heard. It is more nebulous, uncomfortable, and that's ultimately why it's so appealing and productive. Although Western education can boast proud achievements in terms of near-universal literacy and currently record rates of graduation as a proportion of the population, Venki doesn't believe that it's lived up to the flying start it got off too in Classical Athens:

> It's much too narrow and uniform with far too much emphasis on rote learning and regurgitation of facts. In Britain in particular, the curriculum is much narrower than elsewhere. A-levels and even the Cambridge tripos demand cramming and learning to go through a restrictive system instead of a more

discursive, open-ended approach. Narrow training means those trained only ask narrow questions from a mental framework that's been channelled down a narrow path. Those who benefit from a broader training are much more likely to spot relationships between areas that are normally thought of as disconnected. Real-life is much more open-ended than Western – particularly British – education believes it to be. This needs to change.

A bad question for Ramakrishnan is one where, once you discover the answer, it hasn't taught us anything new:

I always challenge my students and postdocs to consider whether, if the experiment they're proposing works, it will have taught us something new. If the answer to a question doesn't generate its own, new, interesting questions, then the original question can't have been that good.

Loaded questions are also verboten as they perpetuate biases rather than challenging those asking them to think about questions as answers. The direction of thought is implicit in a leading question and it's closed rather than open. "We should strive to preserve openness in our questioning beyond anything else, because, when you're open and ask open questions, you're alert to the unexpected, and the unexpected can be truly transformational."

VENKI RAMAKRISHNAN'S TOP TIPS FOR ASKING SMARTER QUESTIONS

1. Always ask yourself: What is it we really want to know?
2. Make sure your questions don't have obvious answers, but at the same time don't generate answers so remote or infeasible that you can't think of how you might make use of them.
3. Be prepared to follow instincts and hunches with your questions, as well as logical next steps.
4. Embrace the explorer's mindset and ask why you're exploring where you are, what you expect to find, and what you'll do if your discovery doesn't fit with the status quo.
5. If answers don't prompt more questions, the original question can't have been that interesting.

NOTES

1   Perhaps the best answer to an exam ever given is almost certainly apocryphal, too. In response to the question on a final year paper in philosophy, I have often heard it said that "someone" wrote simply: "This is" in response to the question "What is courage"? That someone in question is almost always someone in your year who you can't quite remember and everyone immediately lost touch with. Or a minor celebrity or politician for whom the revelation could be embarrassing. The sheer chutzpah, directness, and honesty is always said to have been rewarded with a first or an A. Similarly apocryphal are the following: "Why?" answered by "Why not?" or "Because …" and the exam with no questions, which asked "Here is the exam. Write your own questions. Write your own answers. Harder questions and better answers get more points." The latter is said to have been set by the American economist, Tyler Cowen.

2   This story is told in more detail in my previous book, *How To Be Insightful*, pp. 122–123 and footnotes on pp.144–145.

3   Between the wars, Kenneth went to an elite public (i.e. private) school, Winchester College. Although first and foremost a genuine classical scholar, as happy translating *Times* leaders into Homeric hexameters as the other way around, his passion was art. His drawing master was an inspiring-sounding man of many tales and reminiscences in my father's later years: Reginald "Dick" Gleadowe. Gleadowe taught Kenneth how to draw in perspective and much more besides, and regularly took him and other enthusiastic proto-artists to study typography with Eric Gill at his studio in Ditchling, East Sussex. Gill and his collaborator, Edward Johnston, created some of the most timeless and elegant typefaces, almost always serif-free, including Gill Sans, Johnston (the London Underground typeface), and Joanna. This and my previous books with Routledge are set in Joanna as a line back in time to Gleadowe, Gill, and Johnston via Kenneth. Gleadowe went on to become a Slade Professor of Fine Art at Oxford, though he died before Kenneth returned there in the 1950s.

4   It must be true. *The Guardian* garlanded it with this gong more than 20 years ago. See https://www.theguardian.com/film/2000/nov/01/1

5   After Cummings's inevitable sacking as Johnson's special advisor during the upswing of the second wave of COVID in Autumn 2020, the poacher turned poacher and only latterly gamekeeper regularly attempted to undermine his former boss. In one of his regular Twitter avalanches, he revealed that Johnson has such contempt for the U.K. electorate that he openly refers to the right-wing broadsheet *The Daily Telegraph* as "my real boss". There's more here https://www.bbc.co.uk/news/uk-politics-57854811

6   The full interview between Trump and Jonathan Swan on AXIOS HBO is here: https://www.youtube.com/watch?v=yJIhxKFH9gI

7 Berners-Lee published his paper "Information Management: A Proposal" in March 1989. This is generally agreed to be the moment at which the World Wide Web was born. The original article in full is here: https://www.w3.org/History/1989/proposal.html

8 http://adcontrarian.blogspot.com

9 Another thing I did during lockdown was to become part of an entrepreneur accelerator, run by one of U.K.'s leading retail banks. Some of the webinars run by the entrepreneur accelerator managers were a bit shallow and didn't stand up to detailed scrutiny. What participation in the scheme DID do was provide regular coaching and the mental headspace to work on rather than in the business. And the one area where they knew of what they spoke was mindset. Although it was never called out as Stoicism, the tenets of our regular "Mindset Matters" sessions could have been penned by Marcus Aurelius. I found this to be much more interesting than the faith-based revenue models espoused by some of my fellow entrepreneurs.

2

WHAT DID THE BLOODY GREEKS EVER DO FOR US?

Abstract

The Classics are coming back into fashion, and when it comes to asking smarter questions in the modern knowledge economy, there are few better places to start looking for inspiration than fifth-century BCE Athens. The direct and interconnected lineage of the Socrates, Plato, and Aristotle set the Western tradition of philosophy, science, and enquiry more generally in a direction that has endured for almost 2,500 years. And although a lot of the rough edges have been knocked off along the way – not least by Aristotle in his rejection or correction of some of the principles his teacher Plato held dear – we owe a serious debt to many of the principles they established.

First among these is Socrates's repeated insistence of his ignorance and the fact that the only thing he knew was that he knew nothing. This, the Socratic Paradox, is the perfect starting point for anyone looking to build understanding because it parks all assumptions and prejudices at the door. In so doing, this naïve and open approach liberates us to ask more and better questions rather than jumping to conclusions.

DOI: 10.4324/9781003218470-2

THE LIFE OF STAVROS?

Picture the scene in a parallel universe. Rather than poking fun at how easy it was for cult leaders to gain a following at the time of Jesus under the Roman Empire, the Monty Python team responsible for *The Life of Brian* had chosen instead to lampoon conditions under the Athenian Empire, setting their controversial film a few hundred years before. Huddled together in a secret villa on the island of Naxos, a group of grumpy revolutionaries – the People's Front of Naxos (PFN), perhaps – are complaining about how hard and unfair life is under the Athenians, "taking all our silver ... cutting down our trees". To whip the meeting into a frenzy and inspire action against their imperialist overlords, Yannis, the leader of the PFN asks: "What have the bloody Athenians ever done for us?"

"Democracy?" offers a strangled voice from the gloom.

"Oh, yes, democracy – obviously democracy!"

"Architecture?"

"He's got a point there, Yannis. Where would we be without beautifully-designed temples?"

Others pipe up from around the room. "The alarm clock"/"Trial by jury"/"History"/"Random allocation of citizens to public office"/"Tragedy, comedy – well, the theatre!"/"The lighthouse":

> *Yes, yes, yes, but apart from democracy, architecture, the alarm clock, trial by jury, history, random allocation of citizens to public office, tragedy, comedy – theatre – and the lighthouse ... Apart from that, what have the bloody Athenians ever done for us?*

Silence. A smug self-satisfaction radiates from Yannis in his role as a self-appointed leader of the PFN. He's confident that he's won the argument and galvanised revolutionary action against the occupying Athenians. He's just about to move on to talk about armed insurrection against their parasitic imperial overlords and the dreaded Athenian tax collectors who come to exact their "tribute" each year, when a timid voice pipes up from the very darkest corner of a very dark room. We can just make out the silhouette of Stavros, the film's timid but emerging hero, sitting in on his first meeting of the PFN with the hope of catching the eye of Diotima, a young woman he fancies.

"Erm, phi-philosophy?" he stammers.

Welcome, in this parallel universe, to *The Life of Stavros*.

THE WANING AND WAXING OF THE CLASSICS

There's a lot of misty-eyed romance about classical Athens. In the minds of those who've studied its culture and civilisation directly. In the minds of those who appreciate the way that its literary, philosophical, and even scientific outputs sent ripples – more like shockwaves – through the following 2,500 years, creating the firm foundations of The Western Tradition. Many of the maxims and principles of fair and civilised society have their roots in the practices and writings of some of the finest and clearest thinkers that not only European antiquity but the world has ever produced.

For generations, Latin and Greek – language and literature, history and architecture – were the dominant and in some cases the only courses offered by the earliest, major universities. And even when broader, scientific disciplines developed, students were required to have studied Classics until the end of their school days in order to get onto other courses. The thought of a modern university demanding advanced level Latin and/or Greek as a prerequisite for studying medicine seems fanciful today, but that was very much the case well into the twentieth century in Britain and elsewhere.

Don't get me wrong, I'm not seeking to undermine or underestimate the enduring importance of ancient Greece and Rome. I studied these cultures and civilisations to master's level myself,[1] and as you'll find in this book – and the two other books in this trilogy if you know them – I often draw on the impact and legacy of both to develop principles that enable us to make smarter use of data, in making our questions smarter, in how we surface and articulate insights, and in the stories we tell. We can still unquestionably learn a huge amount from the ancients, and I'm delighted that Classics is currently undergoing a renaissance in primary, secondary, and tertiary education.

In my last year at school in 1985, I was one of just 400 in the country who sat for Greek A-level out of almost 700,000 candidates (see Smithers,

2014). There was a focus on more practical and vocational education in Britain after the end of the Second World War, and, as a result, Classics was increasingly seen as outdated and old school. Science – etymologically simply "knowledge" from *scientia* in Latin – was taking over, from chemistry, physics, and biology, to mathematics, economics, and statistics, and on to sociology, psychology, and neuroscience. With EU membership and movement across the continent freeing up for work and play – remember that? – modern languages were more popular and more useful. Latin and Greek were derided as being "dead" languages, and decreased demand for the subjects from pupils, parents, and employers meant fewer teachers training to teach them.

The recent turnaround in the popularity of the Classics has, I think, three principal causes.

1. **New ways of teaching and learning**. The realisation by universities that you didn't need to have spent all of secondary school studying the languages in order to study the Classics at university. They now realise that students can either learn languages intensively in the first year of a degree course or read them in translation. The rise and rise of Classical civilisation courses in secondary school to General Certificate of Secondary Education (GCSE) and A-level has accelerated this reality.
2. **Faulty logic**. The timeless allure and ongoing influence of these cultures' literature, history, and philosophy on contemporary thought that had become hidden under the apparent inaccessibility of these "dead" languages, particularly Greek with its different alphabet.
3. **Modern media**. The appearance in mainstream culture (TV) of modern superstar classicists, including Mary Beard, Bettany Hughes, Michael Wood, as well as the retelling of ancient myths through modern prisms, from Natalie Haynes to Rick Riordan. Natalie Haynes is particularly important for her feminist retelling of stories from both the Homeric and the Theban epic cycles – the Trojan War on the one hand, the house of Oedipus on the other.[2]

Classics, you see, has had a problem. Almost all tragedy, comedy, epic poetry, and history were written by men for men. Greek and Roman societies were run by men for men. Women – even citizen women – had nowhere near the legal rights, protections, ability to own property or money as men. And the supposedly great democracy of Athens – the birthplace of the very concept – was only great if you were one of the estimated 40,000 citizen men. If you were a woman, non-citizen, or a slave – and slaves and non-citizens are thought to have outnumbered citizens by five to one or more – you were explicitly prohibited from being involved in politics, much of business, or public life. For non-citizens, there was no tradition of getting a formal education to advance yourself, and you lived a kind of a shadow, parallel life.

So, when we reflect on the great legacy – of literature, art, architecture, and particularly philosophy, as we're about to now – it's vital we remember this. This legacy comes largely from a small, highly entitled proportion of just one gender. That sliver of society had the time and luxury to be able to create such interesting thoughts and thinkers because it stole gold and silver from other, weaker city states and coerced others, as slaves, to do their dirty work. We should also reflect not only on who created the work but those for whom they created it and who consumed it: citizen men like themselves.

There's a huge amount that's relevant in the philosophy of fifth- and fourth-century BCE Athens that can set us on the right path to asking smarter questions in our modern 2020s world of fractured dialogue, exacerbated by the cess pit of social media platforms. There's a lot in the dialogues of Plato and treatises of Aristotle and the thoughts reported – by Plato – from the mind and mouth of Socrates. I think it does stand the test of time. But I'm also saying that we should seize the spirit and the ethos of Mary Beard and Natalie Haynes and others. By doing this, we can avoid being misty-eyed about the environment in which this work was created. Because those cultures were very far indeed from what we would consider today to be fair and equal and just.

GENERAL IGNORANCE

John Lloyd is one of the most influential comedy writers in British TV and radio history. His roll call of credits includes *Not the Nine O'Clock News, Blackadder, Spitting Image,* and *Quite Interesting (QI).* Indeed, *QI* is more than just a subversive TV quiz show. With 19 series and almost 300 episodes broadcast since 2003, *QI* is a consultancy, has been a club in Oxford, and remains a way of life for Lloyd. And he's been collecting and cataloguing obscure but *QI* facts – *arcana*; secrets and mysteries, the knowing of which makes life all the more fun – for most of his 70-plus years.

QI the game show has a final round called "General Ignorance", a parody of general knowledge quizzes. In this round, panellists attempt to answer questions that have obvious, widely accepted but incorrect answers without giving these wrong responses. Like the colour-naming Stroop test, this is remarkably difficult to achieve. The round has led to a series of spin-off publications, including at least three titled *The QI Book of General Ignorance*. Separately, in *The Museum of Curiosity* – a long-running BBC radio comedy talk show created and hosted by Lloyd – he styles himself as the Professor of Ignorance at Southampton Solent University, an institution from which he now holds an honorary degree, thanks in no small part to the spirit of intellectual enquiry he encourages from the quizmaster's chair. He was garlanded by Southampton Solent because he asks smarter questions.

Researchers on *QI* are known as "elves". A one-time elf, the Ukrainian-born journalist, Vitali Vitaliev, interviewed Lloyd in 2018 for *Engineering & Technology* magazine. He asked his former boss about his motivations for developing it. Lloyd replied:

> *In 1993, at the age of 42[3], I felt unhappy, powerless and ignorant – a kind of a midlife crisis perhaps. I realised with sudden clarity that, with all my education and experience, I didn't really know anything, like, say, how a tree actually grows. Having been in television for all those years, I had a fairly vague idea of how a TV camera works. That made me think about the power of ignorance – not the arrogant kind, which is just lack of information, but the Socratic 'Even the things I know about I do not know about'. In this respect, ignorance is more important than knowledge, because it drives creativity and encourages learning.*
>
> *I then thought that it would be nice to have a TV show where a bunch of middle-aged comedians would banter about little-known facts, and the audience would laugh and learn while laughing. A good name for such a show would be 'QI' which stands for 'quite interesting', but also, if reversed, for 'IQ', and it could aim to become a media version of the world's first non-boring encyclopaedia.[4]*

Lloyd's account of his midlife crisis of ignorance and his Damascene realisation that ignorance – and the wilful acceptance of ignorance as liberating and the foundation of curiosity and learning – is the first step on the journey to asking smarter questions.

HE CAME FROM GREECE; HE HAD A THIRST FOR KNOWLEDGE

For someone who never wrote anything down – at least nothing that survives from antiquity – we appear to know a remarkable amount about the mind and thoughts and life of fifth century Athenian philosopher, Socrates. Eschewing writing and preferring to talk and ask questions in his lifelong quest to understand the essential nature of the qualities that make people and societies great – truth, beauty, justice; those kinds of thing – we are indebted to his pupil Plato. Everything we know about Socrates comes through the reed pens of others, and almost all of his thoughts and words and deeds are mediated via Plato.

Plato was born in or near Athens in the early 420s BCE, a few years after the start of the era-defining Peloponnesian War with Sparta, which raged – on and off, with summer campaigning seasons and the winters taken off – until 404 BCE. Plato was a pupil of Socrates, but not in the sense that we would understand being a pupil. Socrates didn't run any kind of educational establishment – unlike Plato, who established perhaps the world's first higher education institute in the fourth century in the form of his Academy, where one of his (star) pupils was Aristotle. Plato learned on Socrates's philosophical battlefield, listening to – and doubtless engaging with – his master, as Socrates asked question after question of his interlocutors in his attempt to make sense of the world.

It is thought that, unlike the work of almost all other writers from antiquity, Plato's full body of work survives to the present day. And almost all of his 35 works are written in the form of a dialogue between Socrates and others, usually several others. In no sense should we consider Plato's writings to be verbatim or journalistic reports of actual dialogues with actual individuals, even if they read like that and are often named after one of those with whom Socrates argues and debates: Alcibiades, Meno,

Phaedo, and Timaeus. Doubtless the arguments expressed and techniques of argumentation deployed are a representation of how Socrates went about his days, in public and private spaces, at the gym, walking around Athens, at dinner (or drinking) parties – at symposia.

Plato grew up in a city that held regular festivals and performances of tragedy and comedy, two of the enduring forms of entertainment, if not invented, then certainly perfected by his fellow Athenians. His life overlapped with three of the greatest, the tragedians Sophocles and Euripides, and the jester-cum-satirist Aristophanes. Plato used dialogue to both capture Socrates' spirit of curiosity and enquiry and to bring his approach to philosophical discourse to life for a culture steeped in dramatic dialogue. What is clear from his consistent use of the same genre of philosophical debate is that he believed this form could inspire readers to do the same – to join in debate, use the techniques he was showcasing, and develop arguments of their own. The Socratic dialogues were designed to inform, entertain while informing, and instruct others. When he opened his Academy in the early fourth century BCE, he used his dialogues to recreate the Socratic experience for his students. As a by-product, they keep his inspiration and mentor very much alive. Few – if any – characters in literature say more than Socrates.

BLISSFUL IGNORANCE AND THE SOCRATIC ELENCHUS

Socrates' starting point for philosophical discovery is a technique that sits at the heart of *Asking Smarter Questions*. It's the position espoused by Shakespeare's fool, Touchstone, in Act V, Scene I of *As You Like It*: "The fool doth think he is wise, but the wise man/knows himself to be a fool". It's what inspired John Lloyd, apparently at a point in his life without direction or purpose, to create *QI*. And it's a way of looking at the world and harnessing curiosity that parks assumptions at the door and brings least baggage. It allows arguments to be built – piecemeal – from the ground up rather than deconstructed for their failings from the top-down. Ignorance, the open admission and acceptance of ignorance as the foundation stone for acquiring knowledge, is known as the Socratic paradox.

"I neither know nor think I know" Socrates says at the start of his trial defence in Plato's *Apology*. When asked who was the wisest of men, the priestess at the temple of Apollo at Delphi – the so-called Delphic oracle, where Greeks often went to seek guidance on answering their thorniest problems – said it was Socrates. The reason she gave was not his vast, accumulated wisdom. It was the simple fact that he accepted and embraced his ignorance. The most recent book by British creative advertising guru, Dave Trott, bears a very Socratic spirit – in title (*The Power of Ignorance*) and in content. In a typically pithy and trenchant line in the introduction, for instance, Trott asserts: "Ignorance, properly used with curiosity, allows us to find out things we didn't know" (2021, p.3).

Time and again in Plato's dialogues, Socrates shows how thinking you know something about a subject – even a little bit – can soon see you tied up in knots of contradiction. The Socratic method is known as the elenchus, defined by the newly published Cambridge Greek Lexicon as a "technique of argument for the purpose of disproof or refutation ... examination, investigation (of persons or things); questioning; test, examination, scrutiny, trial (as a means of determining the true nature of things); proof".[5] The elenchus goes like this:

- Socrates asks one of those he's talking to to give their definition of a concept he wants to know more about – truth, virtue, courage. Throughout the Socratic dialogues, Plato has Socrates attempt – using the elenchus – to define the essential nature of such abstract ideas.
- Bearing the initial definition or example in mind, Socrates offers a further characteristic or definition of the concept in question. He then gets his interlocutor to agree with that.
- "Hang on", says Socrates, "these positions are incompatible, and the second undermines the first. Both cannot be true. If we accept the second, we must reject the first, otherwise we're forced to believe contradictory thoughts, and cognitive dissonance[6] is uncomfortable."
- The first definition is rejected, along with other definitions coming from positions of apparent knowledge. This can lead to a sense of

aporía or despair that they're never going to get a definition that satisfies them.

- To get to a working definition that they find acceptable, Socrates and his interlocutors either give up in *aporía* or they start to build arguments from the ground up, seeing what's compatible and what isn't.

It's fair to say that the Socratic method isn't easy, and it also isn't always popular. As Elke Wiss, a contemporary practical philosopher who teaches the application of Socratic dialogue to organisations, says in her book *How to Know Everything*:

> Through this process Socrates demonstrated the other person's unknow-ingness ... and the painful realisation that they weren't as knowledgeable as they thought they were. Since this wasn't quite the outcome they had been expecting from their conversation with Socrates, he ended up rub-bing a lot of people up the wrong way. (p.169)
>
> Asking questions and making room for ... answers calls for courage and vulnerability ... It means abandoning a significant degree of control and letting things happen. (p. 105)

Despite his enduring influence via Plato – and Plato didn't write any dia-logues until after his teacher was convicted of "corrupting the young" and died having drained a cup of hemlock as his punishment – the period during which Socrates was most active in practicing the elenchus was febrile and unpredictable. Wartime Athens at the end of the fifth century BCE shared similarities with our own age of fractured discourse. The contemporary comedian and satirist Aristophanes and later the historian Thucydides used their respective literary forms to caricature and charac-terise the rise of demagogues. These include the xenophobic warmonger Kleon who bears more than a passing resemblance to former president Trump for his bluster, rabble-rousing, and routine deployment of "alter-native truths".

In such a toxic and politically charged atmosphere, it is not altogether surprising that Socrates' uncompromising philosophical approach ended up costing him his life. His canvas was not mediated as ours is by social media platforms and connectivity – comedies and gossip in the citizen assembly notwithstanding. But then, in a direct democracy of just 40,000 Athenian men, it didn't need to be. When Aristotle said in his *Politics* that "man is by his very nature a political animal" – a *zōon politikón* – he didn't mean we were all interested in the cut-and-thrust of party-political intrigue. He meant we thrive by living in a *pólis*, a city state. Because the number of citizen men in ancient Greek city states was so relatively small and manageable, democracy wasn't representative but rather direct.

THE RISE OF REASON AND THE POWER OF HUMILITY IN ASKING SMARTER QUESTIONS

More important than the conclusions about the essential nature of abstract concepts that Socrates did (and often didn't) manage to achieve by using the elenchus, what matters much more is the very real power of humility that his admission and celebration of ignorance offers in asking smarter questions. Indeed, this tenet is so fundamental that it underpins many of the approaches to philosophy, enquiry, science, curiosity, and learning that follow Socrates espousing it and Plato recording and repeating it. Of course, it turns up explicitly at various points across the dozens of dialogues; it turns up implicitly whenever Socrates deploys the elenchus.

Open-mindedness, parking prejudice, and steering clear of assumptions don't throw away previously acquired knowledge. By asking and answering questions in a smarter way, the "assume nothing, consider everything" mantra minimises the opportunity for Confirmation Bias to lead us to inevitable conclusions. That, in turn, encourages greater diversity in thinking. It accommodates more and multiple perspectives. And it widens the net of innovation. Paradoxically, starting from a blank page makes it more likely that that page will be filled with meaningful content. It is also (as we'll see in Chapter 5, "What makes a good question?") one of the foundational principles of the judgement-free approach to using language known as "clean language" (see, for instance, Sullivan & Rees 2008; 2019). Clean language was developed by the psychotherapist David Grove and is to this day much favoured in counselling, coaching, and leadership development.

By channelling our inner Socrates and accepting we don't know the answers when we start asking questions, we reap much more than we sow. Advantages this approach delivers include:

- **Respect from those we're working with**, because we avoid the obvious, simplistic, or hackneyed questions and answers – as Venki Ramakrishnan details in his interview in the previous chapter.
- **Greater engagement on all sides**, with no one operating on autopilot.
- **More time spent productively**; less time spent destructively going over the same old ground.
- **A genuine accommodation of what's come before** – what we know already – but without that dominating discussion. Existing knowledge matters hugely, but our capacity for change and genuine innovation is constricted if what we already know is allowed to dominate or dictate discussions about the future.
- **Balance between where we're coming from and where we're headed to**, navigating a safe course between the questioner's Scylla and Charybdis, the monster on the rocks and whirlpool of debate and discussion.

To consider the enduring impact of the "all I know is that I know nothing" approach to enquiry lived by Socrates, let's consider next the much more contemporary approach of Socratic selling.

TOWARDS INFORMATION SYMMETRY

Socrates was privileged to live a life of philosophical enquiry because he was born a free citizen man in fifth-century BCE Athens. Athens was prosperous for many reasons. It enjoyed an advantageous geographical location on the mainland but at the heart of the Greek world. It had nearby silver mines and good access to flat plains for crops and livestock in the rocky, often inhospitable terrain of the Aegean basin. After the collapse of the late Bronze Age civilisations of the Mycenaean era – the time of the quasi-mythical Trojan War – Athens grew and prospered relatively early, setting in place more advanced and more stable political structures than many other neighbouring city states.

During the Persian invasions of Greece in the 490s and 480s BCE, the *pólis* of Athens was nearly crushed, captured and sacked towards the end of the conflict, and suffered huge losses. But the city state had been smart and instrumental in uniting many of the individual city states into a Pan-hellenic force against the mighty Persians, particularly securing an alliance with Sparta, the military oligarchy whose warriors were legend. Athenian leaders asked: *How might we put together an alliance strong enough to resist our old enemy Persia?* After the Persians were finally defeated in 479 BCE, the Athenians found it straightforward to create an alliance called the Delian League – whose treasury was situated on the central Aegean island of Delos – as a lasting counterbalance to the enduring threat of Persian expansionism.

Always dominated and administered by the Athenians, the Delian League morphed progressively into an Athenian empire in all but name, and the Athenian general and political darling, Pericles, relocated the treasury to Athens in 454 BCE. The gold "tribute" extracted by the Athenians for membership enabled Athens to create the biggest navy ever known in Greece. Of course, it could protect Greece from Persia, but it could also be used to extort more and more tribute from the ever-growing roll call of member city states – as many as 330 at its peak. Individually, they didn't have the strength to resist demands for what was effectively protection money, a state-sponsored Mafia sting. It was also used to fund the building of, among other things, the Parthenon. The mighty temple of Athene Parthenos on the Acropolis came complete with a 12-metre tall chryselephantine (gold and ivory) statue of the city's eponymous goddess and protector. With some justification, critics said that Athens was "decking itself out like a harlot".

It was in this environment and culture that Socrates grew up and had the freedom to become a philosopher. Although it appears from references in Plato's dialogues that he took part in civic life – including serving as a hoplite (a wealthy, well-equipped infantryman) in the Athenian army and in various public offices and duties – for most of his life he lived semi-detached from "normal" society. Contemporary accounts suggest he lived an ascetic existence, not gorging on food or bingeing on wine, not interested in accumulating or holding onto wealth, relatively wealthy as he was. Yet it was the time and location of his birth that enabled him to spend his days asking questions.

That an ascetic, antisocial philosopher should be the inspiration for an approach to sales in the heart of modern capitalism might, therefore, come as something of a surprise. But it was Socrates's humility, gleeful acceptance of ignorance, and his "uncompromising belief in learning through questions" that encouraged Communispond, a progressive U.S. sales training business to develop Socratic Selling Skills, the name it gave to the discipline of customer-centred sales. The principles are summarised in a 2005 book of the same name written by Communispond's Kevin Daley.

Socrates "never assumed he knew what other people were thinking", observes Daley, "and he believed that asking questions of them was the best way to help them reach new understandings" (p.14). It is exactly this kind of lateral transposition of the whole breadth of techniques that underpin how to ask smarter questions, in many different disciplines, that has inspired me to write this book. And it's why I've spent so much of the year before starting out on my own journey to codify these principles, talking to people in many different roles whose success is predicated on their ability to ask smarter questions. You'll find the interviews at the end of each topic chapter.

"Socratic Selling is a discipline that uses active listening and effective questioning to discover customer needs so that the customer and the salesperson can work together to meet those needs", writes Daley. "If you want to master the discipline, you need to put your agenda aside and focus on the customer and her needs ... don't push ... don't lead the customer" (p.29). This approach and its inspiration are so unexpected and a million miles from the stereotype of pushy, "Always Be Closing" sales people featured in David Mamet's play and film *Glengarry Glen Ross*. With its classical inspiration, Socratic Selling also has a lot in common with the "Tell. Explain. Describe". approach favoured by the British Police and described so well by Detective Sergeant Tom Baker in Chapter 8. The planets are aligning, dear reader.

Fundamentally, Socratic Selling is an insight-driven process. It demands empathy. Daley says: "it is based on understanding the customer's perspective, encourages the customer to think out loud and develop visions of the future" (p.35). Again, unlike the caricature of sales folk dripping with snake oil, the process demands the person selling spends more time listening – to answers to smarter questions – than anything else, embracing the techniques of active listening pioneered by the psychologist Carl Rogers. We'll come back to the critical importance of listening in Chapter 7. More than that, Socratic Selling focuses on the *Why?* rather than the *What?*, making it clear that "The customer is not interested in features. The customer is only interested in the benefits those features offer" (Daley, p.41).

At the start of Chapter 1, I mentioned that I've had half-a-dozen colleagues in the past 30-odd years who ask: *What's the exam question?* when taking a brief from colleagues, clients, or collaborators. By far, the most effective sales person and client counsel from that eclectic group I've been lucky enough to work alongside is Andrew Challier. As I read Daley's book, Andrew kept on popping up, apparently on every other page. Andrew is the very quintessence – the Platonic form – of a Socratic salesperson. Before we'd go in to see a new prospective client, he would remind me: "The definition of a good sales meeting is one in which we don't use the sales presentation and the laptop remains closed". When Daley says: "Keep the canned presentation in your briefcase" (p.44), I could have sworn the line was written by Andrew, yet when I asked him, he told me that he had never read Daley's book.

Socrates' mother was called Phaenarete, which means – suitably enough – "she who brings virtue to light". She was also a midwife. In Plato's dialogue *Theaetetus*, Socrates compares his role as an ignorant but smarter-questioning philosopher to be like midwifery (maieutics); his purpose is to bring out definitions trapped in the beliefs of those he's questioning, enabling them to further their understanding. The beautiful thoughts and definitions are inside them, just like a baby in a labouring mother. Socrates comes with no assumptions, no knowledge (apart from the technical knowledge of how to help them out), and with the least possible intervention he nurses them into the light.

I think the metaphor of midwifery is a good one for a light-touch, empathetic consultant of any kind, including those who work in sales. By asking the right, smart questions that enable customers to recognise, clarify, and articulate their needs, successful salespeople do exactly that. It's a theme we'll return to in the interview with Stuart Lotherington at the end of Chapter 6. Indeed, when we spoke, it was Stuart who first introduced me to the very concept of Socratic Selling, although it is not an approach his sales training business SBR Consulting uses. As the American author Dan Pink says in his book *To Sell Is Human*, "We are all in the moving business" – the business of persuading others to take action, to change their attitudes, beliefs, or actions. This is as true of the salesperson as it is of a doctor who wants her patients to take a course of medication to the end of a regimen or a teacher who wants to motivate her pupils to do their homework or revise for an exam.

In the pre-internet, pre-instant search days, salespeople depended on information asymmetry between themselves and their customers to secure and sustain advantage over them. Someone selling cars, for instance, knew what it cost the manufacturer to produce a car – the factory gate price. She knew what the margins were, right down the transactional chain, for national, regional, and city dealers. She knew where she could make a quick buck (on cleaning systems and servicing contracts) and where she could and could not shave costs.

Today, all of that information is available by asking smart questions online, so there is no longer information asymmetry between salespeople and customers. This makes customers much more knowledgeable much earlier in the sales process and places them much closer to the point of purchase before they ever meet or interact with a sales representative. With those unfair advantages removed – with information asymmetry balanced out – salespeople need a different strategy. For me, the Socratic approach is very much more likely to succeed than Alec Baldwin's outdated sales manager, Blake in *Glengarry Glen Ross*, offering a set of steak knives to this week's top seller.

By adopting a position of ignorance about the prospective customer's needs, by asking smart questions that get them to reveal these needs, the salesperson is much better able to focus on benefits, not features. Instead of "ABC – Always Be Closing", the Blake of 2022 would encourage his sales teams "ABQ – Always Be Questioning". Not to mention "ASQ – Ask Smarter Questions". Indeed, as Terry Fadem says in his book *The Art of Asking*: "Questions, by their very nature, are an expression of ignorance, not stupidity. Asking expresses an interest in learning" (p.91).

THE PHILOSOPHY OF BETTER DATA STORYTELLING

Aristotle was born in the early fourth century BCE. His early life is obscure, but it seems likely he made his way to Athens from the Northern Greek City of Stagira at the age of 17 or 18. He enrolled at Plato's by-then thriving Academy, where he learned – live and direct – from Socrates's star pupil. As Oxford Classics professor Armand D'Angour explains in the interview at the end of this chapter, Aristotle was very different from either his master or his master's master. He opened up all sorts of novel lines of enquiry in all sorts of new subject areas, from biology and psychology to logic and linguistics, from ethics and politics to music and storytelling. And although questions were at the heart of Aristotle's approach, he was much more interested than Socrates and some way more interested than Plato in what asking smarter questions can do: yield useful, evidence-based answers.

What's more, with Aristotle's no-nonsense, Northern Greek approach, he wasn't afraid to call out Plato and Socrates when he disagreed with them, both in the conclusions they drew from their philosophy and in their approach. This contrasts keenly with Plato, who tiptoed round his evident disagreements with his master, preferring to put these into the mouths of others and still giving Socrates the posthumous right of veto, or argument, or walking off in a bit of a huff should someone have the temerity to question his role and approach.

Nevertheless, Aristotle was sufficiently inspired by what he learned from Plato that, in time, he founded his own higher education establishment, the Lyceum. The Lyceum was an informal, so-called peripatetic institution. Aristotle's favoured style of teaching was to seek answers to questions while wandering about – *peripatētikós* means "prone to wandering about". Prone to wandering about in and under the *perípatoi*, "a place in which to walk around (especially a colonnade or similar)" according to Diggle's new *Cambridge Greek Lexicon*. This is the approach favoured by many of the most insightful thinkers down the years. They include Mr *Thinking, Fast and Slow* Daniel Kahneman and his long-term collaborator Amos Tversky. Kahneman and Tversky embraced the "walkshop" approach espoused by the early Christian theologian Saint Augustine of Hippo, who declared *solvitur ambulando* – "a solution comes [literally 'it is solved'] by walking about".[7]

When reading and thinking about Aristotle's peripatetic school – also known as the Peripatos, no less – I was reminded of the long-forgotten style of management pioneered in the 1970s by the American computer business Hewlett-Packard: Management By Wandering Around or MBWA. The theory is that if managers randomly sample what's going on in their organisations by simply wandering around, they stumble upon pockets of challenges and innovations that would otherwise remain unobserved unless they had "walked the floor" and asked some naïve but pointed questions.

As you'll know if you've ever worked in an organisation where leaders refuse to walk the floor, the simple act of MBWA not only identifies both difficulties and opportunities. In so doing, it demonstrates to those on the floor – in the front line – that leaders are interested in what the workers are doing. This is precisely the kind of serendipity and positive reinforcement that was so missed and missing from leadership under the recent coronavirus pandemic. As the world becomes increasingly office-based anew – albeit with a hybrid balance between office and home working – leaders would be well advised to embrace their inner Aristotle, get peripatetic, and do more MWBA, asking questions as they go. Tim Johns' pandemic-era book *Leading from Home* goes deeper here.

There are two areas of enlightenment from two of Aristotle's works that I believe deserve special mention at this point in our exploration of what asking smarter questions enables us to do. Both relate to storytelling in general and the ways in which storytelling can be greatly enhanced by the judicious, human, and empathetic use of data. Data storytelling, indeed. The logic of my trilogy of books on "using data better" – starting with this one, the latest of the three – goes like this:

- To make sense of and explain our place in the world – as people, communities, companies – we need to learn how to ask smarter questions. Asking smarter questions yield smarter answers.
- Smarter answers – the right data – enable us to surface and articulate "a profound and useful understanding" of the topic at hand, my definition of insight from *How To Be Insightful*. Insights allow us into the mind, the mindset, the shoes of those we're looking to influence.
- Truly persuasive communication isn't shaped by the odd data point, casual observation, or half-baked thought. Powerful and purposeful stories are rooted in genuine, data-driven insights. Stories that balance the emotional with the rational (and not the other way around).[8]

In essence: Smart questions surface relevant data > Relevant data enable us to surface and articulate genuine insights > Genuine, data-driven insights are the foundation stones of stories that move others to think, feel, or behave differently, not just today but also forever. This equation is true in politics and business, in public and private life.

The first area of enlightenment from Aristotle comes from his short, very readable book *The Poetics*.[9] In this treatise, Aristotle analyses the three forms of popular literary entertainment available to the Greeks: epic poetry, tragedy, and comedy – though rarely for a work of Aristotle's, the section on comedy is almost entirely lost. In the book, he was the first to identify and categorise all kinds of dramatic conventions and devices, from *peripéteia* (reversal of fortune) to *hamartía* (the fatal flaw that leads a tragic heroine or hero to their undoing), from *cátharsis* (purification – removing pity and fear) to *anagnórsis* (discovery).

What's more, Aristotle also codified in *The Poetics* the essential story structure that underpins every epic, every play, every novel, film, short story, boxed set – every story ever well told: the three-act story structure of the set-up, the confrontation, and the resolution. Between each act – and for Aristotle, the acts were the thesis, antithesis, and synthesis – came a turning point. In Hollywood, and notably in the book *Story* and courses run by scriptwriting legend Robert McKee, the first turning point is known as the "inciting incident".

The three-act story structure satisfies us as story-seeking creatures who use narrative structure to help us navigate and make sense of the world. It doesn't just work for dramatic art. It also works for business presentations and pitches, slide decks and proposals for new business. It moves from the past (how a business has been set up) to the present (the pain currently experienced) and on to the future (where the business could be once that pain has been excised – thanks to your natty product or service). It allows us to move from a yesterday (a market overview, say) to today (current trading) and on to a tomorrow (market opportunities).

By analysing epic poetry, tragedy, and comedy – by asking smarter questions about what these creative, dramatic manifestations of the human condition have in common – Aristotle teased out the playbook that informs what makes a Netflix hit and an Amazon Prime flop. His evidence-based framework born of smarter questions truly separates *Squid Game* from almost every series of the sportumentary, *All or Nothing*.[10]

The second area of enlightenment from Aristotle comes from his *Art of Rhetoric*. Here, he gives another three-part prescription of three essential elements of a story well told, three elements that work so well in parallel with the three-act story structure. For a story to move us, it needs a combination of *páthos* (feeling or emotion), *lógos* (reason or logic), and *ēthos* (character):

Páthos: a story needs to move us. It needs to be about real individuals – in Greek literature these can be human or divine, monsters or demigods. Whoever the subject matter, we are made to care about their lives and experiences because we can either associate and empathise with the experiences they go through or be repelled by them. As Kahneman and Tversky's collected body of work has shown us, we make our decisions emotionally, using the evolutionarily ancient, quick-and-dirty emotional brain structures we share with reptiles, birds, and all other mammals. In *Thinking, Fast and Slow*, Kahneman classifies emotional decision-making as System 1 thinking. The almond-shaped amygdala – the brain's emotional barometer – is central to our emotional evaluation of situations (including stories).[11]

Lógos: having made our decisions about whether to listen and engage and then identified whether we like it or not – whether to approach the character of the story or avoid them – through our emotional response, we move into post-rationalisation mode. The emotional brain has no access to language or words. Kahneman shows that we only justify our decisions rationally once we've made them emotionally, using what he calls System 2 thinking. This is only possible for humans and is mediated using the uniquely human cerebral cortices, the wrinkled, bark-like grey and white matter of our cerebral cortices which lie over the ancient limbic and reptilian structures. They're cognitive, slower, and more energy-intensive, activated and potentiated by reason or logic.

Ēthos: stories that move us to action must contain emotion (*páthos*) and rationality (*lógos*), the two critical components of the message. But the messenger matters, too, hence Aristotle's insistence on importance of *ēthos* – the character, nature, or predisposition of the individual giving that message. What we know about them and what we learn about them from what they say help to shape how we receive and act upon the message. Authority figures – gods and kings – may think they command our respect by divine right. But if they're as headstrong as Agamemnon or Macbeth, if they're as arrogant and vainglorious as Zeus or Logan Roy in *Succession*, we will judge what they say and how they say it harshly or critically. Indeed, as arrogant and vainglorious as any of the Roy (or Wamsgams) families, to be fair to Jesse Armstrong and the team that created *Succession*.

SUMMING UP

Aristotle's collected body of work can of course tell us very much more about what asking smarter questions can generate than just these two areas of enlightenment. That said, I do genuinely believe that they are both excellent examples of what his inquisitive approach yielded about both narrative form and storytelling more broadly. More than that, they are also very practical and broadly applicable for the work that more and more of us are required to do in our working lives today. It is estimated that there are in the order of 1.25 billion people actively involved in the modern knowledge economy and up to another 300–500 million who've retired from knowledge economy roles. Taken together, this is more than a fifth of the world's population whose work life has, does, and will depend on the ability to find and use the right data to build persuasive arguments.

The legacy of Aristotle – and of course Plato and Socrates before him – is profound. Profound for what has followed in philosophy, science more generally, and the scientific method. Profound for the tools and techniques we go about finding out answers to questions we don't know. Profound about what constitutes a smart question and what, well, maybe less so.

While some contemporaries of Socrates and generations who have studied him since may have found the Socratic approach to be irritating – particularly when the self-professed ignoramus shows himself repeatedly to be better equipped to enquiry than the expert – his contribution is quite obviously net positive. Starting from a position of ignorance sees an inquisitor build a picture that gradually emerges from the bottom-up rather than a narrative that's imposed from the top-down. It's like a pointillist or impressionist painter whose image is built dot by dot, smudge by smudge. The arrogant, assumptive approach comes with a predetermined story in mind and is more likely than not to ignore relevant, novel, or surprising data, serving up little more than Confirmation Bias. To extend (and possibly torture) the artistic metaphor, it's like drawing outlines and simply painting by numbers, an approach best avoided if you want to create something of lasting value.

As Socrates showed, not knowing and saying explicitly that you don't know is actually quite liberating. And as it turns out, the bloody Greeks did really rather a lot for us when it comes to asking smarter questions.

NAME	Armand D'Angour
ORGANISATION	Jesus College, University of Oxford
ROLE	Professor of Classics

Armand D'Angour is both a classical cellist and Professor of Classics at Oxford University.[12] He is the author of two books on innovation and the ancient Greeks, 2011's *The Greeks and the New: Novelty in Ancient Greek Imagination and Experience*, followed up ten years on with *How to Innovate: An Ancient Guide to Creative Thinking*, an elegant, densely packed, rapid-fire exploration of exactly what it says on the tin. The most recent book includes diverse examples of innovation, from politics to shipbuilding, from military strategy to state-sponsored innovation competitions. We spoke about the ways in which Greek thinkers have shaped subsequent history of thought and science, and the pivotal role that asking questions has played in that influence.

In *How to Innovate*, D'Angour points out that:

> innovative achievement has always been recognized as a feature of ancient Greek society ... various mechanisms can be seen to underlie their inno-vative practices ... such as borrowing and adaptation of external ideas ... [and] ... the cross-fertilizing of disparate disciplines. (2021, pp. ix–x)

He lists some of the inventions of the Greeks of the classical period, from 800 to 300 BCE: "the alphabet ... philosophy, logic, rhetoric, and mathe-matical proof ... theatrical drama, rational medicine, monetary coinage, and lifelike sculpture ... competitive athletics, architectural canons, the self-governing city-state *(pólis)*, and democratic politics" (ibid, xv).

Underpinning the Greek drive to innovate – a drive which D'Angour believes much of classical scholarship has missed or ignored for millen-nia, preferring to think of the culture as essentially conservative – lies the imperative to ask questions. Aristotle's *Metaphysics* opens with the line: "All people desire knowledge by their very nature". In addition to sensa-tion and memory, which we share with other animals, "the human race lives by art and reasoning". This curiosity and thirst for knowledge is what the psychoanalyst Melanie Klein termed the epistemophilic instinct. This instinct is what impels us to search for knowledge, to bring in the good, useful stuff and keep out the rest.

Throughout our discussion, D'Angour focused on Aristotle, his teacher Plato, and Plato's teacher Socrates, whose whole philosophy is that of the questioner:

> Socrates claims to know nothing. Although people make surmises and give examples, he showed that most of us actually know very little about the topics or issues in which we claim to be expert. Socrates' logic is that all we have is questions. Since any answers we give will always be imperfect, never final, we should spend our lives questioning. Which is exactly what Socrates did – spurning the 'unexamined life as not worth living'.
>
> Those who came before Socrates – philosophers lumped together as 'the pre-Socratics' – gave answers and then tried to support their answers with arguments, usually pretty unsatisfactorily. Saying that everything is made of this or that essential element – earth, wind, fire, or water – and then having to justify that is hard work. Socrates (through his life of enquiry) and Plato (through his writing and teaching, inspired by and put into the mouth of Socrates), went against this tradition. Plato took this further, saying that the answers to questions were the Forms – the ideal, perfect, unchanging concepts or ideals underpinning and infusing all qualities and objects that manifest the Forms. Humans can never know them or perceive them clearly, just glimpse them. They exist in another realm that only our souls are in touch with. When we're born and reborn, the best we can hope for is to spend our lives searching for them by asking questions.

D'Angour believes that there's a bit of a vogue for saying that Socrates's approach to philosophical enquiry was irritating – starting from a point of ignorance, asking questions, and showing those he was talking to that their beliefs are contradictory and so wrong:

> You can read a lot of Plato and not get that impression at all. He shows that giving an example – for instance of courage or virtue – is not enough to explain what courage or virtue actually are. What he's demonstrating is that simple, ill-considered answers are not good enough, and that we can only get closer to the truth by asking questions. He was uncompromising is his quest for more universal understanding, though I do appreciate that

*someone who professes ignorance and then gets the better of you in an
argument could come across as frustrating. Being uncompromising is not
necessarily a strategy for winning friends and influencing people.*

As Socrates' trial, guilty verdict, and condemnation to death "for corrupting the young" were to prove at the end of his life.

In *How to Innovate*, D'Angour talks about how ancient Greek philosophers were always "posing disruptive critiques to the ideas and practices
of their predecessors". When we spoke, he went unpacked this further
with reference to Aristotle:

*He came to Athens from the City of Stagira in Northern Greece, and was
much more down to earth. From this empirical perspective, he starts to
shape the scientific method, investigating evidence in enormous detail.
He's interested in looking at the world and understanding how it works –
from biology and zoology to politics and ethics – breaking through from
the realm of the mind which is where Socrates and Plato got stuck. Plato
hinted that his teacher, Socrates, had got things wrong; Aristotle explicitly
calls out precisely where and how his teacher, Plato got things wrong. He
was particularly critical of the limitations and lack of practical usefulness
of the theory of Forms.*

And Aristotle did this, of course, by asking – and answering – progressively
smarter questions.

The classical Greek philosophers left a very powerful legacy, D'Angour
contends, encouraging us to look under every stone and ask smarter
and smarter questions. In the course of just three generations, enormous progress was made that saw the birth of completely new kinds of
questioning and the birth of the scientific method. As he says in *How to
Innovate*: "The fourth century BCE saw the greatest contributions to philosophical thought in Western history … to create a logical and empirical
approach that has influenced all subsequent thinking" (ibid., p.18).

This has also inspired D'Angour's own work, in both music and understanding Greek thinking about thinking and love of wisdom:

*Everything I've ever done or published has arisen from a question: 'What
actually happened? How does it actually work?' I am blessed to have
a questioning mind that looks at material – often material that's been*

presented the same way for generations – and then I notice 'That doesn't quite add up. What's going on here?' Just rolling out the scholarship doesn't satisfy my own curiosity. I'm more interested in what kind of man Socrates really was, in whether it was the act of taking a break and having a bath that led to Archimedes insightful breakthrough.

It's clear to me that D'Angour's spirit of curiosity was first piqued and challenged by studying those writers and thinkers who first set us on the path to thinking about thinking with rigour.

ARMAND D'ANGOUR'S TOP ANCIENT GREEK TIPS FOR ASKING SMARTER QUESTIONS

1. Don't accept the status quo and simply "roll out the scholarship". Question everything.
2. Be prepared to challenge those who come before you, accepting what's useful, rejecting what's past its sell-by date.
3. Cross-fertilise between disciplines. Be inspired by Armand's career-long mash-up between classical music and classical philosophy and literature.
4. Harness the human curiosity instinct and slake your thirst for knowledge.
5. Start from a position of ignorance and fill in the gaps by asking questions, leaving half-considered assumptions and prejudices at the door.

NOTES

1   My most inspirational school teacher who really infected me with the bug for Greek was Bernard Collyer. He taught me from 1981 to 1985 at a state grammar school in unglamorous Aylesbury, Buckinghamshire. Having been out of touch for 20 years after leaving school, my wife started working with his son at the University of Sussex. When I was studying for my DPhil in psychology there, I had the opportunity to meet Bernard again on the day his son collected his own doctorate on campus. We kept in touch and irregularly met for lunch over the next 15 years, together with one of my Greek class peers and oldest friends, William Bentley.

As I was writing this book, it became clear that Bernard's days were num-bered. With my father long dead, there was no one else alive I would have been more honoured to have read this chapter – and pointed out its short-comings. So much of what I know of Greece and the Greeks (particularly the Athenians) and Socrates started with Bernard. It was with him that I first read Plato's *Apology* (for O-level) and *Symposium* (for A-level, an exam in which, much to my surprise and delight, I recorded the best marks in the country that year). In December 2021, I shared the first draft of this chapter with "Mr Collyer", and was thrilled, one COVID-Omicron-threatened evening, to receive this message from my wonderful teacher: "I enjoyed this a lot. I'd be very pleased with myself if I'd written the clear and succinct paragraphs on Soc-rates etc. I'd never have thought, or been capable, of developing their ideas into techniques of selling. But your arguments are very persuasive. I like the touches of humour. I'd love to see a comparison between Cleon and Trump set for discussion in, say, a Cambridge Tripos paper". It is, without doubt, one of the best e-mails I ever received.

2 Natalie Haynes was a student of Mary Beard at Cambridge in the 1990s, and they have performed – including readings from their respective, complemen-tary books – on book promotion tours. Before turning to writing and updat-ing Greek and Roman mythography from a feminist perspective, Haynes was a stand-up comedian for ten years. Working with the BBC, she's combined her deep knowledge and love of the Classics with her innovative feminist per-spective on classical literature, and her stand-up performer's skills to create seven seasons of *Natalie Haynes Stands Up for the Classics*. In each episode, she takes another topic – usually either an author or a character in a classical story – and gives her take and update on it. At the time of writing, these are all available to download or stream via the BBC Sounds app.

3 The fact that Lloyd embraced ignorance as the gateway to knowledge via curi-osity at the age of 42 is particularly poignant. Originally a law student at Trin-ity College, Cambridge, Lloyd befriended Douglas Adams at the Cambridge Footlights Comedy Club, where they wrote and performed together. After college, Lloyd and Adams shared a flat together and for many years worked together on Adams's *Hitchhiker's Guide to Galaxy* radio series, novels, and TV series, with Lloyd often helping Adams through his chronic, relapsing writer's block. In the five-book Hitchhiker trilogy, 42 is the answer to the Ultimate Question of Life, the Universe, and Everything, as calculated by an enormous supercomputer named Deep Thought – planet Earth to you and me. Unfortu-nately, neither Adams nor Lloyd nor any of the characters in the worlds they created knows what the question is. I have no doubt it was smart.

Lloyd and Adams co-wrote a very fine and funny book in the early 1980s titled *The Meaning of Liff*. The premise of the book is to use place names as words for concepts that don't have words. It came complete with a Day-Glo orange sticker which boldly proclaimed: "This book will change your life". So, in *The Meaning of Liff*, Duntish (West Dorset) means "Mentally incapacitated by severe hangover"; an Ely (Cambridgeshire) is "The first, tiniest inkling that something, somewhere has gone terribly wrong" – often an unwanted consequence of being Duntish; and perhaps most prosaically of all, Bures (on the Essex/Suffolk border) is defined as "The scabs on knees and elbows formed by a compulsion to make love on cheap Habitat floor-matting". There's more at https://en.wikipedia.org/wiki/The_Meaning_of_Liff

4 Interview: John Lloyd, professor of Creative Ignorance, QI, *Engineering & Technology*, 09.11.18, https://bit.ly/3ClbGV4

5 Creating dictionaries is a labour of love, a bit like building rail or road networks. Now they're with us, thanks to Georgian or Victorian enterprise, we take them for granted. But the thought of building them from the ground up is too daunting for most to even consider. Generations of classicists – myself included – knew Liddell & Scott to be the definitive Greek-English dictionary. First published in 1843, its most recent update was published in 1940. But a lot – in scholarship and attitudes, definitions and meanings, and our interpretation of ancient Greek society – has changed in the past 80-plus years. That said, the Victorian lexicographers didn't do a bad job in their definition of elenchus as "argument of disproof or refutation; cross-examining, testing, scrutiny esp. for purposes of refutation". But James Diggle's brand spanking new 2021 *Cambridge Greek Lexicon* does a better, more contemporary job to my mind. I was privileged to be taught by both Diggle (Greek lyric poetry) and Mary Beard (a paper called "The Body in Antiquity") in the late 1980s.

6 Socrates never actually talked about cognitive dissonance per se – it wouldn't be discovered until the work of social psychologist Leon Festinger and others identified the universal human need to preserve internal psychological consistency if they are to function, mentally, in the real world. Some lifelong Conservative voters in the U.K. find it incredibly challenging to support the party with Johnson as its leader, although cognitive dissonance didn't seem to be too much of a challenge for 70 million Republicans who voted for Trump in 2020.

Although the psychological discomfort of holding incompatible beliefs took almost 2,500 years to be named, Socrates was an extremely effective, self-confessed gadfly – *múōps* in Greek – who highlighted the uncomfortable reality of cognitive dissonance in philosophical debate.

7 There's a longer exploration of the cognitive impact of walking – as well as running and swimming – and the role exercise as "taking timeout" plays in having genuinely innovative, insightful breakthroughs on pp. 124–126 of the prequel to this book, 2020's *How To Be Insightful*.

8 As in storytelling, so in life. Because – as Kahneman's body of work has helped to establish – we make our decisions emotionally (using System 1 thinking) and only go on to justify them rationally (System 2), we should look to balance the emotional with the rational and not vice versa. In much the same

way, we should aspire to work to live and not live to work. For that reason, we should look to establish a life-work balance not a work-life balance. It's all about getting our priorities right.

9 *The Poetics* is particularly readable in Malcolm Heath's excellent 1996 translation from Penguin Classics.

10 The Arizona Cardinals season is said to be the televisual equivalent of watching paint dry. The Manchester City version is simply a hagiography of coach Pep Guardiola – more of an infomercial or advertorial than a serious piece of documentary making. And the Tottenham Hotspur series, while a study in manager Jose Mourinho's delusions of grandeur and repeated suffering from the Fundamental Attribution Error – claiming all credit for success and denying any responsibility for failure – would be better off being renamed *Nothing*. It turns out that timing is everything. Simply recording thousands of hours in the life of a sports team is much more often narrative free, and it certainly doesn't satisfy Aristotle's prescriptive structure for stories well told.

11 The amygdala – Greek for almond, the structure named after its shape – was the part of the brain I was most interested in for my doctoral thesis in experimental psychology: *You were perfectly fine: The effects of alcohol on memory for emotionally significant events*. See https://bit.ly/3JCLKZ9

12 The best place to see D'Angour's twin passions combined is in his 2012 TEDxOxbridge talk-cum-performance, "Getting in the Flow", https://bit.ly/3GB2caG. Many people, myself included, recommend TED talks. If you've not come across this one before, prepare for your expectations of the genre to be utterly shattered.

3

WHY SHOULD WE EVEN BOTHER
WITH "WHY?"?

Abstract

The questions we ask help us make sense of and navigate the world. One of the most powerful areas in which to start asking smarter questions is the judicious and sensitive use of *Why?*. Why can get to the root cause of an issue. Why can reveal and help to uncover motivation and the all-important *if-and-then* contingencies that reveal connections and causality, both those that are obvious in retrospect as well as hidden third causes.

Educational systems around the world were developed to serve industrialism – to create workers suitable for successive generations of progress through the industrial, cognitive, and now digital revolutions. By that assessment, education was not developed to harness and explode the potential of human curiosity, a true superpower that unlocks creativity. With curiosity and creativity stunted by education, the world of work has done little better. To get back on track, we are at the ideal moment in history for a revolution in education, a new curriculum that harnesses curiosity to unlock creativity. Learning facts by heart helps no one in a world in which

(Continued)

DOI: 10.4324/9781003218470-3

everything the world knows is available with a $100 smart device and a half-decent WiFi signal. Schools of tomorrow should teach critical thinking, curiosity, and creativity. And they should start with *Why?* – with the proviso, acknowledgement, and acceptance that this isn't the only question we need.

WHY "WHY?" IS SUCH AN IMPORTANT PLACE TO START

I must have watched "How great leaders inspire action" – Simon Sinek's talk at TEDxPuget Sound from 2009 – dozens of times. I've watched it alone, for my own education and edification. I've watched it with friends and family. And I've watched it with many, many clients. I often recommend they watch it to prepare for the purpose and data storytelling workshops and training sessions I run. Even if, like me, they've seen it more than once before I recommend they watch it again. I find it always serves as a timely reboot. I should be on points for the number of times I've shared it.

On one level, the talk feels incredibly folksy and homespun. To be fair, it was given at a TEDx event. TEDxes are described by the not-for-profit TED corporation as "local gatherings where TED-like talks and performances are shared with the community", "showcases for speakers presenting great, well-informed ideas in under 18 minutes", and "grassroots ... created in the spirit of TED's overall mission to research and discover 'ideas worth spreading'". It's true that a huge amount has happened since Sinek's first TEDx – to the internet, to TED (particularly its expansion into corporates), and to what we all expect of content delivered online. Not to mention what's happened to Simon Sinek and his burgeoning training and educational consultancy in that time, all centred around purpose and empowering organisations to surface and articulate their *why*.

Yet despite all those changes, there's still something remarkably – as I say – endearingly amateurish about the presentation of Sinek's talk – all 17'48" of it, a suspiciously perfect 12 seconds under the permitted runtime. Sinek is filmed from just a couple of cameras, the long-range camera bleached out and with brightness poorly balanced. He has perhaps one too many buttons undone down the front of his shirt, which is ruched over his belt in a casual and unequal French tuck. His sleeves are rolled-up, workman-like, to halfway between his wrists and his elbows. And he scribbles with a marker pen on a flipchart whose paper looks like it might fall off its hooks at any moment.

Yet despite all of this, "How great leaders inspire action" is the third most watched TED talk of all time, having attracted almost 57 million views at the time of writing – not even half of them from me and my clients. I'm always surprised when people tell me they haven't watched it, but I appreciate that there are lots of things I've never watched too, despite the opportunities afforded by successive COVID lockdowns.

Because Sinek got in there relatively early in TED's mass viewership journey, he's benefitted from the growing use of the platform. Like the compound interest enjoyed by the ancient Livery Companies whose halls pepper the alleys, byways, and bridges of the City of London – many of them 500, 600, 700 years old and more – Sinek's audience numbers have enjoyed metaphorical compound interest. More people saw it early and started to share and recommend it before others' talks. But it's more than that. If his apparently homespun and folksy talk didn't have brilliant content, brilliantly delivered, it surely wouldn't have soared to near the top of the charts and stayed there.

Sinek's central message is that organisations that tell their stories in the order why-how-what – organisations that, in the name of his books, courses, workshops, and numerous copycats, "Start With Why" – are more successful than those that do it the traditional (and now wrong) way round of what-how-why. In less than 18 minutes, he says no fewer than six times, "People don't buy what you do, they buy why you do it". He's spawned or at least catalysed and galvanised the entire, small "p" purpose business. As I argued in Chapter 1, purpose is not just about saving the world – it's much more important than that. It's what makes founders create great companies that do great things and are great places to work; it's what makes employees love the companies they work for; it's what gives us all a reason to get out of bed, haul our bones to the office (or the spare bedroom under "work from home" lockdowns), and greet the unseen with a cheer.[1]

As in data storytelling, when you're looking to build a powerful and purposeful story with data, if you start with "Why?" when you're looking for numbers and statistics to underpin your narrative, you're much more likely to find and use truly relevant data. See www.narrativebynumbers. com for more.

As in the models you use to surface and articulate genuine insights, if you start with "Why?" you're looking to identify genuinely relevant and empathetic evidence to build your profound and useful understanding of those you're looking to influence, you're much more likely to be insightful. See www.HowToBeInsighful.com for more, particularly for details of the STEP Prism™ of Insight framework for surface and articulate.

So in asking smarter questions, if you start with "Why?" – if you know the purpose of the journey you're setting out on, if you know what your objectives are – you're very much more likely to pose questions that will elicit data and evidence, build insights, and craft more persuasive stories. As the veteran journalist and journalism programme director Dean Nelson says in *Talk to Me*: "you have to know *why* you are doing this interview" (p.47). By all means visit the new website for this book www.AskSmarterQs.com and follow its Twitter handle @AskSmarterQs. Truth be told, chapter and verse, very much the small "b" bible of asking smarter question you have in your hands right now.

UNPICKING THE "IF-AND-THEN" CONTINGENCIES OF LIFE

Knowing and understanding why we're doing what we're doing enhances our chances of success, and this is particularly true of asking smarter questions. One of the main reasons why lines of enquiry can go astray is that we don't stop to consider the purpose of our investigation – what it is we hope to get out of it. What this doesn't mean is bringing a whole load of assumptions to the query, assumptions that prejudge the answer or prejudice the process. Far from it. But driven as we are by the epistemophilic instinct – by curiosity to understand what causes what and why things are as they are – we should apply this urge to the very purpose of the questions we ask.

In his book *A More Beautiful Question*, the journalist Warren Berger reports: "According to Paul Harris, a Harvard child psychologist and author, research shows that a child asks about forty thousand questions between the ages of two and five" (2014, p.40). As anyone who's ever raised or even met a child of this age will know, most of these questions start with "why", as these miniature scientists seek to make sense of the world. Almost all children acquire quite spectacularly complex linguistic abilities at around this age, overlaid on and absorbed by Chomsky's Universal Grammar.

The particular flavour of language they acquire is determined by the environment in which they're raised, a function of both geography (where they live) and the language spoken by their principal caregivers (whom they live with). The flavour is irrelevant. Whether it's Cantonese, Arabic, Swahili, or Finnish, pre-schoolers soon come to understand that they now possess an incredibly useful new tool with which to navigate life. Language, for sure, and the raw power of questions in particular.

Before language starts, infants explore the world and seek to determine cause-and-effect contingencies physically. By their actions, we can see the experiments unfold and research hypotheses tested: *What happens if I bite the cat's tail? Will my sister love me more if I pull her hair? What will happen if I put a coin onto the live terminal of that electric plug?*[2] But physical experiments of this sort are hard to do in sufficient volume to learn everything we need to know or want to find out.

This is particularly true when we try to work things out that involve others, when we seek to explore the realm of interpersonal relationships. Our caregivers tend not to leave us alone to explore the world and are usually keen that we don't cause mayhem by trying things out that they know will cause conflict or grief – to us ourselves, and especially between us and our siblings, pets, or playmates. They're bigger, stronger, and nimbler than we are. And although well intentioned, too often they frustrate us by putting a stop to our exploration of the world and hypothesis-testing before we even get started.

This explains why, when language starts to blossom, we lit rip. It's true that caregivers might shush us, ask us not to ask yet another question, or deem some circumstances – the cinema, a wedding service, the doctor's waiting room – to be inappropriate for specific questions or questions in general. Nevertheless, we are more indulged in the questions we ask than the experiments we try to run. Both often test the same hypothesis, are unconstrained, and – from the regulated world of adult and societal norms – ridiculous. But there's much greater tolerance when a preschooler asks what a cat's tail tastes like than when they bite down hard on three inches of fur. Posing a question as a hypothetical line of enquiry shows progress, restraint of impulsivity, and growing cognition.

What's more, as we progressively make sense of the world and work things out with our questioning, our caregivers will smile and nod and say, "That's right!", cuddling or high-fiving us for our cleverness and ingenuity of working things out. Even if the answer generated is in the negative, our ability to draw conclusions based on evidence and the questions we ask is rewarded by positive reinforcement. Like rats pushing levers to receive water, food, or rat-sized lines of cocaine, we seek physical, emotional, and verbal rewards – hugs, smiles, and "Well dones!" Both scenarios represent operant conditioning in action, associative learning where behaviours are encouraged (and discouraged) by rewards and punishments.

THE POWER OF SYSTEMISING AND EMPATHY

Simon Baron-Cohen is a professor in the departments of psychology and psychiatry at Cambridge University and director of the university's Autism Research Centre. Thanks to the research he's led and directed over the past 30 years, he's become Mr Autism. Indeed, since the announcement of the 2021 New Year's Honours, he's been Sir Autism.[3]

Not only does Simon Baron-Cohen run a world-leading research centre that does serious research with very significant impact well beyond academic circles. What his research has discovered – about the effects of foetal exposure to testosterone in the womb, for instance; about the nature of the empathising and systemising dimensions of the human brain – has helped to redefine our understanding of autism. Its real-world impact includes changing policy and practice in the diagnosis and care provided to those with the condition. It has also been a welcome, authoritative, data-driven counterblast to the snake oil peddled by the fantasist Andrew Wakefield, struck off by the U.K. General Medical Council for his made-up nonsense connecting the measles-mumps-rubella (MMR) vaccine to autism.

Baron-Cohen's impact is also evidenced in the popular science books he writes and the public talks and lectures he gives based on his primary, academic research. *The Essential Difference* (2003) created a three-dimensional paradigm to explain what it is that makes men and women different. More recently, he explored what it is in our evolutionary history that means that of all creatures on earth, humans alone invent and innovate. *The Pattern Seekers* (2020) represents, on one level at least, new territory for Baron-Cohen, as he moves from evidence-based, data-driven psychiatrist to evolutionary psychologist.

In the book, he proposes that human innovation and experimentation is driven by "a specific kind of engine in the brain. It's one that seeks out *if-and-then patterns*, the minimum definition of a system. I call this engine in the brain the *Systemizing Mechanism*" (2020, p.12). This mechanism is what enabled "humans alone to become the scientific and technological masters of our planet, eclipsing all other species" (2020, p.13). Curiosity, says Baron-Cohen, is the grinding of the mechanism, the sound of the brain's gears and cogs seeking out contingency and cause-and-effect relationships from what they observe happening in the world. Evolutionary history suggests that the *if-and-then* module – that sparked human innovation and inventiveness – evolved between 70,000 and 100,000 years ago, driving the three different approaches only humans use to solve problems and determine relationships: observation, experimentation, and modelling.

Solving problems by asking "why?" and mapping out *if-and-then* contingencies would not have been sufficient for humans to progress as quickly and dramatically as they did, argues Baron-Cohen. The impact of the Systemising Mechanism was fast-tracked by the parallel development of the Empathy Circuit that "allowed us to think about the

thoughts and feelings of others ... By enabling us to imagine other people's mental states ... we could anticipate what they would be likely to
do next" (2020, p.34). Both of these modules appear to be under separate genetic control, allowing individuals to excel or underperform in
either or both abilities. He goes on to suggest that two networks have
developed, the first:

> supporting **cognitive empathy,** *defined as the ability to imagine the thoughts
> and feelings of another person or animal; and the second* **affective empa-
> thy,** *defined as the drive to respond to another's thoughts and feelings with
> an appropriate emotion ... Cognitive empathy is what primatologist David
> Premark called having a* **theory of mind**. *(2020, p.34)*

A theory of mind, Baron-Cohen contends, allows for flexible decep-
tion, flexible teaching, and flexible referential communication. The
latter enabled us to invent and understand "drama and storytelling,
where we establish a shared topic and describe characters who have
different points of view ... [it enabled us to invent and understand]
humour ... conflict resolution ... use of symbols ... social cooperation"
(2020, p.38). And all of that from developing a hunch that things are
connected and can have an influence on one another, overlaid by the
rapid development of language and the ability to ask *Why?*, *Pourquoi?*,
or *Warum?*; *Perché?*, *Varför?*, or *Pam?*.[4] Not a bad return for perhaps the
simplest question we can ask which returns perhaps the most complex
answers we can generate, explaining cause and effect and not just
coincidence.

WE DON'T NEED NO QUESTIONS IN CLASSROOMS (OR DO WE?)

The curiosity that infants develop may inspire them to ask upwards of
40,000 why-type questions in the three years before they start school, as
they begin to make sense of the world around them in miniature scientist mode, establishing increasing numbers and categories of *if-and-then*
contingencies. As soon as most of them get to school, however, a variety
of factors come into play that squash this curiosity out of them. Indeed,

they don't go on to ask as many why-type questions until after they leave secondary education and head towards university.

Much of the Western (indeed the global) education system is designed to stimulate pupils to generate answers, not questions, the approach that so frustrated Nobel laureate Venki Ramakrishnan in our interview earlier. Rote learning, multiple choice tests, essay questions. Questions, questions, always questions, posed from the supposed position of knowledge (and so power) – the teachers. Answers, answers, always answers from those learning – the pupils. But pupils asking questions in many pedagogical settings are actively discouraged. It can be seen as a sign of disruption or attention-seeking behaviour.

As we will explore in more detail in Chapter 7 in a section called "This is the sound (and neuroscience) of silence", inhibition is a critical aspect of the human brain at the behavioural level, mediated via learning; at the neurochemical level, mediated via neurotransmitters; and at the cognitive level, mediated via the uniquely human cerebral cortices. Complete mastery of cognitive inhibition often doesn't occur until we are in our late teens or early 20s – in part because the grey and white matter doesn't full mature until then – so expecting primary school infants to inhibit their innate curiosity and not ask questions is both unrealistic and counterproductive.

Because the epistemophilic instinct is so strong, schools have had to institute in-class rules that stifle that curiosity drive from the very start, although it's unlikely that either Plato's Academy or Aristotle's Lyceum would have had much truck with such rules, given that both encouraged the asking of smarter questions as a core point of principle. Formal education from the Victorian era onwards, however, has put a primacy on pupils answering teachers' questions over pupils learning by questioning, as we do by our very nature. The negative consequences of forcing children to be seen and not heard unless asked to answer questions is a trope in many school memoirs, leading to the conclusion that, for many, school did not represent "the happiest days of our lives" after all. From the 1970s' anti-school diatribe *That'll Teach You*[5] to the "we don't need no education" recitative of Pink Floyd's concept album *The Wall*, it's a frequent and common refrain.

Four times during *Another Brick in the Wall, Part 2*, the Scottish school-master barks "Wrong, do it again!" and Floyd's lyricist Roger Waters pleads against the system:

> *We don't need no thought control*
> *No dark sarcasm in the classroom*
> *Teacher, leave them kids alone*
> *Hey! Teacher! Leave them kids alone!*

Over-rigid educational paradigms (teachers ask the questions, pupils give the answers) have been reinforced in recent decades by the introduction of core curricula which national and local educational authorities require schools and teachers to deliver. The scope of these curricula are often jam-packed with more topics than many teachers can easily get through in classes of varied (if streamed) ability. This is particularly true because "crowd control" is increasingly demanded of teachers in mainstream state education, with teachers required to keep order in classes and silence – or at least a lid on noise – in classes of 30 and more.

Burgeoning class sizes are harder to control. Keeping 30-plus modern teenagers quiet and focused on subjects they're compelled to study is a challenge for many teachers. This is exacerbated by surging sex hormones, particularly testosterone, which impairs the nascent inhibitory ability of the frontal lobes. It is exacerbated by competitive teenagers looking to score points off teachers and gain esteem in the eyes of their classmates. And it is exacerbated by the apparent epidemic in attention deficit hyperactivity disorder (ADHD) which can manifest itself in the form of disinhibited behaviour, including calling out and disrupting classroom settings.

The blunt chemical coshes of the drugs used to treat ADHD – drugs including Ritalin and Adderall – don't always help either. These drugs increase the presence and so alter the transmission of two key neurotransmitters in the brain: dopamine and noradrenaline. As pupils receive ADHD diagnoses and get used to the drugs, behaviour can actually deteriorate rather than improve – at least from the perspective of a teacher in search of a quiet classroom.

The educationalist Sir Ken Robinson is responsible for the most watched TED talk of all time: 72 million views and rising at the time of writing. "Do schools kill creativity?" (2006) is also one of the most entertaining TEDs, and Robinson's comic timing and delivery – as well as his ability to get distracted by amusing, self-deprecating anecdotes – make it one of the most watchable, too. Robinson's central thesis is the way in which education is structured and run across the world which is designed to squash children's innate creativity and squander their creative talents. Educational systems came into being to serve industrialism and schools operate as a 13-year preparation for university entry. Academic performance, in coursework and exams, has stigmatised being wrong. Marks – particularly high marks – are awarded for being "right" according to the curriculum, not wrong, and although creativity is every bit as important as literacy or numeracy, no one told the establishment. Asking *What if ...?* is at the heart of creativity, but marks are given for answering not asking questions.

In his talk, Robinson reflects that educational establishments around the world all favour academic ability over creativity. The same hierarchy of subjects is common the world over, with mathematics, sciences, and languages at the apex, followed by the humanities, and with the arts routinely bottom of the pile. No school teaches dance or art daily; all schools teach mathematics and literacy on a daily basis. What's more, the curriculum developed in all nations is designed to tell the story of the world according to the ideology of that country, an approach that deliberately excludes or marginalises other countries' or cultures' contributions and questioning that approach is actively discouraged. This reinforces and perpetuates mythographies that are often racist, exploitative, and airbrush atrocities, from imperial exploitation of people (through slavery) and resources (through plunder). The recent breakthroughs of movements such as Black Lives Matter are perhaps starting to redress the balance in the classroom and encourage questioning of outdated imperialist dogma. Mediated exposure to statues of fat cat slave owners being torn down and defaced is stimulating debate in some classes, but for many this is too little, too late.

CRUSHING CREATIVITY OUT OF CURIOUS MINDS

For all of these reasons, the spirit of curiosity that spawns 40,000 why-type questions in most pupils before they get to school is too often squashed into submission. Formal education that favours answers over questions – being "correct" over being imaginative, performance over curiosity – starts this process. In suppressing questions and seeking only supposedly right answers, it has the unintended consequence of suppressing creativity. This, in turn, makes many people believe they are neither creative nor insightful and that creativity is the preserve of a rarefied, special elite.

This is unfortunate, not least because it isn't true. As I show in *How To Be Insightful*, the human brain is a remarkably creative organ, able to combine old and old to make something genuinely new. This is true whether you're working as an actuary or an advertising copywriter, on a trawler or on stage, in a laboratory or in a writer's garret. Every role in every profession has its rules and guidelines – some more critical and vital than others (think oil rig, hospital theatre, or nuclear power station versus call centre, scented candle shop, or consultant). But every role in every profession also has its opportunity for innovation and creativity right through the ranks, with often greater latitude and licence to fail for the less experienced and naïve. As Simon Baron-Cohen says in *The Pattern Seekers*: "Genius is sometimes defined as looking at the same information that others have looked at before and either noticing a pattern that others have missed or coming up with a new pattern that constitutes an invention" (p.71). Doing this often depends on asking questions. Frequently, this requires us to challenge the status quo and – you guessed it – to start with "Why?".

Central to creativity is the phenomenon of *recursion* in human language and thought. As Baron-Cohen observes:

> *recursion, which, according to linguist Noam Chomsky, is the unique feature of human language ... a procedure that includes the procedure itself, and which can be repeated indefinitely ... how, with a finite number of words, we can create an infinite number of sentences ... it's also a critical feature of music. (pp. 120–121)*

Recursion ensures that boxed set scriptwriters, movie producers, musicians, poets, artists, creative crocheters, adult fans of LEGO – hell, even business book writers – can recombine the building blocks of their distinctive medium and never run out of new things to create. But to do so requires curiosity. It requires asking questions. And it particularly requires asking why-type questions that can reveal *if-and-then* contingencies.

If primary school starts the process of discouraging questioning, secondary school turns it into a fine art, particularly in the headlong rush towards public examinations, typically after 11 and then 13 years of formal education towards the end of schooling – General Certificate of Secondary Education (GCSE) and A-levels in the U.K., Scholastic Assessment Test (SAT) in the U.S., the Abitur in Germany. Asking smarter questions is prized and expected by many university courses, though many university teachers are mystified that their students aren't more curious, don't ask more and better questions, and seem so determined to provide answers. When I taught second- and third-year psychology undergraduates on courses as diverse as "Intelligence, Personality, and Thinking" and "The Psychobiology of Addiction", the relentless focus on model exam answers depressed me. On distance and more mature reflection, I'd suggest that disappointed university teachers should reflect a little harder on the schools' education their students have endured as they seek to pass progressively harder exams that secure entry to their institution.

TOWARDS A NEW EDUCATION

Something is rotten, clearly very rotten in the state of education if it discourages curiosity and squashes creativity by design and achieves all of this by putting such a low premium on questioning. So much of what schools education has sought to achieve – particularly the acquisition (and then application) of knowledge – has been made redundant by the internet and increasingly the internet of things. Knowing that Funafuti is the capital city of Tuvalu, knowing that the French for "conjurer" is "prestidigitateur", and knowing the precise arrangement of hydrogen and carbon atoms in a benzene ring ... it's not as if these things don't matter any longer. But rote learning – acquiring and storing fact after data point – are much less relevant than they were 20, 30, 50 years ago.

The world's information – all the facts you could ever need and then some – are stored and available online, returned in a fraction of a second (provided your search string asks the right question, though burgeoning artificial intelligence [AI] is making even that less important). Education and educationalists are at a moment in history when they have the opportunity to recast how we learn and what we learn. Technology, data, and smart devices have brought much of the world to a point where we need a whole new curriculum and a whole new pedagogy. The digital revolution has the potential to pivot the centuries-long focus of education from content to form, from topic-based, thematic subjects we make our children learn to a more useful curriculum based on unlocking and unleashing potential.

Now don't get me wrong. You can't just learn how to learn without having subject matter with which to apply the theory. That would be like having an engine with no fuel source, a body with no blood or food and drink. But for too long, there has been an almost fetishistic disorder among successive government education ministers to get "their" subject at the heart of the curriculum. When Britain entered the EU in 1973, there was an understandable ramping-up of teaching modern European languages in place of their "dead" ancestors: Latin and Greek. It's probably several leagues more important in post-Brexit Britain.

Perhaps the worst offender was the British politician Michael Gove. When he was Secretary of State for Education under the Cameron-Clegg coalition from 2010 to 2014, he insisted that all year 9–11 secondary school pupils should study either geography or history to GCSE level. Gove's special adviser at Education was the quicksilver Dominic Cummings, who later found notoriety running the Leave campaign in the EU Referendum and – for a forgettable 478 days – as chief advisor to Prime Minister Johnson. Gove was sacked in 2014 "amid reports that the government was becoming toxic to teachers"; Cummings slithered off to run Vote Leave.[6] Mandating at least one humanities subject for GCSE may not be the most egregious act of their tenure at Education. For pupils and parents whose hands were tied and choices restricted at the time and since, it is certainly the most memorable. In the words of the chorus of *The House of the Rising Sun*, "And Lord – I know – I'm one".

What subjects would my new curriculum have? In no particular order, I'd suggest the following:

- Mother tongue language, literature, and grammar
- Second language, to appreciate different cultures and traditions and do more than order "Dos cervezas, por favor, Manuel!" when on holiday
- Applied mathematics – particularly applied to finance – statistics, and data storytelling
- Creative expression in any non-verbal format or medium at least once a day
- Coding
- Logic, reasoning, and rationality
- Sports and games, team and individual, as the route to physical and mental well-being
- Meditation, mindfulness, and timeout
- Critical faculty and judgement to develop ninja skills in asking smarter questions

Based on what I've argued already, I trust you understand the majority of subjects on the curriculum of the New Academy-Lyceum. I'd like to draw your attention to two in particular.

1. **Creative expression**. So much of our daily learning and working lives are verbal and cognitive, using language to solve both analytical and insightful problems. Yet we know from the work of Kahneman and Tversky that we make our decisions emotionally using evolutionarily ancient brain structures that have no access to language or data or facts. We only go on to justify them rationally. Encouraging play and expression in a non-verbal medium allows us to access and vent that quite literally vital part of the brain and generate creative, artistic interpretations that can blindside our logical, rational, cerebral cortices. This is part of point of art therapy.

I wouldn't prescribe or mandate the media for creative expression; I'm not the serpentine offspring of Gove and Cummings, after all. It could be dance or music composition or performance, drawing, painting, physical or digital collage, LEGO, pottery, Play-Doh, cooking, making clothes, wood, or metal. I really don't mind. I'd just want those in my charge to be creative cats little and often, at least once a day, perhaps at the start of the day to capture some semblance of the sense that the subconscious has made of yesterday in sleep and dreams. It might also be helpful at the end of the day to begin to make non-verbal associations of that day's input – what things are; what categories they belong to; how things are and are not related and what the relationship is between them; whether one causes the other or vice versa or is there a hidden, third cause; how reliable/knowledgeable is my parent/friend/teacher as a source of information; what's fair.

2. **Critical faculty and judgement**. In a world in which all information is available at the click of a mouse or by pressing a button and muttering into the smart watch on your wrist, one of the single most important facets we all need to develop and develop fast is the ability to call bullshit. Fortunately, there's already a very fine Massive Online Open Course (MOOC) and core text book to help deliver foundation-level critical faculty and it just so happens to be called Calling Bullshit (subtitle "Data Reasoning in a Digital World", https://www.callingbullshit.org). Created by two professors at the University of Washington in Seattle – theoretical and evolutionary biologist Carl Bergstrom and political data scientist Jervin West – Calling Bullshit is a brilliant primer and starting point for learning how to sort the wheat from the chaff.

Many schools in many countries offer critical reasoning or critical thinking courses to many of their pupils. The problem is that, though some educational establishments have realised that this skill is important, they don't signal as much by folding it formally into the curriculum. It's very rarely tested or examined (although it easily could be: *Which of these two data sets/sources do you believe is more trustworthy and why?*), and often these classes are dogged by more animal noises than analysis and seen as timeout during an otherwise packed week. It's not a bad thing to build timeout into the school curriculum, and I'd want to do that in any case through "Meditation, mindfulness, and timeout". Timeout allows our subconscious minds to do their brilliant, creative, recombinatorial thing, joining old and old together and making something new. Schools' failure to take critical thinking sufficiently seriously not only does the skill a disservice, it also undermines it and makes pupils think that if the school doesn't take it seriously, why should they? Yet for me, it's perhaps the most important subject on the curriculum of the New Academy-Lyceum.

THE WORLD OF WORK

What schools begin and many universities refine, the world of work perfects. "Asking out" – pupils repeatedly asking questions that teachers perceive to be disruptive to the rest of the classroom's ability to acquire knowledge, disruptive to their own ability to trudge through the topics required by the curriculum – is often discouraged in schools, from primary schools onward. Yes, there are different approaches adopted by a handful of progressive teaching philosophies – Question-Based Learning being one – but too often and for too long our educational philosophy has been too intolerant of empowering pupils to ask questions.

Success for many working in the modern knowledge economy comes from answering rather than asking questions. Asking questions can be seen as disruptive (as it was in school), divisive, counterproductive – seditious even. Companies have challenges to solve, and the mode of thinking typically valued and rewarded for solving these challenges is analytical thinking: working and working away at the problem, exploring all avenues until the challenge yields to the time and brainpower applied. It's as if management believes that problems are like iron or steel that simply needs sufficient heat and energy applied to bend. And yet many of the most challenging, the thorniest, the most "wicked" problems we face today – from *How can we sell more and more shampoo but do progressively less harm to the environment?* to *What are we going to do to slow down the spread of this new virus before we have sufficient stocks of a vaccine proven to work?* – require the application of a very different mode of thinking. Insightful thinking, the endlessly recursive way of working in which we combine old and old to make new. And for insightful thinking, we need always to be asking *Why?*.

To be fair, the spirit of enquiry and curiosity is to be found in many start-ups, challenger brands, and disruptors. Many of the businesses that didn't exist before the internet – businesses that now dominate markets and stock markets – saw the potential of data and technology to change the means of sourcing and production, delivery and distribution fundamentally and forever. They did this by using the scale the internet provides, the speed, the ability for one-to-one, one-to-many, and many-to-one communication and disintermediation – cutting out the redundant, expensive middle man.

Amazon started out selling books and changed retail forever. Spotify made owning physical copies of music a thing of the past – until the vinyl revival took us back to the future. AirBnB killed travel agents. And Netflix? Well, Netflix started out as a DVD-by-mail rental service that sought to send some shockwaves through Blockbuster's world[7] and ended up changing how we watch and pay for TV and film. Into the bargain, the company became one of biggest studios. The first five years of the Netflix story is well told by co-founder Marc Randolph in his book *That Will Never Work* (2019).

What all of these disruptive disintermediators have in common is the way in which they encourage anyone and everyone in their business to challenge the status quo, to ask why-type questions that often start with *Why – in this category – does it "have to be this way?"* Netflix's "Freedom and Responsibility" philosophy[8] is predicated on all employees' ability to question all aspects of their job – what they do, how they do it – from day one. This fundamentally bottles the curiosity of the entrepreneur within a corporate environment, and Netflix is very definitely a corporate environment these days – $25 billion revenues in 2020 and more than 12,000 employees worldwide.

One of Randolph's touchstones in building the business was legendary scriptwriter William Goldman's maxim about Hollywood: "Nobody. Knows. Anything". He saw this as "a reminder. An encouragement" (2019, p. 203) to relentlessly challenge and question the status quo, to constantly ask *Why?* and in that way, build a better, different tomorrow.

THE FIVE "WHYS?"

Sakichi Toyoda founded the company that his son eventually turned into Toyota. Known as the "king of Japanese inventors", Toyoda's legacy lives on in one critical form: from the perspective of this book as the creator of root cause analysis. Root cause analysis uses simple (but smart) questions to help the questioner work out if the hypothesis or proposal being presented is promising and worth pursuing or ill-considered and destined for the scrap heap. It starts – and ends – with why, and it's a foundational exercise I've run in many different kinds of workshops with clients, from innovation and creativity to insight and data storytelling.

Having become immersed in a common set of data – reports, presentations, research, interviews; whatever is most relevant or potentially enlightening – small groups of five or six take it in turns to present what they believe is the most promising theme emerging from what they've read. It's likely that a genuinely promising emerging theme will have started to form connections – however hazy – between different data points or observations from different reports; old plus old starting to make something new, with the undertones of insight rumbling round the hills of the subconscious like thunder. The other members of the group then take it in turns to turn back the clock and embrace their inner five-year-old and ask *Why? Why? Why?*, infusing the spirit of Warren Berger and asking a more beautiful question, one that starts with *Why?*.

It's important to run this exercise quickly, iteratively, but to do so with focus. If I'm a participant in an innovation workshop and I suggest that a promising avenue for new product lines could be self-cleaning cutlery and crockery, it's no good the others in my breakout room simply ask *Why?* five times. This might be enough for a nimble or experienced player of this game, but to someone new to root cause analysis, we should give them a bit more to work with.

Why #1: Why do you believe this could be a promising new market?
Because it's genuinely new and applies new nanotechnology to a challenge as old as mealtime.

Why #2: Why do you think that consumers would respond well to it?

Because it's an environmentally friendly solution to washing-up that could do away with detergent and the need to heat water for sinks or dishwashers.

Why #3: Why do you feel that this will appeal to the IKEAs of this world who sell dishwashers?

Because, as a premium product, it won't appeal to or be within the price range of all consumers, so there's still a market for crockery and cutlery that isn't self-cleaning, and for dishwashers.

Why #4: Why do you imagine that competitors haven't already made this breakthrough and rejected it?

Because we're pioneers and innovators in this space and have filed and been granted patents for this technology in this and other categories in all the major markets around the world and these were uncontested. If others had created similar applications of nanotechnology, we and our patent lawyers would have come across it in this process of filing.

Why #5: Why do you believe that home and lifestyle bloggers would give it the time of day?

Because it's so new and space age and "Jetsons".

You can imagine similar conversations in the offices of early incarnations of AirBnB, Netflix, or Tesla, but perhaps not at Blockbuster, Kodak, or Nokia. As Dave Trott, one of the leading creative spirits in British advertising from the 1970s to the present, observed of Toyoda's creation recently in the adland bible *Campaign*:

> *The real strength of this method is that it doesn't just provide a solution to the immediate problem, it identifies the root cause, so countermeasures can prevent it happening again. Problems are often symptoms of deeper issues and this discipline stops people jumping to conclusions and getting locked into pre-formed answers.[9]*

A slightly more direct version of the Five "Whys?" is the four "So Whats" used by some in academia to validate real-world impact.[10]

START WITH "WHY"

Another excellent workshop exercise I run regularly that embraces the power of *Why?* is inspired, of course, by the work of Simon Sinek. This can be an exercise to kick-off a workshop or work stream to surface and articulate the purpose of an organisation – and remember: it's not about saving the planet – it's much more important than that. Or it could be a stand-alone exercise to get a workshop about, say, real-world impact of academic research headed in the right direction, getting all participants to focus on their personal motivation. That's exactly how my business partner Saskia and I use it when working with academics.

Either way, as preparation for this exercise, we usually ask all delegates simply to watch Sinek's talk from TEDxPuget Sound 2009 and count how often he says, *People don't buy what you do they buy why you do it* in the talk (spoiler: the answer is six). Then, we ask them to spend a scant 15 minutes writing down a list of candidate purposes for their organisation or business, project or product. In this exercise, we want people to express what it is that motivates them, what drags them out of bed in the morning and gets them to cycle through the elements to their office or lab, what keeps them going when outrageous fortune gets in the way, be it sneaky competitors, unforeseeable world events like a global pandemic, or mean-spirited regulators. Whether we're in the room or on Zoom, working with flipcharts and PostIts, Jamboard, or Miro, we get them to capture and then order their purpose statements using a number of incomplete sentences starting with an active verb in the infinitive. To trigger their thinking, we put up a slide, like Figure 3.1.

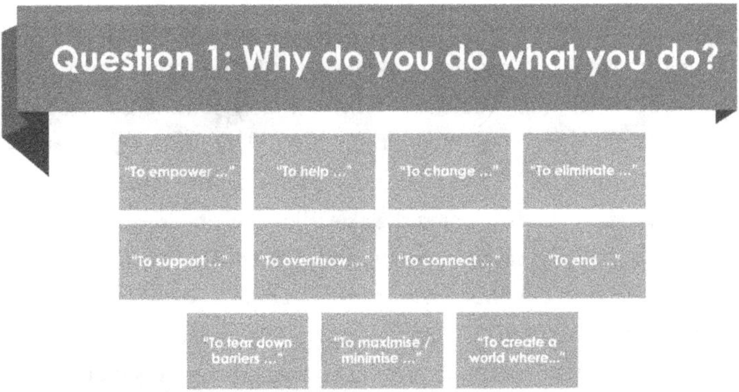

Figure 3.1 Stimulus slide for workshop exercise on purpose – on finding your "why?"

For most people we work with – in business or academia, government or the third sector – they will often have thoughts about their personal *Why?*. They may even have captured it more or less formally within their organisation. But usually, despite the popularity of Sinek's TEDx, books, and courses online and in the room, they won't have gone through this exercise. In the space of just 30 minutes or so, the impact of getting them to focus on their *Why?* has real impact. It's always positive and it can be transformational, a Damascene moment of scales falling from the eyes which makes subsequent decision-making about what to do (and what not to do) and partnerships immediately obvious in a way it wasn't before they'd stopped to think about and articulate why it is they do what they do. Try it. You'll like it.

THE LIMITATIONS OF "WHY?"

Despite my great enthusiasm for *Why?* as one of the best and smartest questions we can ask, it is not universally loved, particularly in the world of coaching. The Dutch practical philosopher Elke Wiss, who teaches the principles of Socratic dialogue to modern businesses, notes in her modestly titled book *How to Know Everything*: "Many guides to questioning techniques advise people not to ask why. That's a real shame, because 'why' is one of the most important questions to ask if you want to gain new insights and deepen your understanding" (2020, p.235).[11]

I agree with Elke that this in unfortunate, but I can also understand the reasons why some are reluctant to endorse *Why?* as the universal question that beats all other questions. *Why?* is widely considered to be one of the most open-ended of all questions. Used right, its intention isn't to close respondents down and it encourages those of whom it's asked to give their rationale underpinning their decisions or opinions. The trouble is that asking *Why?* doesn't always yield open-ended answers. As Wise and Chatfield say in their book *Ask Powerful Questions*, why-type questions can be pointed, accusatory, and closed. For that reason, it can, in fact, create defensive and scripted responses that do the very opposite of reveal reasons why or purpose.

Wise and Chatfield (2017, pp.97–98) give three examples of *Why?* questions that perform spectacularly badly as well as some get-out-of-jail-free alternatives that don't use *Why?*.

Why are you wearing that hat? Even without emphasis or exaggeration on the "that", this is a pretty pointed question, one whose hidden (British) meaning is very close to the surface and intention more like: *Why on earth are you wearing that hat, a hat that any self-respecting person with eyes and a mirror could see is a total fashion faux-pas?*

Their alternatives are the more generous and forgiving: *What do you like about wearing that hat?* and *What is appealing about wearing that hat?* Much more open.

They also give a couple of examples from the workplace. *Why are you late?* is deeply accusatory and filled with undertones of ... *for the fourth time this month, you slacker!* Rather more balanced would be *What happened (that made it difficult for you to get to work [in decent time])?* Likewise, when picking through the bones of a deal gone sour, *Why did you charge so much?* will start a defensive conversation mired in conflict. *How was the pricing structure decided?* pours oil on troubled waters.

As Sullivan and Rees show in *Clean Language*, *Why?* can bring a whole host of baggage, assumptions, and opinions from the questioner to the conversation, turning it from innocent enquiry into full-blown interrogation. Indeed, it's for precisely this reason that I urge those running a root cause analysis – deploying the Five "Whys?" – to add specificity to their questioning and not just ask *Why?* five times. It is telling that in the basic clean language, questions established by the counselling psychologist David Grove, he doesn't feature a single *Why?* in his basic 12 questions. As Sullivan and Rees say:

> What's special about Clean Language questions is that they have been pared down to contain as few assumptions and metaphors as possible. This makes them 'ultra-Open', allowing the speaker the maximum freedom to choose how they will answer. (2008, p.4)

For these reasons, and despite my love of *Why?* and the way Sinek has used this innocent, three-letter word to build a strong and sustainable business, a movement, and a philosophy, I do urge caution in how you use

Why?. Use it as a guiding principle and start with it, for sure. Be careful with intonation and intention and make judicious use of it, avoiding both accusatory tone and language at all costs. It can be incredibly powerful. As Terry Fadem says in his book *The Art of Asking*:

> When you ask the **why** question, you are generally looking for something behind the words you hear … All why questions do not necessarily have to begin with **why,** nor do they all need to be in the form and an interrogative. The 'I am interested in …' approach … is an effective way of eliciting a response. (2009, pp. 156–7)

This is similar to the "Tell, Explain, Describe" approach favoured by the British police, as detailed in the interview with D.S. Tom Barker in Chapter 8. On balance, as Fadem concludes in his section "Looking for Reasons": "If asked in a non-threatening way, *why* is an open question that invites a responsible reply" (*loc. cit.*). What more could we want of a formula for asking smarter questions?

SUMMING UP

It turns out Roger Waters was wrong after all. While we don't need no thought control, we definitely do need some education – just a different type of education, one that harnesses curiosity to foster creativity. Creativity can and is expressed in the arts, from music to dance, literature to Grayson Perry's pottery and rug-making. But creativity is also expressed in analytics, data storytelling, disruptive business ideas. To unleash potential, we don't need top-down, government-imposed programmes that aim to "level up". We need the bottom-up encouragement for all citizens to make best and smartest use of the world's powerful supercomputer that sits between all of our ears.

The brain is the most brilliant, recursive recombiner of old and old that can go on making new for the infinite future. It's why I continue to feel optimistic even when representatives from more than half the world's nations fail to reach a meaningful agreement on carbon reductions and don't ban coal at UN Climate Change Conference (COP) meetings in

Glasgow, as happened a few days before writing this chapter. It's why I continue to feel optimistic despite the fact that – at the time of writing – we're in the second winter of COVID-19 and the world is labouring under a surge of the Omicron variant of the coronavirus. Just look how far and how quickly we've come since the Wuhan wet market fiasco.

What each and every one of the nine billion new brains who will have inherited the earth 100 years from now needs is liberation and encouragement to ask the right questions in the right way. And – with just a modicum of caution – that very definitely starts with *Why?*. As Plato has Socrates say in his (their) *Apology*: "The unexamined life is not worth living".

QUESTIONS ABOUT QUESTIONS – INTERVIEW 3 OF 14

NAME	*Timothy Bishop, QC*
ORGANISATION	1 Hare Court
ROLE	Barrister and Head of Chambers

Tim Bishop[12] is one of the U.K.'s foremost matrimonial finance barristers, frequently handling high-profile and complex divorce cases for the rich and famous. He became a Queen's Counsel (QC) – the top designation for a lawyer in England – in his early 40s, just 20 years after being called to the bar. He has been head of his chambers, 1 Hare Court, for several years.

When we spoke, I was interested to discover the role that asking questions plays in his job, a profession caricatured in popular fiction at least as confrontational and adversarial, with the winners those who ask harder, faster questions.

"To work out the answer to a case – how the money will be distributed – it's really important to have a complete understanding of all the material facts. As barristers in this country," observes Bishop, "we're very lucky. We're provided with information nicely packaged by solicitors. Nevertheless, I always like to ask my clients simple and straightforward questions to secure a perfect understanding of the situation. Experience has taught me what I, the other side's barrister, and the judge are all looking for. I'm also looking for risks and threats that might come down the track."

> *Once we get to court, there's lots of ground we don't need to cover. We don't need to establish every fact, as written evidence is submitted, signed under oath. Where skilful questioning really comes to the fore is when we seek to undermine assertions made by the other side or an expert witness who comes to court. This is how we help the judge to reach an appropriate decision.*

With questioning being such a foundational skill in good advocacy, it is curious to Bishop that the skills of cross-examination aren't taught in more depth at bar school:

> *One lesson you learn early on in court – often through bitter experience – is that you shouldn't ask questions to which you don't know the answer, as this can lead to a loss of control. But – just like bedside manner for doctors – remarkably little time is set aside over in a barrister's education to cover how to ask decent questions. It's often taught by people not in practice which is less than perfect. Perhaps that's why many of us have learned from watching others and then putting that into practice ourselves, starting on small, low-profile cases and learning by doing – and making mistakes – in front of magistrates not high-court judges.*

Preparation is key for Bishop. Questions can be used to establish or challenge factual propositions and this can impact the success of the outcome you can deliver for your client. But without a complete grasp of the facts – secured through questioning – it's quite possible to stray into territories you'd have been better advised to avoid. Preparation extends to knowing the precise physical (or electronic) location of every document or reference you depend on in court. "Fishing around and fumbling through documents completely breaks the rhythm and gives the witness time to work out how they might answer your question. Being on top of your material is critical."

For many barristers – Bishop included – preparation involves not just comprehensive research but also scripting: the questions you're going to ask, the sequence you're going to ask them in, the areas you're going to cover as well as those you're going to avoid. Others do it very differently, deciding on the broad themes they want to cover and going with the flow, extemporising in the moment. "This can be very effective, a reactive and responsive way to catch others out, allowing for *coups de grâce and coups de théâtre*." But this "improv" approach can bear with it the seeds of its own destruction if the other, well-prepared side spots this strategy and decides to take a different route.

Televisual of filmic moments – a "You can't handle the truth!" from *A Few Good Men*, for instance[13] – is incredibly rare under cross-examination. When the technique works, it works by helping to establish in the judge's mind that what's being said is not particularly reliable, that it's been exaggerated, or that there's an attempt to mislead. Like an impressionist painter, a good barrister will use cross-examination to undermine the credibility or plausibility of a witness. "When witnesses contradict themselves, judges become instantly more cautious about the evidence."

Unlike some of the other professions considered in the interviews in this book, barristers often favour building up a story by asking a series of closed questions from which the person being interrogated finds it challenging to deviate, crafting a narrative piecemeal, step by step. Short questions are favoured over long, and barristers who use complex, convoluted questions often make judges glaze over. Not only should the questions themselves be short and easy to understand (aka hard to wilfully misinterpret). Periods of questioning should be short, too. "Going long always reduces the impact," observes Bishop.

Another important tactic in cross-examination is to ask compound questions – questions that include more than one question, one of which may be highly controversial.

> The respondent or witness may try to respond to one part of the question where they feel more confident but completely fail to refute the controversial element. It is then possible to take forensic advantage of that omission, though more experienced judges are not always swayed by this approach.
>
> Cross-examination can be an incredibly important part of a case – like an anvil or crucible where you hammer out and boil down the truth – but there are judges who think it's pointless. They feel it's inherently unreliable, beset by problems of recollection, the emotional stress of the situation, witnesses not understanding the text or the subtext of the moment, and the lawyers playing dirty.

Turning to what makes a bad question, Bishop is certain in his condemnation of leading questions. They suggest an answer based on a presumption. They should be avoided when eliciting oral evidence in court from your clients, but they can be fruitful in cross-examination of the other side. The least useful leading – and closed – question that should form no part of a barrister's armory starts: *Would you agree that ...?* Another no-go (or certainly risky) area is objecting to a question raised by the other side. Not only do judges find this irritating, it also looks like you're covering up.

"Bad questions are also questions asked in the wrong order," Bishop contends:

> You want to establish building blocks in your argument and use questions to cement them together. You need to exude a sense of control and be in control. And it's totally counter-productive to descend into anger or confrontation. We need at all times to remain calm, and in the end, that comes back to preparation. To hit the right questions and ask them in the right order, you simply must prepare.

Destabilising and prejudicial questions are also verboten for Bishop – less for moral reasons, more because they are counterproductive and likely to set the judge against you and your client. And because in niche areas of law, the same barristers are often up in front of the same judge, you can quickly gain a negative reputation for asking simplistic, mean-spirited, unfair questions.

For a centuries-old profession synonymous with wigs, quill pens, and jabots – neck bands – it's perhaps surprising to learn that the explosion in data and technology over the past 20 years has fundamentally changed how barristers ask questions and the types of questions they are able to ask. All work is done electronically, and court papers in the 2020s comprise compiled PDFs and Excel spreadsheets, not leather-bound sheaves of vellum:

> That makes for rather less theatre than before – riffling through papers and pulling out the key document – but it does mean you can do much more sophisticated financial modelling and projections than ever before, crucial to settling matrimonial disputes, and search and find relevant documents in seconds.

Tim ends our discussion with a legal joke about questions.

A solicitor phones up a barrister and asks: "How much will it cost to ask you three questions?"

"Five thousand pounds," the barrister replies, calmly.

"Five thousand pounds!" the solicitor retorts in shock. "That's a hell of a lot, isn't it?"

The barrister says: "Now what's your third question?"

No further questions.

TIM BISHOP'S TOP TIPS FOR ASKING SMARTER QUESTIONS

1. Double-check the answers others give you. Go to the source and get evidence first hand.
2. Cross-examination is a skill best learned from observation and practice.
3. Preparation is everything.
4. Open questions generally trump closed questions, but there's a time and a place for both.
5. Be brief in how many questions you ask and in how long each question is.

NOTES

1 This line comes from the last verse of Robert Browning's poem *Epilogue*. As well as Read The Question (RTQ), Read The Flipping Question (RTFQ), and Read The Flipping Question Again (RTFQA), my father, Kenneth, had specific guidance for very specific types of exams. Though our schooling was separated by almost 60 years, things don't move very fast in the world of the Classics. And one of the most challenging exams any student of Latin or Greek can ever face is the unseen translation paper, an opportunity to show quite how much of these dear, "dead" languages you really understand, by making sense in English of some obscure, recently discovered fragment of love poetry from Sappho or Catullus. It really is a smarter question the examiners are asking you. You may not know the vocabulary or the syntax, but if you're on your game, you should be able to work it out.

And so, whenever I was faced with an unseen translation paper, my father would be sure to say to me before I left the house: "No, at noonday in the bustle of man's work-time // **Greet the unseen with a cheer!** // Bid him forward, breast and back as either should be, // 'Strive and thrive!' cry 'Speed,—fight on, fare ever // There as here!'". And after a consoling hug and a kiss, just before I pulled the front door to, he'd say again: "Greet the unseen with a cheer!" Before my first-year exams at Cambridge, I received a postcard bearing just that stanza, typed in simple, anonymous Courier on his sit-up-and-beg typewriter. The full poem is here: https://bit.ly/31acQFg

2 This last enquiry was suggested by a challenge by Amazon's Alexa voice assistant during the 2021 Christmas holidays in Britain. See this article on the BBC News website – "Alexa tells 10-year-old girl to touch live plug with penny" – from 28.12.21, https://bbc.in/3zpK945

3 Simon Baron-Cohen (see https://www.autismresearchcentre.com/staff/simon-baron-cohen/) is also the first cousin of the comedian Sacha Baron Cohen. Sacha is the creator of comic alter egos from Ali G to Borat and the serial taunter of the British and American far-right politicians and extremists, particularly white supremacists with anti-Semitic views. When Sacha's character Ali G was featured regularly on British TV – originally on Channel 4's *The 11 O'Clock Show* (1998) and subsequently in his spin-off series *Da Ali G Show* (2000–2004) – it is said that Simon grew frustrated when students in his lectures would shout out Ali G catchphrases, from "Rispek!" to "Booyakasha!", patiently informing them that they had "the wrong S. Baron-Cohen". But it is clear from media interviews and their interactions on social media that there is a huge amount of mutual respect between the cousins.

4 These examples are English, French, German, Italian, Swedish, and Welsh. For how to ask *Why?* in more than 100 languages, see https://www.indifferentlanguages.com/words/why

5 *That'll Teach You* was written and illustrated by my uncle John Kirkbride. When the youngest of his children came home from the first day of school visibly upset by the experience, John and his wife Melinda decided that all four of their children should be homeschooled. This was incredibly difficult to achieve in the 1970s Britain – it's only marginally easier today – and the family was subject to regular inspections. The book appeared a few years before Roger Waters's schooldays featured in Pink Floyd's *The Wall*, and I've long suspected some connection or lineage between the two, given the featureless faces of the pupils in John's book that are so reminiscent of Gerald Scarfe's featureless pupils in his cartoons and animations for *The Wall*. As John died of anger and a heart attack in the early 1980s and this thought didn't occur to me until a few years after that, I never got to ask him. It may be a common artistic response to the way formal education treats and can affect pupils that arose spontaneously and in very similar fashion in different stories. It may be that Waters or Scarfe were attracted to or familiar with John's book. Or perhaps

there was a now-lost connection between them. Either way, the similarities are striking.

6 For a forensic analysis of Gove and Cummings's defenestration policy at the Department for Education – repeated in 2019 to "Get Brexit Done" – see Fiona Millar's excellent *Guardian* article from September 2019, "Gove and Cummings honed their dark arts in education. Now they're using them to trash the country", https://bit.ly/3DAXUOV

7 Amazon had the chance to buy Netflix in its first five years and turned it down, having to build its Amazon Prime studio and streaming service from the ground-up having ceded first-mover advantage to Netflix. Much more damaging, Blockbuster video had the chance to buy Netflix in the same period for just $50 million. But Blockbuster was a victim of not being able to ask questions about how the future might be different from the present. At its peak – when Randolph and Netflix co-founder Reed Hastings came a-knocking – Blockbuster owned and operated 9,000 video and DVD rental stores in the U.S. alone, employed 84,000 people worldwide, and had 65 million registered customers. By failing to ask *How might the future be different from today?*, ten years later Blockbuster filed for bankruptcy with debts of more than $900 million. There's a good account of the downfall of Blockbuster at https://bit.ly/32aJOG9

8 The original 2009 presentation explaining Netflix's "Freedom and Responsibility" culture in detail is available to view on Slideshare at https://bit.ly/3FnH5qO

9 See "The Five Whys – A view from Dave Trott", *Campaign*, 21 September 2021, https://www.campaignlive.co.uk/article/five-whys/1726697

10 See Iain Coleman's article "The 4 'So Whats' of Impact" from 22.09.20 on the Impact Science blog, https://bit.ly/3JtFKBX

11 I'm not one to talk given that the third book in my "using data better" trilogy is equally modestly titled *How To Be Insightful*. I just prefer the original title and strapline from when the book was first published in Dutch, which translates as *Socrates in Sneakers* – "The practical, humorous guide full of theory and exercises to have better conversations by asking better questions". In his later, more ascetic days, Socrates was famed (via observations in Plato's dialogues) for never wearing any footwear at all, whatever the weather.

12 https://www.1hc.com/people/tim-bishop-qc/

13 Tom Cruise versus Jack Nicholson? It's worth two minutes and 39 seconds out of anyone's day, even if you only watched *A Few Good Men* last night. Check it out here: https://bit.ly/2YQ8Ybx

4

CURIOSITY DID WHAT, DID YOU SAY?

Abstract

Curiosity is a powerful human instinct that is at the heart of progress and innovation. It is at the root of our ability to both create problems (like climate change) and find solutions (like teenagers staging weekly strikes on a Friday, starting in one school in Sweden, but quickly rippling out across the world). But curiosity needs nurturing.

There are three strategies you can adopt to ensure that the curiosity of infancy is sustained throughout your life and not squashed out of you by school and then work. The first is to embrace curiosity as a way of life. The second is to use divergent thinking exercises to create options. And the third is precisely the opposite – to use convergent thinking exercises to make choices. The drumbeat to all of this is to arm yourself with the ability to ask smarter questions. One of the smartest formulations for asking smarter questions comes from the discipline of Design Thinking, and it begins, quite simply and humbly, with the three words *How might we ...?*.

DOI: 10.4324/9781003218470-4

HOW MANY PAIRS OF SCISSORS ARE THERE IN THE WORLD?

The British comedian and podcaster Richard Herring has a long-running series of interviews – often quizzing comedians and podcasters – known as *Richard Herring's Leicester Square Theatre Podcast* (*RHLSTP*).[1] From 2012 to the time of writing in late 2021, Herring had recorded more than 350 episodes of *RHLSTP*. Essentially a comedy chat show in front of a live audience, from the earliest episodes onwards Herring has always had up his sleeve what he calls emergency questions. He's published several books full of them, and in *Emergency Questions: 1001 Conversation Savers for Every Occasion*, he says that these questions are "designed to turn awkward silences into (occasionally) awkward conversations" (2018, p.1).

"Some Emergency Questions are outrageous, some crude, some surreal, some mundane," he goes on. "Many are just plain childish and silly, but they're not just thrown together (well not entirely) – they're designed to create stories, often ones that even the person telling them won't have thought to tell before" (ibid.). Herring knows himself and his content well, and the self-deprecation of that introduction is well deserved. Most of Herring's Emergency Questions are, indeed, crude, childish, and scatological, and he has an almost overwhelming fascination with limited series of topics, including Shrek, bigfoot, autofellatio, and the practicalities of the horror film, *The Human Centipede* (whether you know it or not, please don't Google it). This isn't to say that that *RHLSTP* isn't very funny indeed. It is. It's just that most of the questions are dumb.

That said, on some occasions during *RHLSTP's* nine-year run to date, Herring has used his generally flippant questioning style and his reliance on Emergency Questions in particular to have his guests voice "some wonderful indiscretions, but also some serious revelations – most famously Stephen Fry feeling comfortable enough to discuss a recent suicide attempt" (2018, p.2). The question that opened Stephen Fry up to revelation was simply *What's it like being you?*, which I do believe is a genuine smart question. More often than not, however, they're just surreal (e.g. *535. Do you see yourself as a pterodactyl or a lawnmower?*) or, as Herring observes, silly.

One of Herring's Emergency Questions – *548. How many spoons do you think there are in Cairo?* – reminded me of a thought exercise I first learned from my half-brother Jeremy.[2] We shared a father – Kenneth – and though we were born more than 30 years apart to different mothers, we were always close. Jeremy was one of the most brilliant, multilayered people I've known. Even though he was also one of the busiest, he was always someone who would always make time to stimulate and attempt to sate others' curiosity. He was the very embodiment of Einstein's maxim: "The important thing is not to stop questioning. Curiosity has its own reason for existing." Part of the so-called brain drain in the early 1970s, Jeremy moved from Oxford to Harvard to become professor of chemistry in 1974. He was soon elevated to fellowship of the Royal Society and numerous other illustrious academic societies and associations. He published more than 250 academic papers and came within a cigarette paper of a Nobel Prize for his work on enzymology and catalysis.

Jeremy was that rarest of creatures in academic circles, a stellar research scientist who went on to become a successful and deftly diplomatic administrator. He was Dean of Harvard from 1991 until his untimely death in 2008. It was said that his job was to raise $1 million a day during his tenure, from alumni and benevolent institutions; he averaged $2 million. In the mid-1990s, he persuaded Bill Gates to start his philanthropic donations early, with a $15 million donation in 1996 to computer science and engineering programmes and a pledge to wire up every dorm room with superfast cable and to provide every student with a computer (even though it had to be Windows-compatible, the gesture was more than generous). This is the same Bill Gates who dropped out of Harvard after just two years of study in 1975, shortly before he set up Microsoft with Paul Allen.

When I was growing up 50 miles from London in the 1970s and 1980s, Jeremy would visit regularly, passing through between this congress and that conference. He'd always make time to help with my chemistry and biology homework. And after dinner, he'd get a twinkle in his eye and ask a seemingly unanswerable question. My favourite and the one that's lodged most firmly in my memory was *How many pairs of scissors are there in the world?* It is a question to which we returned more than once, accompanied by my father and whatever visiting academics Jeremy had in tow.

Asking a question for which there is no obvious data source – particularly 15 or 20 years before Google – is at first, second, and 34th glance challenging. But what this sort of question does is start from a position of Socratic ignorance and allows you to build up a pointillist picture from the ground up, moving from the general to the particular. The starting question is not only Socratic, in that it starts the discussion from zero knowledge. It is also Socratic because it leads to further questions that can help take us towards some kind of resolution:

- When were scissors invented and how quickly did their use spread around the world?
- Did they start as an early industrial or agricultural product and then morph into becoming a tool for domestic use? If so, what was the timeline for that transition?
- What exactly should our definition of a pair of scissors be? Are we including any garden implements or toolbox staples, such as secateurs or pliers?
- How many pairs of scissors do we have in our own house?
- How typical are we of people in our country, in terms of relative affluence, number of people living in our house, ages of people living in our house, hobbies of people living in our house?
- Are some houses likely to have more or fewer pairs of scissors than us?
- How many categories of different types of houses are there in our country, and how many households per category are there – even just approximately?
- How many countries are there like ours – with similar numbers of pairs of scissors per capita – how many are there with more and how many with fewer?
- What are the populations of different countries, giving us multipliers for countries, types of households, and ultimately scissors?
- What professions use scissors in their daily work? Consider hairdressers, clothes-makers, surgeons, and vets, not to mention civic

dignitaries who need giant pairs of scissors to cut through ribbons when opening new day-care centres.

- Is usage of scissors increasing or decreasing? Is this a trend that's reflected equally across the world, in developed, developing, and newly emerging nations?
- Does the current global economic situation mean we're likely to produce more or fewer pairs of scissors?
- How long does a typical pair of scissors last and how often do they need to be replaced?
- What does a typical pair of scissors cost, to make and to buy?
- Can we create an affordability index for a pair of scissors?[3]
- What other calls are there on the metals and plastics used to make the blades and handles of scissors, and the screw that holds a pair together?
- Are there any factors that we should be aware of that might affect the sale and availability of pairs of scissors, from environmental concerns to fashion to a recent spate of stabbings using pairs of scissors?
- Did the invention of left-handed scissors lead to a sudden surge in the number of pairs of scissors?
- Is there any local, regional, or global legislation or regulation that might impact upon the popularity, availability, and cost of a pair of scissors?
- Are scissors threatened in the short, medium, or long term by alternative technologies such as LASER cutters?

Well, there are 20 questions for starters, some of which we raised and considered when we attempted to estimate the number of pairs of scissors in the world, some of which wouldn't even have been considerations to a late 20th-century conversation. One thing Jeremy always forbade us from doing at the start of one of his thought experiments was to make a guess of any kind. As a headstrong, disinhibited teenager, I'd want to make a guess and have all of us write down answers and put them in envelopes and see who came out closest once we'd talked and done some calculations for an hour or two. But Jeremy said a resounding "No!"

He knew – as he explained to me many years later during a family holiday on Cape Cod – that the act of guessing would have biased us. It would have been an assumption that anchored us to skew our answers in a way that would see us answer our questions unfairly. It would lead us to seek out my-side evidence and ignore evidence that contradicted our worldview. As a top-down approach, it would resist anything that went against where we were heading. We'd suffer all sorts of cognitive biases that Kahneman and Tversky and others have identified – Confirmation Bias, Hindsight Bias, Anchoring and Adjustment[4] (the favourite of the second-hand car dealer), and more.

What mattered far more than the destination was the journey. It mattered to Jeremy that we should be curious. We should ask questions to stimulate further questions which might refine the original question in new and surprising ways. We should be open to the possibility, the probability, the almost-certainty that our assumptions would be wrong. As a father and a brother, as a teacher and an administrator, Jeremy was urged on by Klein's epistemophilic instinct. He was a slave to curiosity because of the liberation it brings with it, both a slave and a disciple.

NOBODY KNOWS HOW A PENCIL IS MADE, LET ALONE A COMPUTER MOUSE

In 1958, the economist Leonard E. Read wrote a seminal paper in the journal *The Freeman* enigmatically titled "I, Pencil". The paper argues that there is no one anywhere in the world who knows how to make something as simple as a pencil; no one who has the breadth and depth of knowledge and experience to know how to do everything in the supply chain required to make this humble object. The paper is written in the voice of – bear with me – a pencil, and the pencil considers all of the different steps and stages and degrees of co-operation between experts in different fields that led to its creation. The pencil explains more:

> There isn't a single person in all these millions, including the president of the pencil company, who contributes more than a tiny, infinitesimal bit of know-how. From the standpoint of know-how the only difference between the miner of graphite in Ceylon and the logger in Oregon is

in the type of know-how. Neither the miner nor the logger can be dis-
pensed with, any more than can the chemist at the factory or the worker
in the oil field.[5]

The pencil's point is that there is no controlling force to capitalism and that all the different growers and miners and refiners and shippers in the supply chain know how to play their part, make their contribution, but no one knows how to do everything the entire length of that same supply chain. As the economist Milton Friedman concluded in a 1998 reprint of "I, Pencil": "The miracle of this pencil isn't that nobody knows how to make it. The miracle of the pencil is: how did it get made? The pencil is made of wood that was cut down by a saw ... to make the saw needed steel ... to make the steel needed iron ore, and on and on. Thousands of people – who don't speak the same language, practice different religions, and may very well hate one another if they were ever to meet – co-operate to make a pencil, all without knowing each other."[6]

Asking *Does anyone know how to make a pencil?* is a thought experiment akin to my brother Jeremy's *How many pairs of scissors are there in the world?* In his TEDGlobal talk from 2010, British author Matt Ridley argues that "the engine of human progress has been the meeting and mating of ideas to make new ideas",[7] as he says in the title of his talk, "When ideas have sex". He gives the example of progress from the Acheulean hand-axe made by *homo erectus* from 1.5 million to 500,000 years ago and the computer mouse dating to the 1980s. These two tools are of more or less identical size and shape, both designed to fit the human hand. But that's where the similarities end.

The hand-axe was made to the same design for a million years – the same tool made for 30,000 generations from one substance. The computer mouse is made from "a confection of different substances" – silicon, metal, plastic – and "a confection of different ideas", including transistors, lasers, control of a computer, and so on, in an accumulation of technology. The key to human progress and development, Ridley believes, is the exchange, combination, and specialisation of ideas and technology. And like Read and Friedman before him, Ridley says: "There is literally nobody who knows how to make a computer mouse." In co-operating across time and cultures, humans have created an interconnected global human brain, a construct considerably wiser than any one of us. And there's nothing more likely to stimulate curiosity than seeing what's possible beyond the ken of a single, isolated individual. Contrary to the premature death knell sounded by former British Prime Minister Margaret Thatcher in an interview in *Woman's Own*, there is such a thing as society.[8]

CONVERGENT AND DIVERGENT THINKING

We may be born with curiosity as a primal cognitive urge, but without a little scaffolding and eventually architecture to channel that urge, it can either wither or be stifled. In infancy, when language first comes on and Baron-Cohen's *if-and-then* Systemizing module kicks in, the tolerance and indulgence of parents, caregivers, and siblings helps to satisfy the 40,000 *Why?*-type questions children ask by the time they're five. As seen in the previous chapter, the worlds of both school and work – where it is too often deemed that there are only "correct" answers to some questions, but types of questions are often actively discouraged – are not set up to foster and sustain curiosity.

There are important strategies we can all follow to increase our chances of satisfying our curiosity, three ways we can trigger and stimulate the brain's reward pathways by making it more likely we'll have the breakthrough insights we crave by joining old and old together to make something new; to establish a profound and useful understanding of a person, a thing, a topic, or an issue. Because surfacing and articulating genuine insights is addictive. If we're sufficiently curious and take on board diverse enough stimulus that our subconscious mind can join together in new and unexpected ways, we up our number of genuine eureka moments and get a rewarding hit of dopamine each time we have such a breakthrough. This is mediated through the dopaminergic reward pathway that's triggered by sex and drugs and rock 'n' roll as well as winning at chess, skydiving, and knitting a scarf, though the rewarding hit from an insight is likely to be more like the latter cluster of successes than the former. This makes it less harmful and so more productive.

THING ONE: VORACIOUS CURIOSITY

The first thing we can do to make it more likely that we satisfy our curiosity is to be voracious in our appetite for new and diverse stimulus. Curiosity is not just for this problem you're looking to solve or that brief you've received from a colleague or a client. Curiosity is for life, and not just focused curiosity. As the rock star astrophysicist Neil deGrasse Tyson has said: "No one is dumb who is curious. The people who don't ask questions remain clueless throughout their lives." Giving in to our inner five-year-old, articulating our desire to know whether x caused y, y caused x, or if x and y were the result of a hidden third cause, z, is to exercise our curiosity muscles. The more we use them in pursuit of a particular challenge, the more we use them every day in every way. Curiosity is a virtuous, self-fulfilling cycle.

Crucially, asking questions is not just about asking questions of familiar sources or fishing in the usual ponds for information. In the prequel to this book, my 2020 tome *How To Be Insightful* set out a simple and effective framework for insightful thinking, the STEP Prism of Insight™ (no less). For those without a copy at hand, here's the model for ready reference.

Figure 4.1 The STEP Prism of Insight™ – a simple and effective tool for surfacing insights.

STEP is an acronym (not an initialism) whose component letters stand for Sweat – Timeout – Eureka – Prove. I've explained the framework and how to apply it in *How To Be Insightful* (see Chapters 4–9), so there's no need to go over that again here. It's Sweat that we're interested in. The book advises:

> *Absorb information, perspectives, and points of view from any and every source you can. Listen, read, turn up to events. Talk to people – people who know a lot about the area in which you're looking to solve a problem and innovate, but also those who know nothing about it. Take yourself outside your comfort zone and echo chamber. Seek out stimuli that help to reinforce your hunches, but also stimuli that contradict or are deeply opposed to it. Add some randomness and jitter into your data collection. And be curious forever. Not just for the current brief, today's quandary, this month's challenge. Ensure that the spirit of curiosity fills you always. (2020, p.79)*

From the perspective of asking smarter questions, what matters most is the diversity of stimulus required to make the Sweat phase super effective. If you always look in the same places – be it QAnon and Fox News, Peter Hitchens and Jordan Peterson on the one hand or *The Guardian* and AdContrarian, Christiane Amanpour and James O'Brien on the other – you won't find anything new. You need to be exposed to stimulus that is familiar and unfamiliar, expected and unexpected, confirmatory and contradictory. What's more, you need to be conscious of where on any given spectrum your source falls and – so far as is possible – not bring your assumptions with you when you absorb and muse on that content. Diverse stimulus and multiple perspectives, ideally right across that spectrum, round the back, and out the other side can really help to stretch and shape your curiosity. It's more likely to provide your brilliant, recombinatorial subconscious mind with the input it needs to throw back some truly outrageous mash-ups. And these are mash-ups that might just be insights.

THING TWO: DIVERGENT THINKING

The second strategy you can follow to bolster your curiosity is to make explicit and conscious use of divergent thinking exercises. Divergent thinking is the mode of thinking designed to generate multiple creative solutions, solutions that are "outside the box". Thinking divergently stimulates ideas outwith tightly proscribed expectations. It accepts new stimulus and enables us to create choices. It is precisely the kind of creativity that Ken Robinson was so keen to encourage in his TED talk. Not all or many solutions may be "right" – or, more correctly, helpful – but it's important when running divergent thinking exercises that individuals or subgroups within a whole team don't pooh-pooh ideas, particularly not as soon as they're articulated. In the philosopher Edward de Bono's language, solutions surfaced by divergent thinking exercises shouldn't be "black hatted".

In de Bono's "Six Hat" world, the (metaphorical) wearer of a black hat is cautious (not curious), points out errors or pitfalls of an idea, focuses on the risks, dangers, problems, or difficulties. You all know the sort. If you meet them socially, they'll put you off volunteering information about yourself or contributing to a discussion for fear of being shot down. In a workshop or exercise to develop creative ideas, they'll make you clam up, transporting you right back to school no doubt, and minimise contributions. Rather, all ideas – however lateral or tangential – should be encouraged. To facilitate this, encourage those you're working with to adopt the mindset of the improvisational comedian or actor. In improv, whatever another actor says becomes stimulus to "riff" against. Improv performers see everything as an opportunity, saying *Yes, and* … rather than *No, but* ….
Following are a couple of examples of divergent thinking exercises.

Divergent thinking exercise 1: Adjectives, Verbs, Nouns

If you're a language nerd like me, you may know that organisations – companies, charities, universities, and governments – are incredibly bound by facts. They're not terribly action oriented, and emotion – real stories of human potential – rarely get a look in. If you analyse the language organisations use to talk about the areas or issues they're supposed to be passionate about and count up just the adjectives (which connote emotion; words like "happy", "moderate", and "debilitated"), verbs (which connote action; words like "run", "smash", and "upset"), and nouns (facts, including data and statistics; words like "customer",

"25%", and "aneurism"), there's a remarkably similar pattern, whatever the sector, whatever the issue.

Typically, fully 70% (adjectives + verbs + nouns) are nouns, 20% are verbs, and just 10% are adjectives. This creates turgid, lumpen, fact-filled prose. On websites and social media feeds, in annual reports and leaflets, organisations attempt to browbeat readers into submission with facts, facts, facts; rationality, data, and statistics. Yet as we've already seen – from the works of Kahneman, Tversky, and others in cognitive psychology – we make our decisions emotionally using the part of the brain with no access to language. We only go on to justify them rationally, deploying the uniquely human grey and white matter, our cerebral cortices, which thrive on data and words.

This means that if we want to persuade others to take action, we need to do a much better job of appealing to their emotions. English – and many other languages – find it challenging to construct sentences and paragraphs that are equally balanced in terms of adjectives, verbs, and nouns; it's challenging to write a memo or CEO's statement in the annual report that has equivalent numbers of words connoting emotion, action, and fact. That said, we can do very much better than 10:20:70. It's quite straightforward to redress the balance to 25:25:50. This exercise shows you how.

In groups of 4–6, specify the topic or issue that you're looking to generate ideas for. Spend ten minutes going round the room, generating and capturing the most distinctive adjectives for the topic. No black hats, no value judgements. This shouldn't be difficult to do. People in an organisation think and talk and write about these topics every day. Yet this exercise can feel difficult because participants can feel as if their answers will be judged and they inhibit themselves – those wretched frontal lobes looking to spare their blushes, but at the same time wrecking our divergent thinking exercise. No matter. A good facilitator of this exercise – and the facilitator doesn't need to know anything about the topic to help "midwife" a long list of answers – she just needs to ask: *What are the distinctive adjectives you use to describe <TOPIC? Think about when people experience <TOPIC> for the first time – what about them? How would you describe <TOPIC> to a friend/family member/alien who'd never heard of it before?*

Adjectives, Verbs, Nouns: "social media"

ADJECTIVES (emotions)	VERBS (actions)	NOUNS (facts)
toxic, competitive, happy, sad, angry, fat	search, scroll, doom-scroll, surf, view, read	image, imagination, crime, (self-) harm
overwhelmed, buzzing, lonely, ugly, social	pretend, imagine, boast, show-off, modify	children, child, parents, family, youth
sad, worried, scared, rewarding, rewarded	edit, curate, suggest, live, relive, lie, serve	emoji, thumbs-up, smartphone, iPhone
afraid, exhausted, young, depressed	share, post, doctor, change, erase, delete	Tweet, like, impression, retweet, reward
misunderstood, curious, anxious, sleepless	compete, gladden, sadden, overwhelm	hate, love, picture, words, 280 characters
relentless, conflicted, digital, technical	undermine, disadvantage, irritate, waste	Instagram, Facebook, Twitter, TikTok
in denial, passive, uncertain, sleepless	destroy, vilify, troll, stalk, abuse, hate, hide	WhatsApp, platform, channel, medium
destructive, divisive, resentful, under-age	cannibalise, copy, rip-off, imitate, mediate	media, message, abuse, troll, revenge
annoyed, empowered, challenged, fake	collaborate, create, co-create, enhance	pretence, truth, lie, disinhibition, post, Snap
poisonous, abnormal, concerned, false	embellish, embroider, antagonise, annoy	illusion, friend, enemy, frenemy, time
conceited, vain, challenged, alone, lonely	like, favourite, share, re-post, applaud	time-sink, delusion, reality, (real) life, idiot
browbeaten, cowed, submissive, plastic	celebrate, discriminate, antagonise, spite	death, suicide, regulation, legislation, law

Figure 4.2 Completed Adjectives, Verbs, Nouns template on social media.

Run the full ten minutes and capture the words – on a flipchart or a column of a table in a PowerPoint slide for those running workshops online – so that all participants can see and read them. Capture them as they come out, not ordering or favouring any over any others. Start with adjectives because they're the words that are usually missing in corporate prose. Then do the same for another ten minutes each with verbs for action and finally nouns for facts. Thirty minutes in total for the preparation stage. Above in Figure 4.2 is a template some colleagues and I created recently on social media.

With the long lists of adjectives, verbs, and nouns created, take turns over a further ten minutes to go around the (breakout) room to generate novel sentences using at least one adjective, verb, and noun from the words you've generated. The facilitator should again encourage participants to create as many sentences as they can in a free-spirited and disinhibited way. Again, just as in the process of generating words, some groups can find it challenging to create novel sentences at first; they often say this is because they fear their expressions will be too banal or obvious. Again, encourage them to say the first thing that pops up, simply choosing one word from each column. Figure 4.3 shows the sentences we created using Figure 4.2's adjectives, verbs, and nouns focused on social media. Those in bold are the five we liked best.

Sentences: "social media"

SENTENCES
Young children who use social media share too much of their personal lives in a potentially toxic environment.
Instagram and Facebook encourage vulnerable, misunderstood young people to compete on social media platforms.
Images of self-harm are toxic. The social media platforms do little to moderate such harmful images.
There's no harm in using social media to share happy pictures of your life with family and friends.
Posting airbrushed images of perfection intimidates worried social media users, making them depressed and lonely.
Social media platforms leave little to the imagination and enable users to doctor images and curate lies.
I'm really annoyed and frustrated with Twitter for the fake news and hate it spawns, making a generation doom-scroll.
The lies and fake impressions served up by social media platforms make me feel anxious, browbeaten, and submissive.
It's very hard to take the plastic lives of social media users seriously.
I wish the companies behind social media did more to moderate the overwhelmingly-negative content that fills my feed.
Seeing myself on social media alongside my friends makes me feel so sad, fat, and angry that I want to hide.
The trolls on social media make young people's life a misery, making them think they're abnormal. With friends like this …

Figure 4.3 Completed sentences template from Adjectives, Verbs, Nouns exercise on social media.

Divergent thinking exercise 2: Guildford's Alternate Uses

Leonard Mlodinow is a theoretical physicist who has spent his career researching and teaching at prestigious academic establishments, from Caltech in Pasadena, California, to the Max Planck Institute for Physics in Munich, Bavaria. His extracurricular, non-academic credits include being a scriptwriter for *Star Trek: The Next Generation* and creating the computer games software business responsible for *Aladdin's Math Quest* in partnership with movie actor Robin Williams and director Steven Spielberg.

Mlodinow is also a prodigious non-fiction author, writing books solo and in partnership with collaborators as diverse as Stephen Hawking and Deepak Chopra. This means he's not your typical Caltech theoretical physicist. In perhaps his most-mainstream popular science book – written alone – he set out the neuroscience of insightful thinking with a clarity that no psychologist had managed before him. *Elastic: Flexible Thinking in a Constantly Changing World* is a practical primer in how to free your mind from bounded or frozen thinking, and how to enable it to work at its most agile and recombinatorial peak. He charts the wiring and the activation – the hardware and the software – of unbounded, creative thinking in such a readable and comprehensible manner that *Elastic* is a core text for my new curriculum, detailed in the previous chapter.

One of the simplest, best, and oldest tests of elastic thinking – Mlodinow's synonym for divergent thinking – is Guildford's Alternate Uses. Participants are given a short period of time – I like to give them one or three minutes – to think of as many different ways in which they could use a banal, household object. I give them a free choice, typically of a lace-up shoe, a house brick, or a paperclip. There are no right or wrong answers and the test isn't looking for specific solutions. Alternate Uses measures **fluency** (how many uses identified), **originality** (how different the uses are from the usual function), **flexibility** (how many totally different uses), and **elaboration** (how detailed the uses are).

In a minute, coming up with 15–20 different uses would demonstrate strong **fluency**. Saying a brick could be used to build a house, wall, garage, school, cathedral, and bus shelter wouldn't evidence much **originality**. Saying it could be a paperweight, vase, murder weapon, doorstop, weight for a workout, and barrier on a pet rodent's obstacle course – that's much more original, as is using a lace-up shoe as an impromptu wine cooler when rowing on a lake. First tie one end of a lace to the boat's rowlocks and the other to a loop on the shoe. Then, put the bottle of wine (cork in or lid screwed on, of course) into the shoe. Finally, allow the shoe to float in the water, gently cooling the wine. However hot the air temperature, the water will be closer to a wine fridge than a sauna. That's original, and it's also **elaborate**. And the range of different uses we were beginning to list for a brick earlier this paragraph? That's **flexibility**. I can't take credit for many of the solutions. I've used this exercise dozens of times in the insightful thinking training courses I run, and I'm grateful to my diverse trainees for many of these most excellent Alternate Uses. Particularly the shoe as an impromptu wine cooler while out rowing. That was yours, Stefan.

THING THREE: CONVERGENT THINKING

The third and final strategy you can follow to make curiosity work harder for you is the mirror image of the second: to make calculated, explicit use of convergent thinking exercises. Convergent thinking exercises force us to make choices and narrow down our options, in a sense restricting ourselves to answers that provide "correct" solutions or answers to problems. Where divergent thinking exercises see us zoom out, convergent thinking exercises do the opposite – they make us zoom in. When you're looking to answer a smart question – perhaps with the goal of surfacing and articulating insights – it helps to zoom out then zoom in, repeatedly moving from divergent to convergent thinking exercises, perhaps two, three, or four times when addressing a challenge.

Convergent thinking exercise 1: The Cocktail Party Pitch

Participants in this exercise should imagine they're at a cocktail party. Not a very likely event in the pandemic-burdened early 2020s, you might say, unless you happen to be on the staff of the U.K. Prime Minister Johnson, throwing a series of Christmas parties at Number 10 Downing Street in December 2020 when the U.K. was in lockdown and London classified as Tier 3.[9] Nevertheless, imagine that you are, casting your mind perhaps to the Don Draper era of the TV series *Mad Men*.

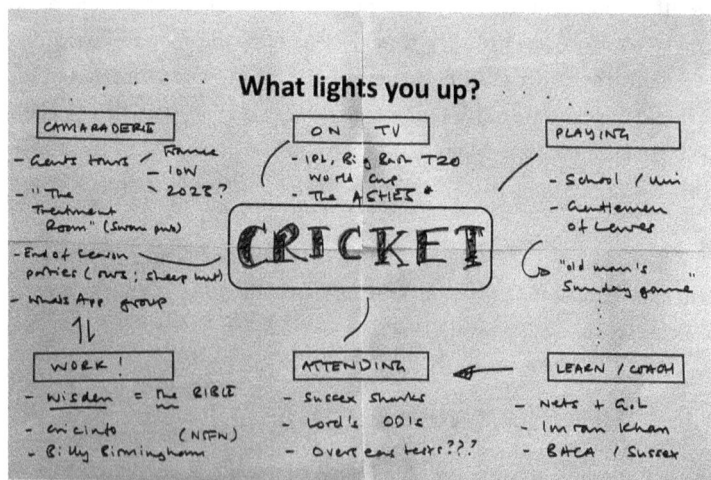

Figure 4.4 Mindmap of the author's passion for cricket, answering "What lights you up?"

Now imagine you need to answer the question *What's it like being you?* or *What lights you up?*, two much smarter questions that elicit much more authentic and rounded autobiographical answers than *What do you do?* Spend 20–30 minutes writing notes for your answer, perhaps in the form of a spidergram – bubbles or circles containing themes and topics you want to cover, joined together by firm lines (denoting a strong connection), arrows (representing a causal relationship), and sometimes even dotted lines (demonstrating a more tenuous relationship). There's one I prepared earlier – on my passion for cricket – shown in Figure 4.4.

Each participant then makes a short presentation – a Cocktail Party Pitch – to the others taking part in the exercise, based on the notes you've prepared. Ideally it will obey the Cocktail Party Rule, which states: "If you want to be boring, talk about yourself. If you want to be interesting, talk about what matters to those who are listening." Participants should speak for a minute or two – agree the timing before you brief participants – and observe how the exercise (magically) enables even those who hate public speaking to make a compelling case. Because they're focused on the topic, they will make choices – convergently – deciding what to include. Just as important, they'll have chosen what to leave out.

Convergent thinking exercise 2: The Pixar Pitch

I first came across the Pixar Pitch exercise from the American business writer Dan Pink.[10] Disney's brilliant cartoon animation studio Pixar insists that the narrative structure of every film it makes can fit – naturally and in no sense forced – into a simple and unique six-cell template. It goes like this:

1. "Once upon a time ..." 2. "Every day ..." 3. "Then one day ..."
4. "Because of that ..." 5. "Because of *that* ..." 6. "Until finally ..."

I've used this template in many different contexts, when training many different disciplines. These include storytelling (generally), data storytelling (specifically), and insightful thinking. As a convergent thinking exercise, it forces those using it to make choices – again about what they include and what they omit. It's focused on a period of time, which can be minutes but is often weeks, months, or years. It has an excellent double, causative contingency ("Because of that ..." immediately followed by "Because of *that* ...").

Once upon a time ... there were two college dropouts called Steve, working all hours in their parents' garages in California.

Every day ... they put all their time and effort into building computers to help the little guy compete with The Man.

Then one day ... they launched and sold 200 Apple Is. They sold ten thousand times as many of the Apple II.

Because of that ... they ensured that Apple became one of the most innovative, empowering companies in the world.

Because of <u>that</u> ... Apple now sells 20m Macs a year but 200m iPhones each year, a decade after Steve Jobs died.

Until finally ... Apple became the world's first $3tn company, worth more than the entire FTSE100. Not bad for two college dropouts called Steve.

Figure 4.5 A Pixar Pitch about Apple.

I find the Pixar Pitch works best when working with teams looking to answer questions – often critical business questions – and they've been fully immersed in all the data, research, and reports about an issue or a topic. Their minds are overbrimming with information, and we want them to see the forest from the trees. The Pixar Pitch by its very constricted nature enables them to do just that. Figure 4.5 gives an example of the Pixar Pitch used to tell a data-rich story about Apple.

DESIGN THINKING

Curiosity and a desire to build smarter solutions are two signature characteristics of the philosophy and approach known as Design Thinking. Design Thinking was developed by the brothers David and Tom Kelley and formalised in the Kelleys' innovation consultancy IDEO and via David's professorial chair at Stanford University's d.school (or design school). Because their methodology works and because they have the generosity of spirit and approach, over the last 20 years of the last century and the first 20 of this, Design Thinking has become an incredibly popular, open access tool for generating multiple, design-solution-led approaches quickly and efficiently.

At the heart of Design Thinking is a five-step sprint, typically run over days, weeks, or months, depending on the practitioner or the urgency of the project. Weeks is normal, though when Design Thinking was the subject of a TV documentary – an ABC Nightline special – IDEO worked with the producers to run a Design Sprint in just a week to create working prototypes of a revolutionary new shopping cart (trolley on the East side of the Atlantic).[11]

The five steps in a classic Design Sprint are: Empathize, Define, Ideate, Prototype, and Test. IDEO's process is so well established and such an inspiration – from Google's own *six*-step variant to the Sprint approach and book by Jake Knapp – that there's no point my rehashing it here. Personally, I believe that Design Thinking takes insights much too lightly. For me, the Empathize step often isn't populated by the high bar I set for insights – profound and useful understanding – but that is, as I say, just my perspective. For me, the STEP Prism of Insight that my business, Insight Agents, has developed is a much more reliable way of generating genuine, breakthrough insights, and that's been proven time and again, from start-ups to global corporates.

THREE MAGIC WORDS

What I really like about Design Thinking is its application of a clearly delineated approach to creative thinking, its rapidity and iterative nature, and the fact that it's rooted in curiosity. If there are any cats in the vicinity of IDEO offices, they'd better watch out. This passion for curiosity is also rooted in the way Design Thinking asks the questions it asks. Most questions under a Design Thinking lens start with the three magic words *How might we ...?* This expression is so open, free of assumptions, and optimistic. It's empowering, liberating, and non-judgemental. It's full of creativity and creative confidence, certain that there is a solution to be found, but open-minded enough not to impose any proscriptions from the get-go.

It asks **HOW** in what way? What are the component parts of a solution that haven't been joined together before? If we are to come up with genuine innovation, we're going to have to fill the hopper of our minds with all manner of stimulus. Some stimuli might be obvious and directly relevant. Others might appear to be totally irrelevant, but once in the brilliant, recombinatorial blender of our minds – both conscious and subconscious – there's every possibility they can be joined together in new and hitherto unexplored ways. "How" opens up potential and closes nothing down, too soon.

It asks **MIGHT**. Might is a modal verb, used with and to govern the base form of other verbs. It indicates and ushers in a whole world of potential and opportunity. Again, it closes nothing down and leaves all possibilities on the table. Experience might matter or it might be redundant. "Might" is mighty powerful in the three magic words of Design Thinking's single most important question, *How might we ...?*

And it asks **WE**. We is inclusive. It's about teamwork and partnership and cross-fertilisation of thinking from many different functions. If you work in a pharmaceutical business, for example, a cross-functional team might be built up of subject matter experts in medical, regulatory, marketing, research and development (R&D), patient engagement, insight and analytics, and on and on. If you work in finance, it could include research, analytics, market making, buy-side, sell-side, brokerage, investment strategy, risk, trading, planning, portfolio management, actuarial, and on and on. "We" is the third powerful word in Design Thinking's super-smart question *How might we ...?*. Here are three examples of questions using the *How might we ...?* formula. This should give you a flavour of quite how and why this is a superior formulation for asking questions that satisfy our curiosity.

How might we convince our customers to use our app more often? (NOT just *What's wrong with our app?* or *Why aren't people using our app?*). This moves from functional, operational issues to unlocking questions about the relationship between customers and companies – particularly service companies like banks – at a much more fundamental level.

How might we accelerate the adoption of cashless payment? (NOT just *Why are people so wedded to cash?* or *What are people scared of?*). This approach has directed PayPal's strategy.

How might we hold politicians to account? (NOT just *Is it possible to stop politicians lying?* or *Why do people believe a word the government says?*). This is the approach and philosophy of the agit-prop protest group Led By Donkeys who use what politicians say, particularly on Twitter, to highlight the lightning-quick hypocrisy of politicians in 2020s Britain.

You know, *How might we ...?* encourages – mandates, even – that multiple perspectives and points of view are factored and baked into problem-solving. The seemingly innocent formulation reeks of possibility and brings to mind the adidas® mantra "Impossible is nothing".

We should paint these words on the walls of every office, factory, and particularly school classroom. We should tattoo it on the inside of our eyelids to help us dream in a fundamentally curious way.

SUMMING UP

Asking smarter questions, free from bias, assumptions, and prejudice, is critical if we're going to tackle the increasing "wicked" problems we face – as individuals, families and communities; as companies, nations, and as a species. Curiosity is the superpower that drives us forward, and by making it a critical tool in our armoury, history has shown that together we can use it to create artefacts as extraordinary as the computer mouse. And even the pencil.

QUESTIONS ABOUT QUESTIONS – INTERVIEW 4 OF 14

NAME	Jane Frost, CBE
ORGANISATION	Market Research Society
ROLE	Chief Executive Officer

Curiosity is a defining characteristic of both Jane Frost and the industry she leads. Since 2011, she's been CEO of the U.K.'s Market Research Society, and before that she had an illustrious career in some of the most curious – and insightful – organisations around: Unilever, Shell, and the BBC. Immediately before joining the Market Research Society (MRS), Frost spent five years working for Her Majesty's Revenue and Customs (HMRC; the tax office), first setting up its customer function and then establishing its digital and social media strategy. HMRC is a critical part of government and one which radically simplified and improved effectiveness under her watch. The golden thread running through her various roles is her passion for customer-led change and innovation.

"You can't get anywhere without questions in our business," says Frost:

Asking smart questions is what we aspire to do, to get to the real benefit we deliver to our clients. We provide the evidence and insight with which they can make informed, strategic decisions. Being curious is the key to asking good questions. Being curious – and being a good listener. If you don't poke at things – and wait to see what happens once you've poked – that's when you can let your assumptions take over. It helps to be good at pattern recognition – spotting trends, anomalies, outliers – and it's also of benefit to be new to a topic. That's an advantage that agencies can have over in-house research teams who research the same topics, issues, or markets over and over again.

Although Frost believes there's no such thing as a dumb question, she believes that there are *trivial* questions, and these are often closed *What?*-type questions. "Asking *Why?* is the fundamental start of everything," she notes:

I've never understood why small children are squashed for asking that. Just imagine if da Vinci had asked **what** the Vatican wanted on the Sistine Chapel ceiling, he might have been told 'gold and red'. By asking 'Why?' he was briefed to glorify God's relationship to humanity, and suddenly creative freedom flowed within that framework. Because he asked 'Why?'.

Frost believes that researchers should start by questioning themselves, not automatically assuming they're right (or, indeed, automatically assuming that they might be wrong). "In social research just as much as commercial research, you need to force yourself out of the 'my worldview' mindset. For a company, there's little point asking about what you're selling. You need to ask about what consumers are buying:

In social research, this is even more important. Here, too much empathy isn't nearly as helpful as being interested. For instance, just because **you** think that you would leave an abusive partner, there's no point asking women in abusive relationships why they haven't left **their** partners. They don't want to make themselves or their children look foolish because they haven't been able to get out – for whatever reason. You need to listen before you ask. A good way to apply this more generally is to alternate qual-quant-qual-quant to be sure you can refine questions and make them truly smart; that you don't overdo or overload the framing, because framing can so easily skew answers. Get the wrong word – particularly cross-culturally – and you can ruin research.

For Frost, market researchers are more likely to ask decent questions if they're well briefed by their clients. Briefs that are too narrow and don't let researchers think for themselves don't get the most out of agency partnerships:

> *Ideally, clients will allow and encourage their research partners to challenge them; to suggest they probe in areas they've never thought about, using methodologies they may think are off-the-wall. We all need frameworks, but we also need freedom within them.*

During the time she's been asking questions for and about the organisations she's worked in, Frost believes that technology has been a boon and a bane. On the plus side, there are many new tools and techniques available to the researcher. These include as neuro-insight, social media listening, and digital ethnography – an approach that adapts ethnographic methods to the study of the communities and cultures using computer-mediated social interaction. On the downside, we have the explosion of data. "That truly is a wasted opportunity," avers Frost:

> *Too many people – researchers and clients – are wowed by the bigness of Big Data – not the smart things it could help them to understand. Too many of us spend too much time just spear-fishing with data rather than asking* 'How smart is our data?' *or better yet* 'How could we get meaningful intelligence from our data?' *Big data sets have also fooled many clients into thinking that the only people who really understand data are technical data analysts, when in fact many more of us in the sector do.*

Overall, Frost is optimistic about the current and future opportunities for the research industry. All sorts of organisations have never needed more clarity on how they can thrive by better serving their customers, particularly in the wake of COVID. With an established track record of asking smarter questions – not to mention a growing armoury of tools that enable researchers to get closer to how and why we make the decisions we do – the U.K.'s £7 billion research, insights, and analytics industry[12] is well set for the bumpy road out of the other side of the pandemic.

JANE FROST'S TOP TIPS FOR ASKING SMARTER QUESTIONS

1. If you want to understand your market, focus on the customer, not the company or product.
2. Flip between qualitative and quantitative research to refine and build smart questions.
3. Question yourself and your assumptions before building any research questions.
4. Park your prejudices and prior experience at the door.
5. Don't be dazzled by the bigness of Big Data. Make it earn its place at the table.

NOTES

1 For many years, I mistakenly thought that all collections of initial letters of words clustered together were called acronyms. I've always been deeply opposed to the use of (what I thought were all) acronyms in any form of communication, particularly from companies, organisations, and brands. Though a time-saving shorthand between colleagues and peers, they are little more than jargon that excludes those not in-the-know from joining in the conversation.

   During the first COVID lockdown, I started a regular series of fortnightly weekend walks with a data analytics guru friend of mine, Tim, up and over the Sussex Downs. As the lockdowns dragged on and merged into one, the walks continued like a regular, dependable drumbeat. On one of these walks, Tim put me right. An acronym – a word made up from the first letters of other words – has to be able to be pronounced as a word, such as ASCII, IMAX, or LASER. Meanwhile, where the letters have to be voiced out individually – as in the BBC, the FBI, or FYI – you have an initialism. Thanks to Tim's clarification and nice distinction, I now get to rail against both acronyms AND initialisms.

   When Herring talks about his podcast in abbreviated form, he attempts to turn the initialism into an acronym by pronouncing *RHLSTP* as ruh-huh-luh-stu-puh. The Apple podcasts link is here https://bit.ly/3n4uOBz

2 There is a largely affectionate obituary to Jeremy in the Harvard University Newspaper *The Crimson* – so often his adversary – here https://www.thecrimson.com/article/2008/4/4/jeremy-r-knowles-jeremy-r-knowles/ He revealed another side of his polymathic self – his love for classical

music, particularly Bach – in his appearance on National Public Radio's *Mad About Music*. A transcript of his 2002 interview with Gilbert Kaplin is here: https://bit.ly/3F5HLRB

3   We talked in these terms in the late 1970s and early 1980s, or at least Jeremy did, several years before *The Economist* formally created its "Big Mac Index". As the editors say on the webpage dedicated to the 2021 index, it was created in 1986 "as a light-hearted guide to whether currencies are at their 'correct' level. It is based on the theory of purchasing-power parity (PPP), the notion that in the long run exchange rates should move towards the rate that would equalise the prices of an identical basket of goods and services (in this case, a burger) in any two countries." For more on a joke that's proved incredibly useful over the past 35 years, see https://www.economist.com/big-mac-index

4   A classic demonstration of Anchoring and Adjustment is to ask two groups of people: "How many countries do you think there are on the continent of Africa?" Then go on to say to one group "I think there are 72" and the other group "I think there are 24". Because you anchor them high, the first group will tend to guess around 50 on average; because you anchor them low, the second group will tend to guess around 35 on average. On the second-hand car lot, a car priced at say £2,999 can easily sell for about £500 less, even if the true worth is closer to just a few hundred pounds. The act of anchoring the potential customer means they feel they've got a terrific bargain if they can haggle the salesman down by a significant chunk of change. This is less straightforward to pull off in the internet age. Today, there is very much less information asymmetry than 20–30 years ago and the market value of any model of any vehicle of any age is available with a simple web search.

5   You can read "I, Pencil" at https://mises.org/library/i-pencil. There's an excellent episode (#236) of *Freakonomics Radio* – the podcast from the dynamic Freakonomics duo, journalist Stephen J. Dubner and academic economist Steven Levitt – from 2016 that tells the story beautifully, titled "How can this possibly be true?" at https://freakonomics.com/podcast/i-pencil/, featuring British writers Matt Ridley and Tim Harford. Well worth the diversion.

6   Milton Friedman on the film on "I, Pencil" in 1980: https://www.youtube.com/watch?v=67tHtpac5ws

7   Matt Ridley's 2010 TEDGlobal talk "When ideas have sex" is instructive on insightful thinking, asking smarter questions, and the way that ideas from different individuals and cultures combine to produce totally new and unexpected concepts, blueprints, products, and whole new categories. See https://bit.ly/3D5YV0g

8   Looking to cut back investment in the welfare state – a trope and complex of policies adopted by successive Conservative governments, from Cameron and Clegg's austerity to Johnson's axing of Universal Credit – Thatcher said that the homeless "… are casting their problems on society and who is society? There is no such thing! There are individual men and women and there

are families and no government can do anything except through people and people look to themselves first." The truth is not only rather more nuanced than that. It's also the polar opposite.

9 At the time of the December 2020 Downing Street parties for dozens of people, official guidance to the public said the following about meeting with others: "You should only spend time in your house or garden with the people you live with. This means you cannot invite people you don't live with over to your house or in your garden unless they are in your support bubble. // You can meet with others in public outdoor places, such as beaches or parks, but only in groups of up to 6 people. // You should maintain social distancing from anyone not in your household or support bubble." Clearly, Johnson's people hadn't got or read that particular memo, even if it was them who wrote it.

10 Pink provides a regular, monthly series of very short instructional videos with hints and tips that are immediately applicable. The "Pinkcast" on the Pixar Pitch is here: https://bit.ly/31iTaiD

11 The ABC Nightline special on the IDEO shopping cart is on YouTube at https://bit.ly/31niq7s

12 Jane's own organisation, the MRS, regularly scopes the scale of the industry. This is 2021's estimate: https://bit.ly/31zCWkZ

5

WHAT MAKES A GOOD QUESTION?

Abstract

The ability to ask smarter questions depends on both content and form, the *what* and the *how*, the message and the medium. Smarter questions need to be created and delivered in the right environment to have their desired impact, and both parties need to pay focused attention to their respective roles in asking and answering questions.

The hallmarks of what constitutes a good question depend fundamentally on the character and disposition of the questioner. These include open-mindedness, curiosity, and pluralism in both stimulus and input – being more foxy and less hedgehoggy. Good coaches often embody these qualities. Characteristics not found in those asking smarter questions include prejudice, a fixed view of the world, and an inability to see a problem from multiple perspectives.

ON THE IMPORTANCE OF BEING MORE FOXY (AND LESS HEDGEHOGGY)

Nate Silver is a titan in the world of predictive analytics. His 2012 book *The Signal and the Noise: Why So Many Predictions Fail – But Some Don't* summarises his distinctive and impactful approach to reading the runes

DOI: 10.4324/9781003218470-5

of data, sticking one's neck out, and estimating where the puck will land. Silver and his team run FiveThirtyEight, an organisation that blogs with fascination about both politics and sport. Since starting up in 2008, they've been variously affiliated to *The New York Times*, ESPN, and now ESPN's sister company, ABC News. FiveThirtyEight is named after the number of electors in the U.S. Electoral College. Indeed, the blog correctly called all but one of the states in Obama's first presidential election victory in 2008 and 50 out of 50 ahead of his re-election in 2012. Things were a little less on point for FiveThirtyEight in the 2016 presidential race – as were so many things in that year of unexpected electoral triumphs by demagogues – but it's safe to say that they were among the least wrong of all pundits.[1]

The current FiveThirtyEight logo is a stylised face of a fox, made up of a black triangle for the nose, a white pentagon for the face, and two conjoined sandy triangles for its ears, reminiscent of an upside-down mountain range. Earlier iterations of the logo were more obviously fox-like, but once you know what the current logo is supposed to be, you can't mistake it for any other animal. That said, because Silver's organisation is focused on insight, intelligent writing, and journalism, the icon can also be seen to represent a pencil. Silver himself has said that the fox has been the blog's enduring mascot because it is "emblematic of FiveThirtyEight's pluralistic approach, as expressed in the old saying 'the fox knows many things, but the hedgehog knows one big thing'",[2] an old saying coined by the Greek lyric poet of the seventh century BCE, Archilochus.

This ancient maxim about foxes and hedgehogs was popularised by the Oxford academic Isaiah Berlin, the founding president of Wolfson College, Oxford. In 1953, Berlin published an essay titled *The Hedgehog and the Fox* in which he categorised a broad sweep of philosophers, playwrights, and novelists as either hedgehogs (who look at the world through a single lens) or foxes (whose worldview cannot be reduced to just one idea). His essay focused on Tolstoy and applied the hedgehog-fox distinction to Tolstoy's great novel *War and Peace*, concluding that the Russian author was a fox by nature but a hedgehog by conviction, and that such a tension was evident throughout the book.

It didn't take long for others to take Berlin's classification seriously – much more seriously, indeed, than the author intended. He subsequently claimed it was a joke or an "enjoyable intellectual game". It certainly captured attention and raised Archilochus' dictum and distinction from obscurity to common parlance. It inspired Nate Silver to celebrate the role of the wily fox in his branding and the declared purpose of FiveThirtyEight. And it regularly crops up in political commentary on both sides of the Atlantic. In the U.K. in mid-2021, Prime Minister Johnson's controversial former strategist, the disgraced Dominic Cummings, described his old boss as neither a monomaniacal hedgehog nor a pluralist fox but rather "a pundit who stumbled into politics".[3] The fox-hedgehog metaphor and distinction has long appealed to Cummings, who used it in a 2015 review of Philip Tetlock's book *Superforecasting: The Art and Science of Prediction* in *The Spectator*,[4] saying:

> *The worst forecasters were those with great self-confidence who stuck to their big ideas ('hedgehogs'). They were often worse than the dart-throwing chimp. The most successful were those who were cautious, humble, numerate, actively open-minded, looked at many points of view, and updated their predictions ('foxes'). TV programmes recruit hedgehogs so the more likely an expert was to appear on TV, the less accurate he was.*

Being foxy – approaching challenges with no single, fixed way of doing things, but instead bringing a quiver full of strategies that might solve a problem – is undoubtedly a characteristic of those who ask smarter questions. Hedgehogs subscribe to a singular, overarching narrative that brings with it all kinds of assumptions and views about how the world is and should be. Foxes, by contrast, are sceptical about the value overarching narratives have in the first place. While hedgehogs approach a world of uncertainty with their fixed *Weltanschauung* and hope that by imposing that the world will somehow – magically – make sense, foxes are keen to get all their evidence in place before they start making sense of things. Foxes are crafty and endlessly inventive, like the hero of the Trojan War Odysseus, whom Homer described as *polúmētis* – "of many devices". The smartest foxes channel their inner Odysseus and use smarter questions and questioning to get ahead.

THE POWER AND WISDOM OF COACHES

I remember clearly the very first session of coaching I experienced with my first executive coach (I had a few over my corporate career, unadvisedly searching for meaning in working for others, but that's another story). Grahame – for that was his name – seemed to do very little other than smile, coax, and cajole me into talking. I was anticipating open questions from him and me making most of the running. But I hadn't really thought about the *how* of coaching. Stuck as I was, I was interested much more in the *why* – getting me out of that rut, giving me renewed passion and purpose.

As we came towards the end of our Friday morning immersion session in a light and airy room on the fifth floor of the London's Royal Institution of British Architects, Grahame motioned me to gather the flipchart pages I'd populated with marker pen hieroglyphics and PostIt notes, in response to various different open questions during I time together. Meticulously, I removed the Blu Tack from each A1 sheet, stacked them in order, and rolled them up. Grahame passed me an elastic band, and I twirled it once, twice, three times around the pages before it was tight enough to twang. And then I handed it to him.

Grahame's perma-grin broadened. "Oh no!" he chortled, benevolently. "These aren't for me. They're for you. It's a really good exercise for you to take these home, not think about the content consciously over the weekend, and then type them up on Monday." "Oh!" he continued. "Perhaps you could email them to me when we're done?" I can't remember what my employer was paying for the course of coaching we'd embarked upon, but it was certainly in the thousands. "What kind of sorcery is this?" I wondered. "He didn't write anything – I did. And now I have to type it all up too?" It made no sense. The tail was wagging the dog. It was as if my bosses were paying this charlatan to tell me the time by reading my watch.

As I headed home to Sussex, welcomed friends for the weekend to ramble the South Downs and drink too much red wine, some of Grahame's *how* slowly dawned on me. Many years (and several coaches) on, I know that coaching yields answers from within the coachees themselves, not according to the prescription, prejudices, or presumptions of the coach. The best of them use smart, open, assumption-free questions to enable their clients to find the answers for themselves, answers that are often hiding in plain sight. And while it took redundancy, a new direction, and the proximate peril of an impossible job to which I was entirely unsuited – plus the very gentle, questioning direction of my very wise wife Saskia, now herself a qualified coach – I got there in the end.

This whole book is predicated on the belief that whatever we do, we do it better if we can pose and ask smarter questions. All the way through, there are examples of smarter (and dumber) questions. The final chapter sets out what I believe to be the best questions in the world, while this chapter and the next are more about the *how* of asking good and bad questions. The *what* and *how* of better and worse questions come from both my narrative exploration of different themes – from classical Greek philosophy to sales, Zen Buddhism to journalism – and from the mouths of those experts I've interviewed, whose jobs depend on their ability to ask smarter questions. Before I spell out in detail what I believe to be the qualities of a good question, the next section of this chapter runs together three interviews, two with coaches and one with a conflict mediator. There are obvious commonalities running between all three as well as some notable differences. What is clearest of all to me is that all three are most definitely foxes and not hedgehogs.

QUESTIONS ABOUT QUESTIONS –
INTERVIEW 5 OF 14

NAME	Tim Johns
ORGANISATION	Orato Consulting
ROLE	Founder and coach

For executive coach Tim Johns, there is a clear distinction between those who fulfil the role of advisor, mentor, and coach. An advisor tells her client what to think and do. A mentor tells her client what she would do if she was her client's age or position, with advice often based on what she did at the exact same, relevant stage of her career. A coach, meanwhile, has an altogether different starting point:

> *A coach starts from one assumption and one assumption only: that the client knows what the answer is to the challenge that they're facing. Coaches don't know what's right for their clients – they can simply guide them and help them to get unblocked and see things their way. This is because, unless someone being coached owns the answer, they won't act upon it.*

In *How To Be Insightful*, the Dutch philosopher and behavioural scientist Eric Bartels told me about the approach used by his consultancy, Inner Why, to identify and articulate organisational purpose.[5] Whether working with start-ups or centuries-old businesses, Bartels et al. start from the self-same, single assumption that Johns does in coaching: that the purpose (the answer) lies within the executives who lead and work in the organisation. Naively at the time, I described Bartels et al. as "idea midwives". Reflecting on what we learned in Chapter 2 about Socrates's heritage (with his mother a midwife) and his comparison of his ignorant but smarter questioning approach to midwifery – maieutics – perhaps my description wasn't so naïve after all. Bringing the beautiful out of sometimes painful and messy labour is the role of the midwife, the philosopher, and the coach.

Coaching is non-judgemental – about the individual, the situation they find themselves in, and the decisions they've made that have taken them to that point. Because it's non-judgemental, it doesn't lead to a proscribed set of solutions. Coaches can't live their coachees' lives for them. What they can do – by asking smarter questions – is help them to find their own solution. "Some say that no-one has a thought until they say it or write it down," observes Johns:

> *so asking questions to elicit answers is a way to help others think out loud. Most people suffer from some form of 'emotional constipation' most of the time – thoughts or feelings that they keep bunged up inside themselves – and good coaches use questions to help those they're working with to become unstuck. The right questions help people reframe or reconsider a situation or an event and this gives them a clearer picture of the way forward.*

For Johns, coaches need genuine curiosity and an interest in others, allied to both empathy and understanding of human motivation and behaviour. Good questions in coaching need also to be non-threatening – "you can't deliberately make people feel uncomfortable, judged, or threatened" – and they need to help coachees get unstuck:

> Many people speak to a coach because they've become stuck: their career hasn't not moved on as they'd imagined it would, they have dysfunctional workplace relationships, they're doing the wrong job, or they're not ready to be promoted. No matter how bright or far-sighted people may be, when they're stuck, all they can see is what's around them, and long-term solutions are hard to grasp.

This is a classic case of failure of Gestalt, of not being able to see the forest from the trees.

To get people talking, it can be as simple as asking what they want to talk about, but if you're stuck, it can take three or four sessions to be able to articulate what you want to talk about. This can be frustrating and make some feel as if they're going round in circles. This is where a model or framework, powered by questions, can help. One that Johns favours is the GROW model.

G	Goal	*What do you want to get out of this?*
R	Reality	*What are the most important factors that have led you to get stuck?*
O	Options	*What might you do to make things better?*
W	Will	*What effort are you prepared to put in to change?*

The right kind of non-judgemental questions can give those being coached sufficient emotional distance from the situation in which they find themselves stuck. For Johns, there is a truly magic question in coaching that can introduce that necessary distance. One version asks: *If you knew the answer, what do you think it would be?* That can lead to rapid – sometimes instant – unblocking. If not, having them project into the mind of someone they respect is often helpful. Try asking: *Who's the brightest person you know/the person you most admire? What would they tell you about how to solve the challenge you face?* Almost without exception, one of these two approaches will yield a passable, practical response. The act of projection depersonalises the blockage and the coach's response to the respected friend's imagined answer is then simply: *So, could that work for you?* By shifting the frame of reference, they're often at last able to visualise and analyse the scenario that's frustrating them, without having to think about it. This magic question truly is a great unblocker, and a variant Johns often uses to great effect in unblocking is: *If you had a magic wand, what would you do next?*

Johns also favours open questions in coaching, questions that don't return monosyllabic grunts, but rather encourage coachees to explore the issues in greater depth and operate under uncertainty. "It's important to focus on what's being said as well as what's not being said," encourages Johns:

> *generating self-awareness and reflection about the situation at hand and the range of possible options. That means listening – really listening – and taking people seriously; giving them the time to explore the issues. Listening demands not responding, embracing and enjoying silence, and allowing them to fill the silence with their own thoughts or observations.*

Like many coaches, Johns has his niche. His happens to be senior corporate executives. This is in part because of his long experience in the corporate world – at Unilever, Sainsbury's, and BT – and in part because of the nature of referral, from one corporate client to the next. But as a coach rather than an advisor or a mentor, Johns is confident he could coach executives from any sector:

> *Whether you're running a consumer goods business or a division of the national health service, you face the same kinds of challenges – stress, anxiety, feeling out of control, human relationships, feeling undervalued, overlooked, or ignored for promotion. These are the realities of the world of work. If you're looking to frame and ask smarter questions as a coach, what matters much more than sector-specific knowledge is humanity and*

empathy, understanding of how people get blocked and the questions to ask to get them unblocked.

Trained in the Meyler Campbell school of coaching, Johns is ambivalent at best about some of the most frequently used tools of his trade:

The explosion in data over recent years has given many coaches unwarranted confidence is psychometric tests. Yet just because a popular tool like Myers Briggs has been administered millions of times and there are vast lakes of normative data doesn't mean we should be confident in it ... particularly if it's not a particularly reliable or sensitive tool.

Too often, Johns has found that individual profiles vary over time and change as people get more senior or fulfil different roles. "So much of personality is dependent on context." He continues:

We can be professional extraverts but personal introverts, and Myers Briggs can't cope with that. Also, sensing and intuition aren't opposites – you can be both, but not according to Myers Briggs. As Dan Pink suggested in To Sell Is Human, *we're all ambiverts, depending on context. For me, it's astrology for people who went to business school. Coaches depend on it way too much. It's like smoking in the 1980s and 1990s – we knew it was no good for us, but many of us did it anyway.*

Johns' fundamental beef with Myers Briggs is that it reduces people to a set of rigid, mutually exclusive criteria and then uses these criteria both to judge others and also to excuse or indulge unacceptable behaviours:

because that's what we're like. Rigid criteria and judgment are antithetical to coaching. It's the same with the slapdash chucking about of neuroscience. We need much less personality profiling and bogus, often wilful misunderstanding of electrical and chemical reactions in the brain – ideally none at all. We need much more open, empathetic, non-judgmental questioning, questioning that allows and empowers those being coached to find the answers for themselves.

TIM JOHNS'S TOP TIPS FOR ASKING SMARTER QUESTIONS

1. Start from one assumption: that the person you're coaching already knows the solution.
2. Avoid questions that are judgemental or make those quizzed uncomfortable or threatened.
3. Reframe questions as if asked to the smartest person you know/the one you most admire.
4. Enjoy the sound of silence and allow the person you've questioned to fill that silence.
5. Stick to questioning approaches that you know work. Don't steal others' like a magpie.

QUESTIONS ABOUT QUESTIONS – INTERVIEW 6 OF 14

NAME	Pip Brown
ORGANISATION	Conflict Insights
ROLE	Director

Pip Brown is a conflict mediator. She helps warring parties to sort out disputes by helping them to see all sides of the battle in which they're embroiled. Having worked for many years in conflict environments from Mogadishu to Islamabad, five years ago she retrained to redeploy the skills she'd developed on the global stage to solve personal disputes. A Samaritans' listening volunteer for more than 20 years, Pip has long understood the value of asking smarter questions over giving advice, opening up a space in which apparently unbridgeable differences can be resolved. By helping all sides involved in a conflict broaden their perspective, conflict mediation allows them to notice and reflect on material facts or feelings from which their total immersion in the dispute had blinkered them. In this way, it is more likely that an accommodation can be reached because everyone can see what needs to change to allow them to move on and put the conflict behind them.

Just as disputes between countries and companies often up end in the courts, so conflicts between individuals are also frequently resolved by lawyers. The trouble is, when a conflict gets to court, the only winners tend to be the legal profession. Conflict mediation is an alternative to calling in the lawyers – an alternative that is often cheaper, quicker, and less stressful. Good questions in conflict mediation are open not closed, questions that unlock and open up issues and don't narrow them down to simple factual yes/no, black and white answers. "We're looking to prompt reflection and self-reflection, open up dialogue," notes Pip:

> *For the conflict negotiator, this means posing simple, open questions that encourage all parties to consider the issues from multiple points of view, shutting up, and actively listening. It means giving the conversation space to breathe. A frantic, frenetic interrogation is totally counter-productive, as all parties will have experienced that for too long in the period of active dispute, before they start working with a conflict negotiator.*

Pip's work often involves disputes between neighbours, frequently around noise and the aggravation that other people's noise can cause. Starting a process of mediation with both parties in the room can be counter-productive, and Pip tends to hold individual meetings with each party separately as she learns the objective facts and subjective interpretations of the case. Then, she'll hold joint meetings:

> *It can be very powerful to hear the story from one another in a calm and controlled environment, to learn what the situation is like from the other person's perspective; to understand what the consequences of our behaviour are on others, but in a less charged, less emotive atmosphere than the actual moment of conflict.*

The aim of mediation is to reach agreement on a dispute, and if people who have hitherto been at loggerheads agree to work with a conflict mediator, that's a good sign that they want resolution rather than continuing conflict. But it's not the mediator's responsibility to agree what resolution looks like, just as it's not a coach's responsibility to find a solution and unblock the challenge that a coachee is facing. "You manage a process that can lead to resolution," says Brown:

> And while it is possible that peace and harmony break out thanks to your intervention, it's unusual for mediation to feel like a completed journey. More often, there's been an improvement in understanding, stress is reduced, and there's no need to progress to legal proceedings.

For Pip, there are five principal characteristics of a conflict mediator who asks good questions.

1. **Curiosity** – a genuine desire to find out what's happened, what the impact's been. "It's so important to come into mediation without assumptions. Your curiosity must be open-minded, or else you'll ask closed, prejudicial questions that reinforce tired, heated arguments. You need to start broad and only go narrow when people give a clear indication that they've been heard."

2. **Active listening** – allowing all parties to tell their stories, actually hearing what they say, how they say it, and taking note of what they don't say, too.

3. **Empathy** – "It's critical – so important. It's very hard to be an active listener if you don't actually empathise with the person that you're listening to. For me, empathy is a much-misunderstood quality. There's a huge difference between 'best intentions' sympathising, which often comes across as paternalistic, and the ability to step into the other party's shoes, empathetically."

4. **Patience** – "You need to give others the space, time, and respect necessary to process and work through what's going on. It's not up to me to dictate the pace at which they might want to volunteer information."

5. **Emotional intelligence** – when conflicts have escalated to the extent that they require the intervention of a conflict negotiator – perhaps the last chance before involving lawyers – emotions are always running high. "Inexperienced mediators can miss potential trigger points, and there's a rich potential for types or lines of questioning that can exacerbate a conflict."

By contrast, questions that are closed, incurious, loaded, or leading are likely to be inflammatory. So, too, are questions asked with a tone that's disrespectful, one that belittles or undermines participants in the mediation or moves on to the next question before everyone's said their piece:

One sure-fire was to get all parties on edge is to ask questions that presume or assume a specific response rather than give them the opportunity to tell their story from their perspective. Closed questions signify indifference, disregard, and disinterestedness. They tell all parties that you're not interested in exploring the issue and that you're just looking for resolution – any resolution – rather than reaching a genuine accommodation.

PIP BROWN'S TOP TIPS FOR ASKING SMARTER QUESTIONS

1. Use questions to open up space in which unbridgeable differences can be resolved.
2. Ask open questions to prompt reflection, self-reflection, and facilitate dialogue.
3. Resolving disputes takes time and patience. Don't close down questioning too soon.
4. Questions asked in a calm, controlled environment can yield more meaningful answers.
5. Ask questions that give everyone the opportunity to answer at their own pace.

QUESTIONS ABOUT QUESTIONS – INTERVIEW 7 OF 14

NAME	Rob Varcoe
ORGANISATION	Rob Varcoe Consulting
ROLE	Founder and coach

For Rob Varcoe, a career and leadership development coach, questions play a pivotal role in his practice. He finds that it's often the combination of open and closed questions that proves most effective:

> *They're really important, to get people talking, but they're not the be-all and end-all. Listening, setting the right tone, building personal relationships – these all matter too. Without a firm grasp of these skills, you wouldn't be able to ask the right questions at the right time – or, indeed, avoid asking the wrong question at the wrong time.*

Varcoe believes that really powerful questions are inherently simple. Bad questions are complex, clusters of questions, questions that answer themselves, or questions so closed that they only have one possible answer. Leading questions are also a no-go area:

> *If I ever hear myself saying during a session, the first or twenty-first – 'I think the answer to the problem we are discussing is x', I'll know I've failed. You are not your client. You have no responsibility for answering their questions, no ability to do it, so you never should.*

Varcoe usually begins an engagement with a new client by asking questions such as *What would be different for you if the coaching was to be a success?* This allows the client to set parameters for success. Often, he will also set his clients an autobiographical exercise in which – in 500 scant words – he has them pick out significant points in their lives and careers to date:

> *This exercise is really another kind of open-ended question – self-consciously so – and it generates a broad array of different types of answers. Because executives are used to analytical thinking cultures, clients will often ask me: 'Did I get this right?' when of course there are no right or wrong answers. It's deliberately open, and it helps to make them feel reflective and to focus on what matters for them. In doing so, it fundamentally kick-starts the journey to self-awareness.*

Varcoe understands the impact of flexing between open and closed questions, from *What do you want?* (more open) to *What will you do to achieve or address that objective?* (more closed). Like an effective pyrotechnician, Varcoe favours lighting the blue touchpaper and then standing well back.

"Open or closed, you have to ask your question, close your mouth, and give your clients the opportunity, time, and space to talk." Like Tim Johns, Varcoe is confident that his approach can work in any sector. And like Johns, Varcoe works more in one sector than another (advertising for Varcoe, corporate executives for Johns).

For Varcoe, even a coach at the top of their game has to earn the right to ask questions, and to do that you need to be quiet and listen:

> *Being quiet isn't just about buttoning your lip until it's your turn to ask another question. To build a relationship and build trust, you have to really listen, hear, and interpret your client's responses. If they contradict themselves about, say, their aspirations for the future and how they think they can get there, you need to point this out to them – in the most appropriate way, having previously checked what level of challenge they are comfortable with. When you do that, it can really blow their mind, as up to this point they have probably been operating in their own echo chamber. The simple act of listening well and feeding back what you've heard can surprise them;* 'Wow! You were actually listening to me!'

Varcoe has learned his trade, technique, and process from practice and the application of intrinsic common sense:

> *I've earned my spurs from thousands of interactions with business and non-business people over the years. Being immersed in session after session, you start to join the dots and see common patterns, allowing you to anticipate where clients are going and how you can help them. You earn the right to ask them the next question by virtue of all the other coaching questions you've asked before. This is what enables you to create the right environment in which those you're coaching can answer their own questions.*

Working with senior leaders, it is incredibly powerful for a coach to give these individuals permission to admit that they don't know everything:

> *The more senior you are, the more people report to you – and it can be hundreds of thousands, directly and indirectly – it's just not possible to know everything about every aspect of your role. At the same time, it can be considered to be weak to admit that you don't know all the answers. Really effective leaders build really good teams around them and are able to reflect that they can't possibly know everything that all of their reports do.*

When they speak to me as someone who is independent of the company, I think they find a terrific sense of release from pressure if and when I ask them questions that allow them to confess that they don't know everything. We co-create a safe space where – through simple, smart questioning – they can admit to that. Once they've done that, they can find it much more straightforward to work out the best way forward.

Varcoe ends our discussion with three powerful and interconnected observations:

1. Empathy is the hallmark of a good coach, but you need to resist the temptation to stray too far from empathy to sympathy. "Coaches can and should sympathise with the struggles their clients are facing but can't get too close. The point to remember is how can you be most useful to your client in the situation they are facing. You can ask about a situation or person, show that you've listened well, and empathise. But spend too long sympathising without looking for a way forward, and you cease to be useful." This is such a strong echo of conflict mediator Pip Brown's perspective.

2. "As soon as you think you've asked a brilliant question, stop yourself. Make it simpler. Remember that less is more and being a great coach is not about showboating with a great question. Leave a lot more space for the answer than you think you should and be quiet. Your client will remember you for the space you gave them to come to their own conclusion, not how devilishly clever your question was that took them there."

3. Certain questions can only be asked of certain people at a certain time, and it takes experience to know what you can ask of whom and when. An example of this is a question such as *What's the one thing you really don't want me to ask you?* "For someone who's robust, confident, and knows where they're headed, that can be a truly transformational question. But for someone who's insecure, uncertain, and isn't comfortable being challenged, it could send them into a spiral. A good question has the potential to deliver incredibly rich insights. But equally, it can be destructive at the wrong time with the wrong person."

With each of these observations – each clearly hard-learned – Varcoe is emphasising the need for the coach to be led by the client and the circumstances of their situation rather than relying on a set of favourite questions. As he says: "You have to earn the right to ask questions, not impose them."

ROB VARCOE'S TOP TIPS FOR ASKING SMARTER QUESTIONS

1. Content isn't necessarily king in questioning. Listening, tone, and relationships matter too.
2. Keep questions simple, avoiding complex and cluster questions that answer themselves.
3. Be ready to flex between open and closed questions, moving from generality to specificity.
4. Don't rely on a favourite set of questions. Be led by the client and their circumstances.
5. Learn when to ask which questions through practice. You have to earn the right to do this.

TEN WAYS TO ASK GOOD (AND BETTER) QUESTIONS

1. Be open not closed – within reason

All of the experts we've met so far – and many of those we're going to meet in the coming chapters – are convinced of the benefits of the open question. Open questions tend to park their assumptions and prejudices at the door. They don't anticipate what the person being asked the question is going to – or should – answer. And they encourage respondents to build a narrative and share all relevant information. Open or open-ended questions seek out answers in paragraphs and more, not monosyllabic, closed-off grunts. Provided the language used to ask open questions is "clean" – in the terms outlined in Chapter 3 and according to the principles established by the counselling psychologist David Grove – there's nothing inevitable about answers to open questions, and often something quite surprising about them. Because of their lack of prejudice – literally "judging before (the question is asked)" – open questions are more likely to reveal respondents' inner thoughts and feelings, motivations and desires.

To make the most of the inner whys that open questions can reveal – particularly when they're given sufficient time and oxygen to work their magic – it is perfectly acceptable to follow-up open questions with the polar opposite: closed questions. As we've already seen from Queen's Counsel (QC) Tim Bishop, when seeking to establish a specific order of events and chain of causation, a series of rapid-fire closed questions can be beneficial. This piecemeal approach to narrative building is also possible when – as coach Rob Varcoe just explained – an open question followed by a closed question can be incredibly helpful in moving from the general to the particular.

Some examples of open questions include:

- Why do you say that?
- Can you give me some examples of what this feels like?
- What might you be doing in the future?

2. **Encourage those you're questioning to open up and tell a story**
   As soon as humans acquire even relatively crude linguistic ability – as soon as the Systemizing module posited by Simon Baron-Cohen kicks in and we start looking for *if-and-then* contingencies – we use story and story structure to make sense of the world. For most of us, this starts around our second birthday. Open questions are a brilliant way to encourage those we're questioning to tell us a story, to frame their knowledge and experience in a way that we can learn from it. Not everyone is a natural-born storyteller, following Aristotle's thesis-antithesis-synthesis, three-part story structure with every answer given to every question. But in the audience – when we're listening to answers to questions – we appreciate responses that do that.

The implicit overlay of narrative structure is useful for checking the consistency and veracity of the stories that people tell in response to open questions. Whether you're a journalist seeking to hold a mendacious special adviser to account[6] or a lawyer in court looking to cast doubt on witness testimony, a story that doesn't add up can be clear evidence of a respondent being "economical with the actualité", as the former British Trade Minister Alan Clark was found to have been over the sale of arms to Iraq.[7] We'll meet one of the simplest and best approaches to getting people to open up and build narratives when we meet Detective Sergeant Tom Barker in Chapter 8, where he details the "TED" model that sits at the heart of British police force's open questioning technique:

- Tell me a bit more about ...
- Explain to me ...
- Describe that to me in a bit more detail ...

3. Learn to love the sound of silence

Storytellers need an audience, and the answer to a smart, open question needs to be heard – properly heard. As Rob Varcoe details particularly keenly in our interview earlier in this chapter, once a questioner has asked their question, they should be quiet for as long as the respondent needs to give a full answer. For many of us, conversation and dialogue is a competition and we're only quiet for as long as we can't think of anything to say ourselves, including the next question. Reciprocity and turn-taking is one thing – no one enjoys spending time with a monologuer – but interruptions don't allow for a full and considered response, made without pressure or harassment. For one, constant interruption is rude and disrespectful. More importantly, it doesn't take the questioner off transmit mode and put them into receive. If we're perpetually thinking about what we're going to say next – how the crumbs of the responses we hear match or jar with our own opinions or intentions – we're not able to truly hear what our respondents are saying.

What's more, many people cannot stand the sound of silence. If you ask a question and let it hang in the air, most people will fill that silence. In the case of a celebrity profile writer, this could lead to some inadvertent juicy gossip. With a police officer taking a statement from a witness or suspect, it might reveal a contradiction that gets the investigation closer to the truth. And for a salesperson looking to negotiate a new contract with a customer, it could reveal the counter-offers that the customer has received from the competition. These and many other truths can be revealed purely by learning to love and respect the sound of silence.

4. Listen – really listen in order to hear

Once you've asked a smart question, it can be incredibly easy to miss the true import of the answers you receive. As we've just explored, learning to love the sound of silence and not preparing your next question or statement while others are speaking is the first step on the journey to listening and really hearing what the respondent is saying. But buttoning your lip is only the first step to truly, actively listening. Your lips may be closed, but your mind may be in over-drive; your face may look as serene as a swan gently gliding over a millpond, but the electrochemical blancmange between your ears may be distracted and not paying attention.

To assess the relevance, significance, and veracity of an answer to your question, you must of course pay attention to the words used in the answers you receive. This will help you to spot consistencies and inconsistencies with what you already know and from what you've learned from other sources. It will help to build up or wear down the credibility of the respondent, depending on whether what they're saying chimes or jars with established facts. Assuming you've been careful enough not to ask a loaded, prejudiced question, be careful that you don't allow your prejudices to bias what your hear so that you build up a selective picture. Truly active listening not only hears and encodes what is said, it also observes and takes note of what isn't said, of tone and timbre of voice, of body language, of eye contact (or not), and of direction of gaze. This is one of the challenges of using video conferencing software – the default means of meeting during the pandemic – a topic that we'll return to in Chapter 7.

5. Be oblique[8]

George H.W. Bush was the 41st U.S. President, serving a single term from 1989 to 1993. When pressed on matters he didn't want to address, Bush developed a reputation for evasiveness. Not sneaky evasiveness and pretending to answer a question or that politician's stalwart of answering the question they wished they'd been asked or had been prepared for by their handlers. If Bush didn't want to answer a question, he'd acknowledge it and say he didn't want to engage. On one infamous occasion, he is said to have responded: "It's a very good question, very direct, and I'm not going to answer it." Blunt, Bush-like directness is not necessarily the best strategy when it comes to asking smarter questions.

If Bush had come up against the journalist and author David Sedaris, he might have had a tougher ride. In his MasterClass on storytelling and humour, Sedaris extolls the practice of being oblique in your questioning.[9] If you want to find out someone's views on disability, Sedaris recommends that you ask: *Do you know many people in wheelchairs?* If he wanted you to know how someone else is coping with their ailments or illness, he'd suggest: *Do you know many doctors?* And if you just want to get a conversation started, rather than asking *How are you?* or *What do you do?*, Sedaris favours a truly oblique formulation like *When was the last time you smacked a monkey?*

6. Keep it simple

The smartest questions are often also the simplest. There are many ways in which you can make a question overly complex, and we'll cover some of these in more detail when we consider what makes a bad question in the next chapter. According to the Flesch-Kincaid methodology, which grades the relative simplicity-to-complexity of language, any sentence that contains more than 30 syllables is hard to hold in working memory. (Like that last one, which contained 55 syllables, though I crave your forgiveness: it's much harder to hold onto meaning of spoken rather than written sentences and questions.)

Here are five simple rules to help you keep it simple:

- Keep your questions short – fewer words and shorter words
- Don't ask several questions in one – so-called cluster questions or cluster bombs
- Avoid the passive voice, choosing to use the active *Did the cat chase the mouse?* over *Was the mouse chased by the cat?* The passive takes longer to process and so is easier to ignore
- Steer clear of (complex) metaphors to make your language as clean as possible
- Favour concrete expressions over abstract, for example, *The dog chased the ball* is quicker and easier to understand than *Her canine companion bounded after the spherical plaything*

7. Be curious. Always

The epistemophilic instinct drives us on as a species – we have a thirst for knowledge and understanding, impelled forward by the *if-and-then* Systemizing module. In a world made weary by wave after wave of coronavirus, any of us could be excused for being worn down by the fruitless curiosity we've expended, from doom-scrolling mortality data to navigating the sequence of tests required to be allowed to go and return from holidays. Paradoxically, despite heightened anxiety, sleeplessness, and increased mental health issues, the instinct appears to remain undimmed by COVID. If anything – with millions forced to find new ways of making a living and forging relationships – the future is bright for human resourcefulness driven by curiosity.

It's important to cultivate curiosity as a way of life and a state of mind, not just to switch it on and off to address today's challenge, this month's brief, next year's plan. Be curious. Always. And be curious with no particular goal in mind. Fill the hopper of your subconscious with what interests and diverts you – as well as the opposite, from familiar, favourite sources as well as those which you loathe. You never can tell when the planets will align and apparently unrelated connections will impel you to ask that smarter question.

8. Park your assumptions at the door

Humans are brilliant regularity detectors – spotting patterns, learning from those patterns, building rules. This facility helps us pluralise nouns and avoid lions. It enables us to save time by establishing chains of contingency and automate processes. But it also encourages us to create cognitive shortcuts – heuristics or biases – that ensure we make predictably irrational mistakes. Marketing strategist Richard Shotton lists "25 behavioural biases that influence what we buy" in his book *The Choice Factory*.

When seeking to ask smarter questions, it's important to slip from apparent unconscious competence to conscious competence and think about what it is we're asking and why, not simply to ask it. To be a truly smarter question, you need to park your assumptions, prejudices, and prior experience at the door. It's too easy for questions to be shaped by biases and what we know already, a topic we'll cover in much more detail in Chapter 10 when we consider just how sensitive a question should be. The one exception – the one assumption you should bring with you – is that those you're asking are likely to already know the answer themselves. This is clearly very true in the case of the coach and the conflict mediator, as we've seen in the interviews in this chapter. But it's also true more generally.

9. Challenge the status quo

Just because we've always done something in a particular way is no reason we should carry on doing it like that. The litany of billion-dollar businesses out-evolved during the digital revolution – with Blockbuster and Kodak replaced by Netflix and Instagram – are testimony to the benefits of challenging the status quo. When it comes to asking smarter questions, challenging the status quo is the flip side of the coin that encourages you to park your assumptions at the door. The status quo is built of assumptions and experience that served us well … right up until today. So, if you're looking to build and ask a good question, be sure that you seize the opportunity to do things differently.

10. **RTQ! RTFQ! RTFFQA!**

As we've explored in this section, particularly when considering the virtues of the sound of silence and the imperative of actually listening in order to hear what people say and mean, the question-answer two-step involves concentration from both parties. It's perfectly straightforward to ask a smart question that yields a dumb answer. If the respondent isn't concentrating – if they're racing ahead to think what they might ask in return – they can miss the opportunity to give the question the attention it deserves. My father Kenneth's three-part exam advice – given in the increasingly urgent initialisms RTQ! RTFQ! RTFFQA! (Read The Question! Read The Flipping Question! Read The Flipping Question Again!) – demands you read the effing question at least three times. Before you start to answer a question, turn it over in your mind at least three times. Respondents as well as questioners have the imperative to embrace and learn to love the sound of silence. If it's a simple, smart, open question – one driven by curiosity and seeking out a narrative response – turning it over three times in your mind before you answer it won't hold you back for long. And if you really do decide to RTFQA, you can guarantee a smarter answer.

SUMMING UP

The coach's mindset can help you ask smarter questions. Ten strategies from the smarter questioner's interrogative playbook include:

1. Be open not closed – within reason
2. Encourage those you're questioning to open up and tell a story
3. Learn to love the sound of silence
4. Listen – really listen in order to hear
5. Be oblique
6. Keep it simple
7. Be curious. Always
8. Park your assumptions at the door
9. Challenge the status quo
10. RTQ! RTFQ! RTFFQA!

NOTES

1 FiveThirtyEight's eve of election blog from 8 November 2016 gave Hillary Clinton a 71.4% chance of winning the presidency and Trump a 28.6% chance, a 302–235 win in electoral votes. See https://projects.fivethirtyeight.com/2016-election-forecast/

2 See "FiveThirtyEight's New Logo, by the Numbers", *Emblemetric*, 24 March 2014, https://bit.ly/3y6YYYQ. The original epigram reads: πόλλ' οἶδ' ἀλώπηξ, ἀλλ' ἐχῖνος ἓν μέγα – "the fox knows many things, but the hedgehog just one big thing".

3 "Boris Johnson a pundit who stumbled into politics, says Cummings", *The Guardian*, 21 June 2021, https://bit.ly/3Ewd34b

4 "A review of Tetlock's 'Superforecasting' (2015)", Dominic Cummings's [sic] Blog, 24 November 2016, https://bit.ly/3Gjtu4t

5 The interview with Eric Bartels is on pp.113–115 of *How To Be Insightful*. A different and fuller version of that discussion can be found at https://insightagents.co.uk/finding-our-inner-why/

6 The former BBC Political Correspondent, Laura Kuenssberg, made good use of this approach when grilling disgraced former special adviser to Prime Minister Johnson, Dominic Cummings, in a televised interview in June 2021. See https://bbc.in/30N10AZ

7 See "Economical with the actualité", https://bit.ly/3J5p2Zp

8 In 1975, musician Brian Eno produced a wonderful set of cards promoting creativity called *Oblique Strategies: Over One Hundred Worthwhile Dilemmas*. Three I just drew at random from my set read: *What to maintain?*, *Remove specifics and covert to ambiguities*, and *Discard an axiom*. Get your set from www.enoshop.co.uk and draw one a day. Whether you act on it is – of course – entirely up to you.

9 https://www.masterclass.com/classes/david-sedaris-teaches-storytelling-and-humor

6

WHAT MAKES A BAD QUESTION?

Abstract

Asking questions just because you're in a forum or an environment in which questions are asked is no guarantee that the questions you ask will be smart. One of the biggest impediments to asking smarter questions is the baggage we bring with us to the crucible in which they will be aired and answered. This baggage can take the form of assumptions, prejudices, and self-interested blinkers that mean asking questions can become a "political" act and not primarily designed to satisfy curiosity or work on a challenge.

In this chapter, we explore ten ways to ask bad (and dumber) questions. By becoming increasingly aware of the follies, foibles, and failures of bad questioning technique, it is possible to use the flip side of these biased strategies to ask smarter questions yet.

ENLIGHTENED SELF-INTEREST?

There was trouble brewing in the U.K. for the alcoholic drinks industry in the late 1980s. This was the result of a combination of a series of long, hot summers; increasing affluence; more widespread availability of cheap alcohol, particularly beer, most notably lager; and media reports

DOI: 10.4324/9781003218470-6

of alcohol-fuelled violence across the country. The Thatcher government banned alcohol in football grounds – or at least "the consumption of alcohol within view of the playing area" – in 1985 in an attempt to curb football hooliganism. Nevertheless, town and city centres on Friday and Saturday nights were increasingly becoming booze-soaked, no-go areas, spawning regular horror headlines.

In 1987, an article appeared in *What's Brewing* – the monthly publication of the Campaign for Real Ale (CAMRA) – which included the first use of an alliterative description of the perpetrators, and it came to dominate political, media, and public debate for years to come. The Lager Lout had been born. The following year, British Home Secretary Douglas Hurd – the politician responsible for making sure that all communities are kept safe and secure – jumped on the Lager Lout bandwagon. He made a speech after an interview demonising "young people with too much money in their pockets, too many pints inside them, but too little self-discipline".[1] It was a culture satirised to great effect by the comedian Harry Enfield and his distilled essence of the Lager Lout, the character Loadsamoney.[2]

Politicians love an enemy, and it wasn't long before blame was being shifted from the Lager Louts themselves to the brewers responsible for popularising the lager craze and then the alcoholic drinks industry more broadly. The principle of vicarious liability was threatening to float across the Atlantic, particularly with multinational mergers in the drinks industry. Vicarious liability holds manufacturers (in this case brewers) and distributors (in this case pubs, which were at the time mostly owned and operated by the same brewers) responsible for the actions of those allowed to over-imbibe, even after they left their premises. It had been used to good effect by the neo-prohibitionist Reagan administration to raise the legal drinking age from 18 to 21 in many U.S. states, together with the offer of Federal funds to rebuild state highways, provided the legal drinking age went up.

At first, the U.K. drinks industry panicked, but then it calmed down. It quickly decided it needed to establish a long-spoon, quasi-independent organisation that could address the social issues associated with alcohol. With sufficient distance from the industry, this organisation could work in partnership with Government departments, health education bodies, the police, and others involved in mopping up after its customers had one (or ten) too many. Better yet, it could divert the attention of potential regulators and legislators like a table magician, showcasing the good works it was doing through alcohol education for tweens and teens and training for staff in licensed premises.[3]

At the time, there was a dynamic set of relatively young but senior executives at drinks giant Guinness, the company that had recently acquired a major liquor business called United Distillers. The takeover had been mired by a share trading fraud which bolstered Guinness' share price and so enabled it to run a successful bid. The Serious Fraud Office brought a successful case against Guinness and secured large fines and prison sentences for senior management and their advisers. Guinness had purged its leadership team and adopted a clean slate, promoting younger executives faster than it otherwise would have. In a move designed to show investors, regulators, and Government that it had cleaned up its act, Guinness, more than any other drinks company, focused its public relations and public affairs efforts on the social aspects of alcohol. It did so much earlier and with more zeal than its competitors who addressed these issues, too. This legacy of fronting up to social issues is still evident more than 30 years on with Guinness – now in the form of Diageo.

As a result, Guinness executives, including its strategic affairs director Peter Mitchell, had the imperative, focus, and energy to urge the seven other biggest booze barons to join in setting up The Portman Group. This was one of the world's first social aspects organisations and its declared goal was to "promote sensible drinking, reduce alcohol misuse, and tackle alcohol-related harm". The early success of Portman meant it was a model soon copied around the world, from the Century Council in the U.S. to the DIFA-Forum in Germany. Often, these bodies had the same global corporate members as Portman, supplemented by local companies – big brewers in Germany, wine producers in Australia, and so on.

By making the industry part of the solution and not just the cause of the problem, they hoped to make punitive regulation and legislation less likely. The Group was unapologetic that it existed in the enlightened self-interest of the industry. It appointed Dr John Rae – an ascetic, media-friendly, former headmaster of Westminster College – as its first Director.

The total staff was just seven and the directorate was just three strong: Rae, Director of Strategy, George Winstanley, and – in the middle 1990s – me, less than half the age of either colleague and charged with looking after the Group's communications.

It was great fun being at the cutting edge of the early evolution of corporate social responsibility (CSR). Not lip service CSR embedded within a company, a route that many have since pursued and found that it did little more than make people inside the business feel warm. No. In the intention of the founding funders at least, creating a quasi-independent organisation to help address the social ills brought about by too much or inappropriate use of its products, the drinks industry was attempting something genuinely pioneering.

It was also the working environment I found to be the most formative for developing and honing my own skills and practice in asking smarter questions. Part of this was because of my colleagues. Rae's head magisterial demeanour and approach often saw him behave like the most generous and engaged coach, encouraging his small team to work out the answers to the challenges they faced. He'd set big *How Might We ...?* questions and then give his colleagues the time, resources, and partners to try to answer them. *How might we make a meaningful contribution to reducing the incidence of under-age drinking? How might we take the government's anti-drink-drive campaigns to hard-to-reach recidivist drink-drivers? How will we know if we're having an impact on the issues we're addressing? How might we measure and report our impact transparently?*

Big questions with minimal unhelpful prejudices or distracting assumptions – these were the kind of questions that played to Winstanley's considered, strategic mindset. After graduating from Selwyn College, Cambridge, in the mid-1950s and completing his National Service, Winstanley spent many years working for the Foreign and Colonial Office in Bechuanaland Protectorate, South Africa's land-locked Northern neighbour. As it moved towards independence in 1966 (when it became Botswana) and stability, Winstanley was instrumental in helping to craft and implement a constitution for the newly emerging nation. Often hailed as one of Africa's best success stories in the postcolonial era, at least a part of that is the result of Winstanley's keen ability to involve and empower multiple interest groups in a common endeavour – though he was too modest to ever acknowledge that.[4]

Thanks to Winstanley's nimble experience in statecraft, working alongside him at The Portman Group was like having a super-empathetic guide on call. We were active at a chaotic hotchpotch of an intersection – between the drinks industry, government, health educators, academics, anti-alcohol lobby groups, parents whose children had been killed by drink-drivers or alcohol poisoning, and pro-temperance campaigners. His ability to see the bigger picture and simultaneously accommodate multiple points of view was first class, and often he gently nudged me towards a much smarter answer to the challenges Rae had set us. I couldn't have done it without him.

Every month, we three had the privilege of sharing and refining our programme with the most senior executives of the U.K.'s eight biggest drinks companies at an 8am, first Wednesday Council meeting. Being the early 1990s, all eight were white, British, public school-educated men. Even though all eight were notionally in the same industry, there were obvious fault lines and nuances of difference in what they were prepared to do and be seen to do to tackle alcohol misuse. The spirits companies were keen to harmonize taxation on alcohol across all different types of drinks, which would have meant a sharp increase in taxation on beer. The brewers didn't like this. They also rejected the spirits companies' desire to lobby the British government to cut the legal drink-driving limit, from its idiosyncratic 80 milligrammes of alcohol per 100 millilitres of blood (0.08%) to the European norm of 50 milligrammes (0.05%). Unlike the brewers, you see, the spirits boys didn't own any country pubs, so drivers drinking less in pubs wouldn't impact their profits nearly as quickly or directly as it would the brewer-pub owners. Clearly, self-interest could only be enlightened if it didn't gratuitously damage the bottom line.

These and other "wicked" problems sharpened my appreciation for what makes a good – and a smarter – question. Paradoxically, the in-committee behaviour of many of the chief executive officers (CEOs) sat around Portman's Council table also taught me an awful lot about what makes a bad question. I was the Group's director of public affairs in my mid-to-late 20s – a prematurely elevated title, for sure – and this was the first time in my career that I'd seen such senior executives in action so regularly. I'd expected these gods sitting at the top of an industry to be super-impressive in everything they did. From the way that some of them asked questions, however, it soon became clear that some senior people actually use questions neither to satisfy their curiosity nor to work something out. Rather, they used – and squandered – their question quotient for purely for "p", political, reasons.

Let's consider the wasteful approach of six of these CEO types. It being the early 1990s, they often puffed out their incontinent queries shrouded in clouds of early morning cigarette and cigar smoke.

1. **Mr First Question** – an inconsequential, off-topic enquiry but deliberately pitched on an issue that would have to be recorded, designed purely to ensure their name appeared first in the minutes. *Don't you think we should review directors' remuneration most urgently?* First in the minutes, demonstrating to shareholders and internal stakeholders that they took this social responsibility thing seriously, even if their question had nothing to do with any aspect of social responsibility at all.

2. **Mr "I Always Ask This Question"** – usually from one of the spirits companies, wanting to focus attention on taxation equivalency or the opportunity to score political points. *As it's nearly Christmas, why don't we urge the government to review the drink-drive limit?* The question may not make the minutes, but it would lead the beer barons to fug up the room with smoke spluttered and coughed from exasperated lungs.

3. **Mr Not-So-Enlightened Self-Interest** – *When are you going to realise that country pubs make all their profit from people who have a couple of drinks too many and then drive home perfectly safely on empty country roads?* When you'd heard it once and acknowledged the source, it was much more a statement of the bleeding obvious, driven by bottom-line concerns before considering the safety or well-being of the general public, the industry's own – and heaviest-drinking – customers.

4. **Mr Answer As A Rhetorical Question** – when cornered or forced to consider an issue that clearly wasn't in their company's commercial interests. *Well, would you lobby for a policy that's going to hit your profits hard?*

5. **Mr Show-Off** – dressing up a question as an opportunity to name drop. *As I was asking Her Majesty – as comparatively recently as yesterday – don't you think we should invest more in educating teenagers about the dangers of having one too many?*

6. **Mr Gratuitous Interrupter** – when a Council member hadn't been heard for some time, he'd often wait until one of us on the directorate was reporting to our funders and then use a question purely to draw attention to themselves. This failure to obey the Cocktail Party rule,[5] this absence of empathy, this demonstration of a lack of understanding of the rules of reciprocity in dialogue, this lack of courtesy – it would always throw the speaker off course. And it would always come in the form of a question. *Yes, but hang on – haven't you heard we tried this in the States and it failed?*

Rather than captains of industry, the behaviour and wilful misuse of substandard questions by some of those who sat around Portman's Council table made me think that they were more like a collection of bumbling corporate Mr Men. This affliction was certainly not suffered by all or even most of those we served, and some of the tricks from the dirty half-dozen outlined above were deployed by the same individual. But I did find this forum to be more enlightening about how not to ask smarter questions and what can motivate us to do this. It was the yang to the yin of working with such fine questioning colleagues as the dear, departed Rae and Winstanley.

SATURDAY NIGHT'S ALRIGHT FOR QUESTIONING

For approaching 50 years, America's finest emerging comedic talent has had a regular weekly showcase on NBC's *Saturday Night Live* (*SNL*). The careers of stars as diverse as Eddie Murphy and Julia Louis-Dreyfus, Bill Murray and Tina Fey and dozens more besides have been propelled forward by appearances on *SNL*. One performer whose talent has faded since his untimely death in 1997 aged just 33 – from that classic comedy staple of a cocaine and morphine overdose – is Chris Farley.[6]

Farley played a number of different, recurring characters on *SNL*, but perhaps his finest creation was playing "himself" as the bumbling host of

The Chris Farley Show, the chat show within a show. In this comedy vehicle, he would interview A-list celebrities using some of the very worst, ill-thought-through questions that failed to elicit anything of interest or note from some of the hottest guests imaginable. Celebrity victims – of course in on the joke, but always dead panning and looking increasingly irritated as the interview progressed – would sit and listen as Farley listed the films or TV shows or albums they'd created. Sometimes, Farley would become inexplicably side-tracked by random other celebrities, like a dog whose attention is grabbed by a passing squirrel.

Remember when you were in <THAT SCENE> in <THAT MOVIE> and when you said <THAT LINE>? he'd ask. The star – be it Martin Scorsese, Jeff Daniels, or Paul McCartney – would look bemused and offer an *Err, yeah?* Invariably, Farley's nervous, bumbling persona would simply reflect on his own question by saying: *That was awesome!* This was his only style of question (simply listing and asking the star to corroborate his recollection and then commending them for their awesomeness). His only way of operating was to completely waste the opportunity to quiz some of the most creative talent on the planet. That – of course – was the point. Farley was very much in the mode of Messrs 2, 4, and 6 from The Portman Group Council.

Asking dumber questions is not just about the *how*, of course – the personae adopted and the approaches taken to ask questions. It's also very much about the *what*. For the rest of this chapter, we'll consider the very worst strategies you can use with the questions you ask. In some cases, these are the opposite of the principles set out in the previous chapter where we considered "What makes a good question?" But many of the principles of asking dumber questions throw more light on how to ask smarter questions than simply holding up a mirror to last chapter's guidelines on good practice.

TEN WAYS TO ASK BAD (AND DUMBER) QUESTIONS

1. **Close down the options of your subject at every turn**
   Where open questions encourage those you're questioning to open up and tell a story, closed questions tend to surface monosyllabic

answers that aren't terribly enriching or enlightening. Closed questions include those that start when, what, where, who, is/are, do/ did, and have. They can yield useful information – and as Queen's Counsel (QC) Tim Bishop showed us in Chapter 3, they can be used tactically to follow up more strategic, open questions and establish a key set of facts or a logical argument. But as a tool for getting to the why behind the what, they're of limited value. They might yield the answer yes or no, Jane or Steve, last Thursday or 2001 BCE. They might generate a shrug or an *I dunno*. Or they might generate silence. What you can be sure of is that the answer will be shorter than the question and that's entirely the wrong balance.

Closed questions can also set the mood and expectations of the person being quizzed. As Wise and Littlefield say in *Asking Powerful Questions*: "If you ask lots of closed-ended questions, the experience will feel more like an interrogation" (p.115). These authors either have little experience of what actual interrogations are like or they've fallen prey to the mediated, soap opera version of how effective interrogations are actually run, as we'll see from the interview with police Detective Sergeant Tom Barker in Chapter 8. In that discussion, Barker gives details of the open, exploratory power of the "TED formula", where interview subjects are invited to Tell, Explain, Describe the events under investigation in an open and elucidatory fashion.

2. Lead the witness with directions and assumptions

Journalist and teacher of journalism Dean Nelson observes in his book *Talk to Me*: "Good interviewers must be aware of their biases as they head into an interview and must be equally ready to abandon or at least adjust // their assumptions as the interview progresses" (pp.27–8). Time and again in this book we've seen evidence of how damaging – how counterproductive – it can be to allow your questions to be tainted by your assumptions. Indeed, I'd go quite a bit further than Nelson about interviewers needing to simply "be aware of their biases". They need to park them at the door and not allow them to affect or infect questions at all. Coaches Wendy Sullivan and

Judy Rees encourage us to root out assumptions from our questions altogether, using metaphor-free, clean language.

Coaches Tim Johns and Rob Varcoe – as well as the conflict mediator Pip Brown – emphasised the critical importance of using neutral, assumption-free language in working with coaching clients and parties to conflict in our interviews reported in the previous chapter. *When did you stop beating your wife?* is the caricatured stereotype of a loaded question chock-full of assumptions. So, too, is *Did that bloody cat kill another bird?* compared with the altogether more innocent query *Can you describe to me what happened in the garden this afternoon?* As Elke Wiss, the contemporary practical philosopher says in her book *How to Know Everything*: "many of our questions aren't questions at all. They are messages in disguise" (p.244). If you're planning to use questions for that end, at least do so consciously.

The Latin language had two innocent-looking words grammatically designed to bias answers – *num* and *nonne*. A *num* question saw the questioner impose their belief that *Surely such and such happened, didn't it?*, while a *nonne* question was the opposite – *Surely such and such didn't happen, right?* Fortunately, the words died with the language, although the desire to impose assumptions on questions sadly did not. Elke Wiss defines a category of assumption-driven questions as "But questions", giving a couple of *num/nonne* examples: "'But don't you think Maya should have responded differently?' or 'But don't you think the layout of the report needs changing?'" (p.245). As she concludes: "The underlying message of a but question is: I already have an opinion on this, but I'm not coming out with it directly" (*loc. cit.*).

3. **Be insensitive to the impact that your questions can have**
   Questions phrased wrongly, clumsily, or with a total lack of awareness of diversity and the equal rights of all people can radically undermine their power and impact. They can generate anger or hurt from those questioned and negatively bias responses because of the negative biases they contain. If you are insensitive to the impact that your questions and their wording can have on issues as diverse as

ethnicity, race, gender, sexuality, sexual orientation, age, disability, neurological status, religion, and marital status, your questions will more than likely be dumb and the answers they yield worthless. We'll cover the issue and how to address it in Chapter 10.

4. Keep your mouth open and your ears closed

Too often – as with the Portman Group Council members picked apart above – people ask questions not because they're curious or genuinely interested in finding out meaningful answers to smart questions. Too often, there are political reasons for asking questions, to be seen to be active. Too often, although the questioner may fall silent and appear to allow the other party to answer, the questioner isn't listening to or evaluating the response. Rather, they're preparing the next question which – while it might appear to be related to the previous question or even the answer being given – won't be listened to either. Learning to love to the sound of silence isn't (just) about politeness and etiquette. It's also about understanding what smarter questions can achieve given half a chance by giving measured responses their deserved consideration.

5. Be as obscure and complex as you possibly can be

The explanation that requires the fewest possible assumptions is usually the correct one. So states Occam's razor, the philosophical principle of parsimony named after the 14th-century theologian William of Occam. The same is true of questions. Simple questions are the best. They're the best because their intention cannot be concealed. They're the best because they cannot confuse the person of whom they're asked. And they're the best because they don't allow for cherry-picking the easy parts and ignoring the more difficult ones.

That said, if you want to ask a dumber question – a question whose answer will be neither dependable nor useful – make it as complex as you can. Use unfamiliar jargon, abbreviations, acronyms, and initialisms. Make it unclear and word it ambiguously so that it seems like there are hidden meanings implied (even if there aren't). Ask multiple, cluster questions and nested questions with interrelated contingencies. Use abstract not concrete language. Favour the passive voice over the active voice. Make liberal use of litotes, the ironic and rhetorical figure of speech that expresses understatement by using a negative to affirm a positive, as in: *I didn't dislike the play.* Ask a question about which you know very little with all the confidence of a world expert.

If you're on the receiving end of complex, unclear questions, adopt a policy of zero tolerance and refuse to answer them. Use your own, crystal-clear questions to push back and demand clarity before you give a response. Try *Which of these questions would you like me to address first?* or *What do you really want to discover?*

6. Open your arms wide to cognitive biases

Our own biases, opinions, and assumptions should not be part of a smarter question. There's just too much data in the world for humans to be able to attend to and process every incoming stimulus properly. This is not just a function of the explosion in digital data over the past 25 years, though that doesn't help, particularly in terms of messages from media and commercial communication. No, this is a function of the extreme complexity of the world around us and the limited – if brilliant – processing power of the human brain. To allow us to function without pausing for extensive analysis of every sensory input, our brains have developed a broad array of cognitive shortcuts (aka heuristics) that allow us to appear to process much more sensory input data than we actually can. These heuristics or cognitive biases ensure that we can make decisions in real time. They also lead us to make predictable mistakes.

So, if you want to ask a dumber question, you could do worse than welcoming in the cognitive biases that lead to predictable mistakes in decision-making, including the Availability Heuristic (assuming that because you've heard lots about shark attacks recently, they must be commonplace), Anchoring (meaning we are unable to deviate far from others' estimates), and Confirmation Bias (seeking out evidence that reinforces your beliefs or assumptions and not evidence that contradicts it).

7. **Over-promote the role of experience and expertise**

The pre-Socratic philosophers (and many who've come since) believed in the primacy of expertise, experience, and previously acquired knowledge. Socrates was among the first to assert – or at least among the first to be recorded having asserted – "All I know is that I know nothing". As we considered in Chapter 2, the Socratic paradox is a brilliant starting point for asking smarter questions, and its application ranges from philosophical enquiry to consultative sales strategy.

Building questions from a position of domain specificity can be severely limiting and is the very antithesis of the approach taken by many entrepreneurs, disruptors, and their venture capitalist investors. Being bound by history, the status quo, and *How we do things around here* didn't serve Blockbuster or Kodak very well, and they won't serve you well either, as you look to develop and pose smarter questions. Be more Netflix and Instagram, though be sure you don't adopt Instagram's apparent tolerance for images of self-harm. That helps no one and harms many.

8. **Ask the same question again and again until you get the answer you want**

Just after Tony Blair's first landslide election victory brought a humiliating end to 18 years of unbroken Conservative Party rule in the U.K., the former Tory Home Secretary Michael Howard was interviewed by the BBC's attack Rottweiler, Jeremy Paxman. In an interview on the network's flagship news analysis programme *Newsnight*, Paxman grilled Howard about his apparent threat to overrule the Director General of the British Prison Service Derek Lewis.[7] A parochial enough issue. But it's an interview that's gone down in the annals of political TV interviews because in less than ten minutes, Paxman asked Howard the same question – *Did you threaten to overrule him?* – a dozen times. Howard refused to answer the question time and again, trying – unsuccessfully – to reframe the question onto his own terms.

Neither man covers himself in glory – Howard for his refusal to engage on a question which he clearly has no intention of answering because it would compromise him, admit a significant failure, and torpedo his bid to become party leader in the wake of election catastrophe; Paxman, because he's fallen foul of Einstein's supposed definition of madness – doing the same thing (asking the same question) again and again and expecting a different outcome. While it's easy to feel contempt and revulsion for Howard for his political misjudgement, it is equally easy to think that Paxman should have altered his questioning strategy, however calmly and gentlemanly he repeated the question.

9. **Don't be afraid of losing your cool**
However difficult a question may be to answer – because it may reveal culpability or guilt or because it opens up bad memories of personal trauma – it is never acceptable for the person asking the question to lose their cool and attempt to browbeat the other party into submission. Insistent though Paxman was with Howard in the example immediately above, the interviewer never lost his cool. Crime and police fiction – in novels, films, and TV shows – often has police or lawyers, in the interview suite and in court, losing their cool, thumbing a table, and raising their voice to a shout; to ask a question emphatically. As we'll learn in Chapter 8, this is not how police ask questions of suspects, victims, or witnesses. In the interests of both delivering natural justice by securing convictions of the right suspects only, the questioning strategies trained into police detectives always demand that officers remain calm and in control. If you want to ask a dumber question, lose it and lose it early.

10. **Be sure your questions get tactical as soon as possible**
We are rational, analytical creatures. Many jobs in the modern knowledge economy – from market research to academic enquiry, sales to medicine, journalism to coaching – depend on practitioners using analytical thinking techniques to solve problems. Solving problems has a powerful gravitational pull towards the tactical and away from the strategic. Yet analytical thinking is not the only form of thinking that is valuable in the workforce. Insightful thinking, where we join old and old together to make something new, to create a profound and useful new understanding of a person, issue, topic or thing, is also incredibly

valuable. The trouble is, with so many roles in so many career paths predicated and rewarded on the basis of solving problems, analytical thinking is our preferred way of thinking and so more practiced and more highly valued than insightful thinking. What this means is that our thinking – and our questions – get too tactical, too soon, and often stop when a workable (if unimaginative) solution is proposed. This approach misses a whole step. If you want your questions to be smarter – if you want them to surface, articulate, and incorporate genuine insights – you could do worse than reading my previous book, *How To Be Insightful*.

SUMMING UP

Dumb questions give questioning a bad name. There are ten approaches you can follow if you want to make sure you ask bad – dumber – questions, namely:

1. Close down the options of your subject at every turn
2. Lead the witness with directions and assumptions
3. Be insensitive to the impact that your questions can have
4. Keep your mouth open and your ears closed
5. Be as obscure and complex as you possibly can be
6. Open your arms wide to cognitive biases
7. Over-promote the role of experience and expertise
8. Ask the same question again and again until you get the answer you want
9. Don't be afraid to lose your cool
10. Be sure your questions get tactical as soon as possible

QUESTIONS ABOUT QUESTIONS – INTERVIEW 8 OF 14

From *Death of a Salesman* to *Glengarry Glen Ross*, from telemarketers who call in the middle of a family supper to the bombardment of targeted digital advertising, sales has a bad reputation. With some justification, the worlds of advertising and public relations are reviled by the media, even though they depend on both professions for much of their content and revenue. The tang of the "snake oil salesman" tag often makes executives whose roles evolve to include sales baulk at the challenge. But as I've discovered from Stuart Lotherington – having been trained by him and his organisation over the past decade and particularly from our recent interview – sales done right is a million miles from the caricatures too many of us carry around with us. It can also tell us a huge amount about how to ask smarter questions.

NAME	Stuart Lotherington
ORGANISATION	SBR Consulting
ROLE	Managing Director

Stuart Lotherington runs SBR Consulting, a company that helps organisations improve sales performance. Unlike many coaching, training, and development businesses in the sales space, SBR encourages its clients to take the consultative approach to sales, an approach characterised by asking smarter questions. Like a general practitioner (GP) looking to determine the fundamental reason why her patient has made an appointment or a business consultant seeking to understand the market dynamics of a prospective new sector, SBR enables those responsible for selling products and services of all kinds to drive engagement into the sales process through thoughtful, focused interrogation.

Lotherington explains:

> All the consultative sales models encourage salespeople to focus on the three core players and relationships in a client engagement: (i) **Them** – the client and their needs, (ii) **You** – the offering you provide, and (iii) **Us** – how you and they can work together. These are the three component parts on the sales journey, viewed from a constructivist perspective. Constructivism – one of the four grand theories of learning – builds up, step-by-step. It's like when children learn mathematics. They can't learn multiplication before you've mastered addition.

For Lotherington, the same is true in sales. There can be no "Us" before "Them" and "You" and no "You" before "Them".

How realistically, can you talk about anything you could offer to a prospective client until and unless you first understand what their needs and pain points are? All the features and benefits in the world are irrelevant if you don't know what kind of help they need, what kind of distress they're in that your product or service could meaningfully address.

In a typical first sales engagement, Lotherington recommends spending 30–40 minutes of an hour-long meeting, in-person or online, asking questions to gather insight into client needs. This will vary depending on the technical details of what's being sold, but for those selling consulting services, questions (and answers) should always dominate discussion. SBR has trained more than 75,000 people in this approach, and it pays off. Lotherington knows this from client success stories, repeat business, and word-of-mouth recommendation. He also knows it from the success and growth over the past 20 years of SBR, which very definitely practices what it preaches.

"To start with, you have to keep your questions simple and clear," advises Lotherington:

You want to invoke a response that's more than a word. That doesn't necessarily mean an open question (though it often does). A good first question opens up a dialogue and can guide the future path of the conversation. If it becomes clear that what you are offering is in some way outside the scope of what they usually do, an agile salesperson who's really listening will look to reframe the discussion. This can involve drawing on your knowledge or what the person has said previously, or else making reference to insight you may have gathered ahead of the meeting. You might say, for example: 'Talking to the CEO of company X, they mentioned that supply chain issues are playing havoc with their delivery schedules. How are you handling this kind of pressure in the market?'.

In terms of an attitude or approach that characterises salespeople who ask good questions, Lotherington believes there are two critical dimensions. The first is the pre-approach – the planning part; thinking of what decent questions might be and how to ask them. The second, more challenging aspect is when you're live and engaged with a prospect. This is when you need to be a good and active listener, using the answers you're getting in real time to frame both subsequent questions and dictate the selection of the products or services you offer in the context of that prospect's declared needs.

Lotherington explains more, using two analogies:

> *Effective questioning in sales is like a dance, where you take people around a dancefloor, structuring their thinking, and helping to frame that thinking with your questioning. And it's also like football. If you go all-out to shoot on goal every time you get the ball, you won't score. You have to skilfully draw the defence out (the client's limited beliefs) so that you can open up goal-scoring opportunities (to make a point that hopefully provides an 'A-ha!' moment for the client). With any proposition you're looking to sell, questioning helps you understand where you want to get to. In therapy, it's all about being neutral and non-judgmental; in sales, it's all about helping the prospect conjure up the right imagined future in which they can understand the real benefits of your proposition.*

Often, those selling products or services will find themselves in a position where they're entering a new market, an industry sector about which they know very little. Lotherington believes this is largely irrelevant. "You'll never know as much about their specialist area as they do," he observes:

> *but it's not too hard to pick up key data or trends. Clients are less interested in your knowing everything about their sector – that's their job. They want you to be expert in what you do, how you can help them. More often than not, they're interested in social proof – third-party validation from others of your customers – that what you offer makes a real difference. The first question – perhaps* 'Tell me about your business and how you're doing in the current market' *– makes a profound impression. But it's the second question that really matters. The sale is made in the questioning more than in the solution itself. There's a required mindset shift, to flex from technical knowledge to quality questioning, to show your expertise and take people on that journey with you.*

When it comes to the qualities of a bad question, Lotherington says that "closed" is the quick answer:

> *In reality, a bad question bears all the hallmarks of the opposite of a good one. If you can demonstrate you haven't listened ... if you've focused on details that are irrelevant or close their thinking to a specific point too soon in the conversation (limiting the wider conversation) ... if you've got out of your depth and can't understand the answers ... if you've made them*

feel uncomfortable – say by getting too personal, too soon – all of these approaches are likely to kill any prospect of a sale before it's even got started.

We close our conversation with a discussion about the impact of the pandemic on the sales process. Lotherington has observed – in SBR's own sales process and that of its clients – that there are now more sales meetings and more qualification necessary before closure:

This can be challenging, because it means more, shorter, bitty meetings that before might have all happened in the room in one or two sessions. But – as with so many aspects of Covid – we're all learning to adapt to the new dynamics of sales over Zoom or Teams.

STUART LOTHERINGTON'S TOP TIPS FOR ASKING SMARTER QUESTIONS

1. Be like a doctor in your questioning: be consultative.
2. When starting a new partnership, ask questions about Them, You, Us – and in that order.
3. Dedicate two-thirds or more of your first engagement with a prospect to asking questions.
4. Don't feel you need to be a world expert in your client's sector. Use questions to learn.
5. The first question makes an impression, but it's the second question that really matters.

NOTES

1 There's an excellent account of the phenomenon on Boak & Bailey's beer blog titled "Panic on the Streets of Woking: Rise of the Lager Lout" at https://bit.ly/30wbIvN

2 As a measure of how Enfield judged the mood right, his record *Loadsamoney (Doin' Up the House)* peaked at number four in the U.K. charts. ICYMI, you can still watch it on YouTube, even though it predates the platform by almost 17 years, at https://bit.ly/3JA4Or5

3   In the 2020s, Big Tech is using the same "table magician" strategy – showcasing pioneering work it's doing in one area to divert attention from scrutiny of more dubious practices. Facebook's creation of a new parent company and rebranding as Meta in October 2021 and its decision to focus its energy and others' attention on the so-called metaverse is a very powerful example of this approach in practice. While regulators, legislators, and many consumers rightly accused Facebook – sorry, Meta – of doing too little to police and remove content that foments hate and division and threatens psychological well-being by failing to remove images of self-harm from its platforms, particularly Facebook and Instagram, Facebook says: "Yes, that's all under control now, but look at this shiny new metaverse over here. Isn't THAT exciting?" My fellow podcasters and I from the Small Data Forum called Meta out on this in our November 2021 episode "From metaverse to pyroverse", at https://bit.ly/3BZBxAl. Although the podcast focuses on contemporary uses and abuses of data big and small in politics, business, and public life, I recommend students of how these themes emerge over time go back through the archives of the podcast, but perhaps particularly the show notes that Thomas Stoeckle and I take it in turns to write. OK, Thomas outwrites me about 2:1.

4   Winstanley died in 2014 and we lost touch just after the turn of the millennium, five years after we stopped working together. In his retirement, he found the time and energy to tell many compelling stories about his time in Bechuanaland in his book *Under Two Flags*, long since out of print but worth seeking out. At a time when there is much reflection and deserved criticism of the exploitative nature of British imperial history, Winstanley's tales of his role in helping set Botswana up for success post-independence are worth a look.

5   The Cocktail Party Rule states: "If you want to be boring, talk about yourself. But if you want to be interesting, talk about what matters to those who are listening". See Chapter 6 of *Narrative by Numbers*, particularly pp.115–117.

6   Although I've watched a lot of *Saturday Night Live* over the years, I wasn't familiar with Chris Farley's chat show host persona. I'm grateful to Dean Nelson – the author of *Talk to Me*, the journalistic guide on "how to ask better questions, get better answers, and interview anyone like a pro" – for introducing me to Farley. I've scoured the corners of YouTube and elsewhere and gorged on all remaining interviews. You can view McCartney under the very feeble Farley microscope at https://bit.ly/3qVv489.

7   Gluttons for punishment can relive Jeremy Paxman asking former Tory Home Secretary Michael Howard the same question a dozen times at https://bit.ly/33TW6Dq

7

DOES SILENCE AND LISTENING MATTER?

Abstract

Being able to suppress the natural human desire to fill silence with words is an integral aspect of our ability to ask smarter questions – and learn from the answers we receive. But growing to love the sound of silence and allowing those we're questioning as much time and space as they need to answer our questions is not easy. It takes skill, practice, and self-control, not least because inhibition of inappropriate behaviours is something we have to learn twice as we mature. This happens first as we acquire and become skilled with language in young childhood and then again after the onset of puberty. But it's worth it, for the quality and depth of answers that someone given the gift of silence will produce compared with someone hassled and harried into answering.

DON'T BUTT IN, BACK OFF

We first met coach Tim Johns in Chapter 5 when we considered what makes a good question. Tim produces a frequent but irregular series of super-bite-sized vlogs under the soubriquet "The Man in the Hat", where

DOI: 10.4324/9781003218470-7

he shares nuggets of coaching wisdom in just a couple of minutes.[1] In a December 2021 vlog titled "Be quiet", Tim advised:

> As coaches, we are trained to speak less, to say less, and to listen more, because interrupting and giving your view doesn't help the process of helping other people to find their own solutions. It's through the silence and allowing other people to talk – and the listening – that the true answers can be got at. So, I think every now and again we should embrace what Will Rodgers, the American actor said, which was: 'Never miss a good chance to shut up.'

In addition to our natural ability to ask questions driven by the innate epistemophilic instinct, by now you should also have started to pick up a set of new tools and techniques that enable you to ask smarter questions. And when we put effort into crafting questions that we believe will help us satisfy our curiosity, we need to give those to whom we ask these questions sufficient time and respect to answer them as fully as they want to and are able. To empower them to do this, we need to turn transmitters off and receivers on. In falling silent, we give ourselves the opportunity to listen – to actively listen and to actually hear – what the other person is saying. Falling silent and remaining that way has two big benefits:

1. It allows the other person time to gather, consider, and express their thoughts and give your question the attention it should deserve.
2. It encourages them to exhibit the near-universal human distaste for silence and fill it with answers that may be more revealing than they imagine

Yet in our world increasingly run at warp speed, silence is all too rare. We don't actively listen. We get side-tracked and distracted by our own thoughts. We fail to focus on what the other person is actually saying. We butt in and interrupt them, picking up on titbits – words and phrases that trigger associations – and seek to answer our questions for them. We rush in with the next question before the previous one has been properly addressed. For many people, it's as if the back and forth of dialogue is a competition about who can get the most words – most questions – on the conversational ledger. Many of us find silence awkward and unnatural and behave as if we think it's a monumental waste of time. The irony is that if we fail to embrace silence and wait for a considered response, we'll only end up having to ask the same question again because the other person won't have answered fully. Even if they've got close to doing that, our disinhibited interruptions will mean we haven't attended to that response and it won't have registered with us properly. So, in fact, it's interrupting that wastes time, not silence.

Interrupting also means we fail to attend to the metamessages, body language, facial expressions, and other paraverbal signals others give off. The human brain is remarkably good at paying attention to more than one sensory modality at once – what people are saying and how they're saying it. Yet if we overload our processing capabilities by thinking of the next question or smart thing to say or actually interrupting, we make it very much less likely we'll catch the elements of the other person's response that matter. Attempting to transmit and receive at the same time is the inquisitorial equivalent of trying to pat your head and rub your stomach simultaneously: almost impossible to achieve for sustained periods without one action or the other becoming dominant and the other suffering and failing. To extract the most from that response, we need to pay focused attention – looking at and looking interested in the other person, mirroring their body language and postures, maintaining eye contact, and perhaps taking notes. Interrupting and obviously thinking about other things doesn't deliver focused attention. Rather, it results in unfocused inattention; a blurred impression of understanding, but that's nowhere near enough.

In the summer of 2021, *The Guardian*'s advice columnist started a series of eponymous podcasts called Conversations with Annalisa Barbieri. In an article discussing the podcast in the paper's *Weekend Magazine*, she said:

> Listening, I discovered, wasn't just about waiting for the other person to stop talking, or asking good questions, or even not interrupting. It was about really hearing what the other person was saying, and why they were saying it. Being interested, but also curious. Sometimes that means looking for what's not said, what's left out, which words are used to mask emotions that are hard to acknowledge. Likewise, good listening is about approaching what has been said as if you've never heard it before. Put simply, it's about paying attention.[2]

CAN WE CHAT ON ZOOM OR TEAMS?

Increasingly, conversations are taking place online over video conferencing platforms. In part, this has been enforced by the two years of the coronavirus pandemic, with the majority of the world's knowledge economy workers spending most of 2020–2021 working from home. While pandemics don't last forever (even if their novelty and uncertainty makes it feel like that), it seems certain that five-day-a-week office jobs will be the exception rather than the rule from the mid-2020s onwards. Too many of us have experienced too many life/work balance benefits – and in that order – to go back to what office life was like before SARS-CoV-2 rose from obscurity in late 2019.

What's more, lockdowns and enforced working from home have finally and forever demonstrated that it's not necessary to have everyone in a meeting or workshop in the same physical space. With sufficiently skilled chairpersons and moderators – and for sure a lot of work needs to go into upskilling those who fulfil these roles – the past two years have clearly demonstrated that what matters is bringing the talent together in a way that gives everyone the opportunity to make their contribution. We've always known this can be done in person. We now know that it can be done remotely or in a hybrid compromise, some in the room, others online.[3]

The death of the "everyone together for a meeting or workshop" culture also has some unintended benefits, the biggest of which are human and environmental. I well remember being invited to fly to Jakarta to give a 15-minute presentation at the end of a three-day workshop, only for that wrap-up session to be cancelled because previous sessions had overrun. That's flying almost a third of the way around the world not to give a presentation, days of avoidable jet lag, and weeks of disruption to family life – before you even stop to consider the carbon footprint. Yet in the past two decades, everyone-together workshops became the way of doing things, until the pandemic made that impossible. Did the workshops stop? Far from it. Did they cease to produce the outcomes required of them? Nope. They pivoted online overnight.[4] There were new dynamics, of course, and it's harder to run interactive and creative exercises online than it is in the room.[5] But post-pandemic, it's going to have to be a really special meeting that has to be run in the room when everyone at all levels of seniority has seen what is possible on Zoom or – at a stretch – Teams. And all of that without jet lag, family disruption, and unnecessary travel.

That said, running all meetings and workshops over video conferencing platforms is not without its disadvantages. People are so much better in three dimensions, and genuine, enduring human interactions benefit from at least some time being spent together in real life (IRL). Much of what has been achieved in pandemic-era meetings and workshops has cashed in on relationships forged before lockdowns, even if many people have started new jobs and run events with new colleagues they've never met in the past couple of years. The other major disadvantage of not meeting in person has been the almost complete disappearance of water cooler moments. We've lost the randomness of two or three people meeting in the lunch queue by sheer serendipity and then six months later working together on a new project, the germ of which was hatched when X passed Y the plate of samosas. For pathological connectors and lovers of the chaos of opportunity like me, this has been one of the most frustrating aspects of working from home. I know I am not alone.

What's more, there are very real challenges of running a job – a career – over video conferencing tools. Because of different personal circumstances, domestic arrangements, and personality types, many people don't feel sufficiently confident or comfortable to attend video meetings with their camera turned on, either all the time or some of the time. This makes building team dynamics and rapport much harder – not least because colleagues may suspect that camera-off associates are either not attending to the session, are doing something else (emails, writing an overdue report, or playing Sudoku on their phone), or are only "there" out of a sense of duty. Even when cameras are on and there are no "You're on mute" moments interrupting spontaneity, there's a two-dimensional stiltedness about online meetings that's hard to overcome. Again, this is in part mitigated by an experienced and agile facilitator or host, but there are limits to what even the best can achieve. Overlay all of these challenges to attention on those identified in the first section of this chapter on questioners' repeated failure to shut up, and it's clear that focused attention – active listening – is a challenge for dialogue IRL and online, with the ability to read paraverbal signals hampered and often exacerbated online. It's even worse for leadership, but that's another's story.[6]

ON LISTENING ETIQUETTE AND NETIQUETTE

Whether you're asking questions in person or mediated via video conferencing software, it's important that you monitor and seek to actively inhibit your behaviour and desire to butt in and cut others off once you've asked a question. If you don't allow them to complete their response – if you rush them and make them feel they're in a competition – most likely you'll achieve five things. None of them are desirable and none of them further the aspiration of asking smarter questions.

> First, you'll put them on edge, and that makes them likely to rush their response and give a more obvious, more straightforward answer that doesn't require much thinking through.
>
> Second, you'll show that you're not interested in what they're saying and are more interested in the sound of your own voice and your opinions than theirs. Above anything else, it's damnably rude.
>
> Third, in demonstrating your lack of interest in what they're saying, you're undermining the potential power of your question. If it is genuinely smart but you can't be bothered to hear what the other person has to say, they'll dismiss it as trivial when they may have thought it was actually quite interesting.
>
> Fourth, you'll turn the conversation into a "cage fight not a climbing wall", to use the vivid metaphors of Julia Dhar's TED Salon talk, "How to have constructive conversations". A cage fight can only end one of two ways. Both are bloody and neither are constructive or smart.
>
> And fifth, you won't be able to process, turn over in short-term memory, or consolidate into long-term memory whatever it is you've allowed them a few seconds to say. What you say will mingle with what they've said and turn into meaningless word soup.

In his book *Socratic Selling Skills*, Kevin Daley observes:

> *Most people have two states in a conversation: speaking and waiting to speak. Waiting to speak is a bad listening habit. If you're waiting to speak, it means you're thinking about what you want to say, which means you're not listening. (p.79)*

Socrates may have been irritating because he asked tough and smart questions of his interlocutors, but one thing that he (or the version of him that comes to us via Plato's dialogues) can't be accused of is failure to listen or failure to give his interlocutors time to answer him in silence. They might become irritated or frustrated when Socrates points out that what they've said in response to a first question contradicts what they've said in response to subsequent questions. What that shows is quite how keenly he was listening to their answers, not that they didn't have sufficient time or head-clearing silence in which to compose their responses.

THIS IS THE SOUND (AND NEUROSCIENCE) OF SILENCE

In her novel *All Rivers Flow to the Sea*, Alison McGhee observes:

> *You are most powerful when you are most silent. People never expect silence. They expect words, motion, defense, offense, back and forth. They expect to leap into the fray. They are ready, fists up, words hanging leaping from their mouths. Silence? No.*

As we've seen, silence is the perfect complement to asking smarter questions. If we want our smarter questions to have the desired impact and yield more interesting answers, we should learn to love silence. It's a quality and environment central to the domain of meditation, a topic which we'll cover in the interview with Zen Buddhist Sensei, Tania Turner, at the end of this chapter. Having posed our query, we should then shut up, allowing the other person the time and space to think of a response. Silence turns the five points in the section immediately above on their head.

1. Silence allows the other person the time to think through and articulate a smarter answer in their own time, not to some draconian, breakneck timetable of competition.
2. It shows you are interested and are prepared to make the time to hear them out.
3. You give your question every opportunity to have maximum impact.

4. Silence turns your dialogue into a climbing wall, not a cage fight, enabling both parties to look for conversational handholds and footholds pressure-free. This is especially true for the one answering the question, and it'll be the questioner's turn again soon enough anyway.
5. By embracing silence, you'll remember what they say. You'll be able to rehearse in your short-term memory's phonological loop the answers you receive, holding them there until they begin to pass into long-term memory.

It's amazing what you can achieve by simply putting a sock in it, closing your mouth, sitting back, and listening – actively. Not a bad return on investment for doing nothing. Well, almost nothing. In order not to do something, you need to inhibit that behaviour at a cognitive, behavioural, and below all at a neurobiological level. Inhibition is just as important a biochemical process as excitation – indeed, it's perhaps even more important. In the human brain, there are more than 60 different types of neurotransmitters. Most neurotransmitters are excitatory, including some of the most common and well known, such as histamine, epinephrine, and glutamate; the latter is present in more than 80% of synapses, the connections between neurons.

Dopamine – involved in the reward circuitry, pleasure, attention, and movement – can be both excitatory and inhibitory, depending where and how it's used in the brain, while serotonin is inhibitory. Anti-depressants of the so-called selective serotonin reuptake inhibitors (SSRI) class work to combat low systemic levels of serotonin. They do this by blocking (inhibiting) the reuptake of this neurotransmitter into neurons once it's been released into the synaptic cleft, with consequent beneficial effects on mood and emotion. By far, the most common inhibitory neurotransmitter is gamma-aminobutyric acid (GABA), which is found in an estimated 10–20% of neurons. GABA is the yang to glumate's yin, and the brain has many complex interacting ways of turning the metaphorical volume up and down, depending on the brain function in question. The brain and the behaviours it mediates are a delicate balance of excitation and inhibition and it takes time – years – for each brain user to get the balance right, particularly as balance exists at the complementary levels of neurochemistry, behaviour, and cognition.

Younger children often find it hard to inhibit and suppress behaviours that some adults deem to be inappropriate in "civilised company". This can include behaviours such as "blowing raspberries", swearing, shouting, putting the cat down their pyjama trousers, or poking their grandmothers' breasts. With time in the world – and sometimes chastisement or a Paddington Bear-style "hard stare" – most children learn to inhibit behaviours that are deemed to be inappropriate. Again, this is based on brain users overlaying complex, cognitive processes, including learning and memory, on the complex neurochemical blancmange that sits and wobbles, fizzes and pops between their ears. Simply waiting for tweens to become teens and teenagers to mature into adults doesn't remove or even slow down inappropriate or taboo behaviours. Indeed, the swirling maelstrom of hormones unleashed at puberty and throughout most of the teenage years can radically disrupt inhibition that seemed to be sorted before puberty, confusing everyone, particularly parents.

In part, this is by emotional design – biologically speaking, to make their own independent way in the world, teenagers need to become as securely detached from their parents and carers as they were attached as vulnerable infants. There's an evolutionary, biological logic behind every *I hate you!*, *You just don't understand me!* teenage temper tantrum, sometimes more frightening than those from the Terrible Twos because teens are often physically stronger, faster, and more agile than their parents, unlike most toddlers. In part, this is by physical design. Inhibition is controlled structurally by the prefrontal cortex, the uniquely human, grey and white matter, full of folds and crenelations, wrapped on the outer surface of the whole brain like the bark of an ancient, gnarled tree but doesn't fully mature until humans are in their early 20s.

It was damage to the left prefrontal cortex that caused god-fearing Phineas Gage to become a potty-mouthed navvy when a tamping iron – used to pack down gunpowder for blasting rock to make a railway cutting – exploded and was propelled through his jaw and out of the top of his head, cauterizing the wound as it sped into the sky taking 10% of his grey matter with it. When he'd recovered from the trauma, this polite Victorian boy became "gross, profane, coarse, and vulgar, to such a degree that his society was intolerable to decent people".[7] He lost his inhibition and couldn't control his behaviour, making him much like many people when they ask questions. Asking smarter questions requires us to self-consciously inhibit our inner, post-accident Phineas Gage.

SUMMING UP

So, if you want to give time for your smart questions to germinate, root, and grow more interesting answers in the minds of those you're asking, act like the great interviewers act: consciously inhibit your desire to talk and avoid filling the silence with nervous verbiage. Be like David Frost when he interviewed disgraced President Nixon in 1977: ask your question and let it have its impact.[8]

In his multimillion-selling book *The 7 Habits of Highly Effective People*, Steven Covey's fifth habit is "Seek first to understand, then to be understood". By having the self-control to allow your interlocutor to answer your question, you're being much more than polite and showing a proper appreciation and understanding of the rules of conversational turn-taking. You'll get much more than a better answer to a better question, even if that is the principal benefit of posing a question and then falling silent. By not showing your hand first but rather asking the other party to show theirs, you'll find yourself in the dominant position of knowing what they think and believe when they don't know your views.

QUESTIONS ABOUT QUESTIONS – INTERVIEW 9 OF 14

NAME	Tania Turner
ORGANISATION	Zen Buddhist school of meditation
ROLE	Sensei

Tania Turner has been a practicing Zen Buddhism for almost 20 years. She recently received transmission and the official designation of a

Sensei, a person authorised to instruct others in Zen Buddhism. The lineage of those from whom she has received instruction encompasses two of the three traditions or sects of Japanese Zen Buddhism, *Sōtō* and *Rinzai*. Having known Sensei Tania for almost twice as long as she's been practicing, I've observed with great interest how her practice has enriched and deepened her experience of life. In conversations over the years, it's become clear that questions are central to her practice. Meditating on questions (known as *kōans* [unsolvable enigmas]) provokes doubt and tests a student's progress. In Turner's lineage, there are around 700 *kōans*.

"*Kōans* are questions through which Zen Buddhists practice," says Turner. "They invite you to be incredibly intimate. You aren't able to answer them with our usual dualist way of thinking. You have to let go of that way of approaching questions and, by doing that, another approach develops."

Well-known *kōans* include: *What is the sound of one hand clapping? How do I stop the sound of a distant temple bell? How can I take a five-storey pagoda out of a teapot? Does a dog have Buddha nature?* I wonder what Buddha nature is, and Turner tells me:

> *Actually, that's another kōan in itself: 'What is Buddha nature?' It's like describing what's on the menu without eating, a conceptual understanding but one without experience. When you think about yourself, you think of your name, how you identify yourself, how others see you, yet none of those are who you are. They're labels. We usually have a sense of ourselves as a solid person – flesh and blood – but that, too, is a delusion. We're not as solid and separate as we think we are, and the practice of meditating on kōans helps us to realise the truth of this.*

Turner acknowledges how frustrating it can be to bring the Western analytical thinking mind to address *kōans*:

> *You just have to sit with it. Because we're trained and brought up to think in a particular way, you find yourself approaching it using the usual framework. But that doesn't work and you can feel like you're banging your head against a wall. But, in time, that drops away. Then the kōan embeds itself in you, it works with you, and you become one with it.*

Bernie Glassman, the Jewish American Zen Buddhist *roshi* – master – maintained that "questions are more alive than answers" and that you have to sit with a *kōan* until it plunges you into a sense of openness. With no fixed ground to stand on – no established frames of reference that we normally have to rely on – you can then go into the unknown. This is why, Glassman maintained, there is no yes or no answer to a *kōan*, making a *kōan* the most open a question can be.

As initiates and trainees start working with their teachers, all meditative work is focused on answering a progressively more challenging series of *kōans*. A teacher will direct a student to the particular *kōan* they're going to work on. The student writes it down and learns it. You sit with it in focused meditation sessions, but all the time, too. "It becomes part of you," observes Turner. "You may not be constantly thinking about it consciously as you might try to solve a conundrum in everyday life, but it's there." When a student feels she's made progress, she meets with her teacher. She sits outside the teacher's room, a bell rings, the student goes in, says her name and practice, and presents her reflections on the *kōan* to her teacher – not an answer as such. The teacher may ask further questions about how she sees the *kōan* and decide whether or not the student is ready to move on to the next *kōan* in the series prescribed by the lineage. Each one can take many months of sitting and meditation to address.

Turner says that the purpose of asking questions – posing and addressing *kōans* in a very specific and prescriptive order:

> is to see your Buddha nature and understand that it's not separate from others; to see the interconnectedness of all beings and things, sentient and non-sentient; to properly appreciate your non-position in the world. In the Western tradition, we're so consumed with confirming and validating ourselves. We constantly look to secure ourselves – and Zen Buddhist practice helps you realise that we can't. The process isn't about negating or denying yourself, but appreciating that we are not this constant fixed thing.

Zen Buddhist practice is very much more about the journey than the destination. A critical part of that journey is listening. When you sit with a question – for hours, weeks, months – you listen to it. It is only by listening to it that the "right" answer – the appropriate response – can arise. "Usually when we listen to a question, we're immediately ready – too ready – to jump in with an answer, based on our experiences, assumptions, and prejudices. But when we really listen, something else happens."

> *To study the self is to forget the self. When the Buddha Dharma and my life are separate, when I do not see that my life is the one body, that is delusion. When I see that they are together, this is so-called enlightened life.*
> **Dogen Zenji, 13th century Japanese Zen Buddhist priest**

Those who ask good questions in Zen Buddhism, Turner believes, have come to realise that they are already enlightened and that enlightenment is nowhere else but here. From experience, she knows that it can be foolish to try to hold on to those all-too-elusive moments of enlightenment because they are so fleeting. "The more you bear witness to the ungrounded ground, the more you become fluid and flexible. Not just in addressing *kōans* but also in addressing the challenges of everyday life."

Turner believes that Zen Buddhist practice has made her life more tolerable, "but only sometimes! It's called practice for a reason," she asserts:

> *because you keep having to come back to it. Every day. And although I still have my neuroses, my dissatisfaction doesn't bother me nearly as much as it used to. Practice also makes it easier to tolerate circumstances: when you're hot, you're hot; when you're cold, you're cold. You realise that you can't change circumstances to satisfy yourself.*

Like Stoicism, Zen Buddhism enables practitioners to understand that they can't change events and they only have power to control their reactions to them. Like Socrates – perhaps an unwitting early practitioner of this practice – Zen Buddhists' "beginner's mind" is understanding that we are ignorant. After an hour talking with Sensei Tania, the Socratic paradox doesn't feel anywhere near as paradoxical as once it did.

> *The bad news is you're falling through the air, nothing to hang on to, no parachute. The good news is there's no ground.*
> **Chögyam Trungpa, Tibetan Buddhist master**

As we come to the end of our discussion, Turner concludes that there is something about the process of questioning in Zen Buddhism that changes the practitioner. "It trains you in being flexible, being open, not landing on one particular answer, then letting go of it. You learn not to attach yourself to anything." She has found this particularly beneficial during the pandemic. "I've coped much better than I feared I might. My practice has enabled me to be so much more compassionate towards myself – even if I've been struggling to deal with it."

When we'd finished our discussion, Tania said to me – self-effacingly, but also rooted deeply in her practice and tradition: "I don't know if any of that made any sense, and if I didn't, I've probably done a good job."

I'll say!

TANIA TURNER'S TOP TIPS FOR ASKING SMARTER QUESTIONS

1. Let go of the usual dualist approach to answering questions.
2. Sit with questions to come to realise that we can answer them in another way.
3. Allow the questions that you're working on to become part of you – not necessarily consciously, but always permit them to be with you.
4. Use questions to help you understand the interconnectedness of all things.
5. Enjoy the journey over the destination, particularly the role of listening to questions.

NOTES

1 See Tim Johns' YouTube Channel at https://bit.ly/33uMijj. The December 2021 video "Be Quiet" is at https://bit.ly/3ER6EB3 and features "The Man (not cat) in the Hat" in a particularly fetching new trilby.

2 "Be interested, be curious, hear what's not said," Annalisa Barbieri in *The Guardian*, 24.07.21 – https://bit.ly/3pKUSCY

3 Before the COVID omicron blip, the excellent Brighton Chamber ran a stellar event called Hybrid with both speakers and attendees in the room and mediated online. It's an excellent example of what technology and a bit of wit can achieve. Suitably enough, one of the speakers was Robin Shattock, Professor of Mucosal Infection and Immunity at Imperial College. See https://bit.ly/3JtAXjF

4 Reflecting on the first nine months of life under the pandemic, Jill Dougan, sales and marketing director at Centrica, told marketing investment experts Ebiquity:

> *The one thing that COVID did for us is show us that we can be really fleet of foot – we can be agile. We had thousands of people WFH [working from home] overnight. If we'd tried to do that through a transformation programme, it would never have happened.*

5 During the course of 2021, I ran several dozen workshops for clients online, often spanning at least three time zones – the U.S., Europe, and India; Europe, India, and the Far East. Now that we know that the infrastructure has sufficient bandwidth and stability to support the knowledge economy online, there's no ramming this particular genie back in the bottle.

6 See Tim Johns' 2020 book, *Leading from Home*.

7 I tell a fuller version of the Phineas Gage story in *How To Be Insightful*, pp.59–62.

8 Ron Howard's 2008 film *Frost/Nixon* is a gripping tale of British talk show host David Frost, seemingly out of his depth in interviewing former President Nixon. In a series of interviews, however, Frost and his team sealed the fate of how history will remember Nixon. The cliché "hoist by his own petard" has never been more apposite, with Nixon underestimating the ability of Frost to ask smarter questions, including *Why didn't you burn the [Watergate] tapes?* and *Are you really saying that the President can do something illegal?*. See https://imdb.to/3EECW12

8

CAN WE GO OVER THAT IN FORENSIC DETAIL?

Abstract

There is a lot we can learn about how to ask smarter questions from the tools and techniques deployed by those required to operate in situations that have the highest stakes. What a hostage negotiator asks a terrorist or bank robber can determine whether hostages live or die; whether a siege ends with avoidable loss of life or calmly and quietly. But it's how the hostage negotiator asks questions that are even more important.

The same is true for police detectives looking to build a coherent and accurate picture of the facts of a serious crime. They have to do this despite incomplete evidence and suspects, victims, and witnesses who may all be reluctant to share an objective account of what happened, each for their own reasons. Again, it is how detectives ask that must be got right before they focus on the what. The golden threads running through the questioning style and techniques used by those operating in life-and-death situations are calmness, empathy, and preparation. These have broad application. Even – or perhaps particularly – to you.

DOI: 10.4324/9781003218470-8

UPPING THE STAKES

The veteran journalist Dean Nelson says in his book *Talk to Me*: "Interviewing isn't just asking a bunch of random questions to random people. It's a guided conversation" (p.147). The more professions we meet for whom asking smarter questions helps to define their success, the more applicable I believe the tools and techniques we're picking up along the way can be for all of us – at home every bit as much as at work.

As barrister Tim Bishop told us in Chapter 3, the way that lawyers prepare, sequence, and deploy questions in court can have a profound impact on the outcome of legal proceedings. It's perfectly possible for the same set of material facts in a case to be presented and marshalled differently by different lawyers and for the same judge or jury to reach and different conclusions. The *what* matters, but the *how* REALLY matters. Bishop's expertise is matrimonial law – dividing the spoils of marriage fairly when a partnership is no longer sustainable. It's fair to say that the techniques and principles of this area of law are echoed and mirrored in many jurisdictions' contract law that governs disputes between individuals, corporations, governments. Wherever a case needs to be built, evidence presented, and the parties in a dispute required to answer questions set by lawyers acting for both parties, the tone and content of these questions can help to shape the outcome.

This matters from the perspective of natural justice. Societies set laws to permit behaviours or actions they believe are fair and unlikely to unduly harm or compromise the interests of others. They also set laws to prohibit other behaviours and actions that are unfair and likely to harm or compromise others' interests. When societies first emerged, these were often based on moral codes set down by religious leaders. In many Western nations from the Enlightenment onwards, there has been a formal and self-conscious decoupling of church and state, although nations as diverse as America and Afghanistan have seen laws passed as recently as 2021 that are driven entirely by religious dogma. From the state legislation in Texas designed to outlaw abortion as early as six weeks[1] to the reimposition of Sharia law by the returning Taliban,[2] where church and state are not separate in the early 21st century, the laws passed are often designed to suppress women's rights and entrench patriarchal views of the world and strategies for government. Fortunately for natural justice, today these are very much the exception rather than the rule, and for the most part most legislation is driven by morality and fairness for all and the overwhelming appeal of natural justice.

As Conan Doyle had Sherlock Holmes say A Study in Scarlet, "What you do in this world is a matter of no consequence. The question is what can you make people believe you have done." In this chapter, I am less interested in whether individuals or corporations have access to smarter lawyers than those they face in court. In an ideal world, everyone would be able to afford equally good legal representation, even if that might lead to legal stalemate. The world is far from ideal and there are celebrated cases or areas of law – notoriously drink-driving and libel in the U.K. courts – where whip-smart lawyers have prevented convictions for their celebrity clients or secured super-injunctions that keep their charges out of the papers. For the purposes of this chapter, I'm more interested in the *what* and particularly the *how* of questioning in a legal context. I'm keen to assess what we who aren't in court or high-stakes genuinely life-and-death negotiations every day can learn from those who are. And before we take two perspectives from the British police service, let's get inside the head of former FBI hostage negotiator Chris Voss.

NEVER SPLITTING THE DIFFERENCE

Whenever hostages who are U.S. citizens are captured and held against their will by kidnappers, the U.S. government is represented by trained negotiators who work for the Federal Bureau of Investigations (FBI). From 1984 to 2008, Chris Voss worked for the FBI, rising to the role of a leading international kidnapping negotiator. He spent his days (and many nights, often several at a stretch) negotiating with bank robbers and terrorists. He was trained by the FBI, at the London Metropolitan Police Force's Scotland Yard headquarters, and at Harvard Law School.[3]

When actively engaged in the field, Voss led teams who sought to bring hostage situations to a peaceful end, avoiding both harm – including death – to hostages and payment of ransoms in cash, in kind, or in personnel to kidnappers. Often, Voss negotiated directly with kidnappers. Hostage situations that end peacefully – with kidnappers releasing hostages without violence or bloodshed – routinely end with arrest and usually imprisonment for the perpetrators of these very significant crimes. Nevertheless, it is the job of the hostage negotiator to effect a negotiated peaceful end in a way in which the kidnappers do not lose face and certainly are not humiliated. To achieve this requires negotiators to be trained to ask questions to an extraordinarily high standard and to practice what they learn flawlessly, repeatedly, and calmly. Most importantly, they must do this under the most intense pressure, because one wrong move and innocent civilians who simply went to the bank to pay in a cheque or took a flight to visit their grandchildren, can end up as collateral damage. Dead.

Having worked on more than 150 international hostage cases – including 15 years on the New York City Joint Terrorism Task Force – in 2007 Voss left the FBI and created the Black Swan Group, a company specialising in the application of negotiation skills for business. Voss has codified what he learned in his 25 years with the FBI in an excellent book called *Never Split the Difference*. He has also brought these lessons to life in a couple of very watchable online courses via the MasterClass platform.[4] I won't attempt to summarise Voss's comprehensive negotiation toolkit, but I do think it's worth our considering a selection of the key tools he identifies in his book, online courses, and consultancy work:

- **Tactical empathy** – by keeping your own projections and assumptions out of a negotiation, a skilled negotiator inhabits the other side's world and sees things from their perspective. Voss describes tactical empathy as "emotional intelligence on steroids" and says that negotiation is "the art of letting others have your way". At first reading, tactical empathy sounds cynical; when you read or hear Voss's application of tactical empathy in life-and-death situations – achieved through other tactics, including mirroring and personalising negotiations – even cynics lose their cynicism about the approach. We've already considered the role of empathy (and the follies of sympathy) in asking smarter questions in previous chapters. Voss's approach simply systemises what for many can be a nebulous human quality.

- **Mirroring** – this sees negotiators repeat the last one to three words of what the other party says: the actual words they use, very definitely not your own synonyms for them. Having mirrored the language of the other party, you then fall silent and allow them to reflect on what you've said in response to them. The fact that you've used their own words makes them feel heard and understood and more likely to negotiate.[5]
- **Late night FM DJ voice** – by speaking in a deep and low, soft and calm voice with downward inflection, the other party feels reassured. It's a great analogy, as any insomniacs will attest.
- **Labelling** – another tactic designed to make those you're negotiating with feel listened to, which enables negatives to be diffused and positives reinforced. Rather than accusing or stating the other side's position, using labelling a negotiator uses phrases such as *It looks like* … and *It seems as if* …. If you get it right, you'll allow them to agree; if you get it wrong, it'll allow them to correct you, but with minimal damage done.
- **The accusation audit** – negotiators on both sides of a crisis are often afraid to speak out loud the worst possible outcomes of that situation. By naming them, however, you acknowledge them, remove some of their power, and can then move on.

There are many other techniques in Voss's full toolkit – from framing, humility, and assessing the impact of paraverbal signals to personalising (introducing yourself/using your first name), taking the consultative approach highlighted by Stuart Lotherington in Chapter 6 by using calibrated questions, and unearthing what Voss calls Black Swans (critical data that changes everything). Reading his book or completing his online courses will introduce you to them in detail and in a very practical, approachable format that will dial up the effective *how* quotient of the questions you ask.

I believe there are three aspects to Voss's approach that make it so compelling. First, it's been developed in some of the toughest field situations in existence; as the subtitle of his book puts it in its call-to-action: "Negotiating as if your life depended on it". If it can work with terrorists, kidnappers, and bank robbers, it can work in a sales pitch; if it works in life and death, it works in life and work. Second, it's very well thought through, and the tools build on one another in complementary fashion. And third, its humility and calmness are characteristic of the questioning strategies favoured by the police service, as we'll see in the next two interviews.

Voss's approach to bargaining is also hugely refreshing. Although the book is called *Never Split the Difference*, bargaining isn't its principal focus. But as he says in the book, "I'm here to call bullshit on compromise right now", and he identifies how unsatisfactory a compromise solution can be and the importance of deciding on your sticking point (on price, concessions, etc.) beyond which you will not go before negotiations begin and moving up (or down) in ever-decreasing increments (20%, then 10%, then 5%, then walk away). His approach to negotiation reminds me of two of the techniques I've picked up from the U.S. sales training consultancy, Sandler:

- The first is the upfront contract. At the beginning of an exploratory sales meeting, you agree how long you'll talk (say 40 minutes), after which you'll review the discussion and agree whether or not you have a basis to proceed to a further engagement. Make sure that after 40 minutes, you fulfil your obligations of that upfront contract and review where you've got to.
- The second is to exhibit vulnerability – like a dog showing its neck to another – by saying: *There may or may not be a fit, but let's review the discussion and see if there is.*

Both of these approaches – tried and tested like those in Voss's armoury – show no desperation. And both of them are liable to send otherwise cynical, sceptical prospective clients into a buying frenzy. As Dan Pink says in his book *To Sell Is Human*, "we are all in the moving [persuading] business". Setting out an upfront contract and exhibiting vulnerability are very potent motivators for those being sold to. Like Voss's black swans, they tell prospective clients the vendor is so confident in their offer – of products or services – that, to some degree, they're indifferent as to whether they make a sale today or not. Overplay this and it comes over as arrogance; play it right and it's like catnip.

CALL THE POLICE!

Having considered the role – and particularly the *how* – of asking smarter questions in hostage negotiation and as used by lawyers, I was keen to find out the ground rules of questioning favoured by the police. In the U.K., the police are responsible for determining how evidence is assembled and presented for crimes that come to court, providing fuel for the prosecution by the Crown Prosecution Service and for the state to prosecute wrongdoers and law-breakers.

Crime fiction is one of the most popular genres of literature in many countries, particularly the U.K. and the U.S., and crime dramas dominate mainstream TV, the movies, and streaming TV services, from *Hawaii Five-O* to *Brooklyn Nine-Nine*, from *Killing Eve* to *Only Murders in the Building*. The behaviour and techniques of many fictional detectives are often over-excited caricatures of oppressive, intimidatory, coercive shouting. Your inner TV critic may be disturbed to learn that this is not best practice or indeed practiced at all; your inner seeker for natural justice will be relieved to learn that the approach trained and used in the contemporary British police service is very much more considered and Chris Voss-like than what Brits of my generation experienced when growing up and watching *The Sweeney*, *Juliet Bravo*, and *The Bill*.

I spoke to two police detectives at very different ends of their careers, both from the North England. Chris Gregg served in the West Yorkshire Police, rising through the ranks from police cadet in 1971 to head of West Yorkshire Criminal Investigation Department (CID) by the mid-2000s. He was responsible for creating the Homicide and Major Enquiry Team for that county's police force, a Team that helped to restore public faith in the service in the wake of the failures surrounding the Peter Sutcliffe case in the 1970s and 1980s. I also spoke to Detective Sergeant (DS) Tom Barker from North Yorkshire Police, who leads teams of detectives today who gather and present evidence in more serious and acquisitive crimes. What I found speaking to both was that asking smarter questions – the *what*, yes, but particularly the *how* – is central to the police doing a more professional, more successful, and more equitable job on behalf of the communities they serve. As with the learnings from hostage negotiation, so in police detective work. There are many admirable and applicable tools and techniques that we would all do well to adopt and apply in our day-to-day existence, at work every bit as much as at home.

QUESTIONS ABOUT QUESTIONS – INTERVIEW 10 OF 14

NAME	Chris Gregg, QPM
ORGANISATION	West Yorkshire Police; Axiom International
ROLE	Former Detective Chief Superintendent; Former chief executive officer (CEO) of Axiom International

Chris Gregg is the former CEO of Axiom International, a British company operating globally that delivers strategic capacity-building programmes, institutional and public sector reform, peace-building, and national security development. Before co-founding Axiom in 2010, Gregg enjoyed a distinguished first career as a detective with West Yorkshire Police. Following a period of service spanning four decades, he was awarded the Queen's Police Medal.

Gregg became a police cadet straight from school in 1971, joining the force three years later as a probationary cop in his home town of Huddersfield, West Yorkshire. In 1978, he changed direction to become a detective in the Huddersfield CID. "Finding out who'd committed the crimes and why always seemed like the more interesting end of the job to me," he notes. West Yorkshire was – and remains – one of the biggest English police forces, a mix of urban and rural, taking in the big metropolitan areas of Leeds and Bradford as well as other large towns. Major crime became his expertise, and in time he was promoted to Detective Superintendent in the role of Senior Investigating Officer (SIO); it is SIOs who run murder investigations. By 2005, he was a Detective Chief

Superintendent of West Yorkshire Police, and he went on to be Head of CID for the entire force.

It was in this role that Gregg established the Homicide and Major Enquiry Team (HMET) which he led successfully until he left the service. The HMET developed a strong reputation for solving crimes – including cold cases – under Gregg's leadership, but it's safe to say that West Yorkshire CID hasn't always smelled of roses. Indeed, after its repeated failure to catch the serial killer Peter Sutcliffe – the so-called Yorkshire Ripper, who was interviewed and released nine times during a five-year investigation in the late 1970s and early 1980s – the force's reputation was in tatters.

When we spoke, I wanted to find out more about the role of asking questions in police detective work in general. I was also interested to learn more about the importance of smarter interrogation in how Gregg rebuilt the culture, effectiveness, and reputation of West Yorkshire CID; in how he helped to turn the force into one of the police service's shining lights. For although the Ripper case was unprecedented and presented a unique set of challenges, the force evidently failed on a number of fronts. And when institutions fail as West Yorkshire Police had failed, it can be incredibly challenging to get back to where it had been, let alone rise – phoenix-like – to become a beacon of best practice.

QUESTIONS FOR INVESTIGATING AND SOLVING CRIMES

Asking the right questions and listening is critical in investigative work. Gregg observes:

If an interviewee – especially a criminal suspect – gets a sense that the interviewer doesn't fully know what they're talking about, or isn't properly prepared, this will very likely be picked up and can result in the suspect actually controlling much of the interview. While you'll never know as much about what happened as a guilty suspect – you weren't there, after all – you've got to be as prepared as you possibly can be, as the tiniest bit of detail can make all the difference in ensuring you remain in control. It starts with being fully on top of the facts, and then requires you to ask smart, logical, and structured questions that ultimately join the dots.

Interviewers are well trained and use a staged process, which first involves planning and preparation, a degree of rapport building, encouraging an uninterrupted account of events, followed by clarifying and challenging, and finally closing. Interviewers will generally favour open questions as an interview builds. Much better to ask *Can you tell me where you were at 10pm last Thursday evening?* (open) than *I understand you were in the Black Bull pub on the High Street at 10pm last Thursday, weren't you?* (closed). Closed questions can quickly close a suspect interviewee's responses to single-word responses, the opposite of what the interviewer is trying to achieve.

Gregg believes that there's no single approach that characterises interviewers who ask the sort of questions that enable suspects to confess, but it's impossible to overemphasise the importance of listening. Good listeners make good interviewers. "Don't be on transmit mode when you should be on receive," urges Gregg:

> There is no one size fits all approach to interviewing suspects, and while the nature of the crimes committed and what's being recalled can be terrible, it's critical to maintain a professional, non-judgemental, and respectful approach throughout. We're all human and the accounts heard and crimes investigated can be truly appalling, but the interviewer must always set emotional feelings aside during the interview process.

Preparation is key. Every step of every interview needs to be well structured. Before major crime suspect interviews, specialist-trained interview advisors sometimes assist interviewers to plan and prepare. This helps officers work out, for example, at which point to introduce certain evidence – such as DNA or CCTV footage, fingerprints or phone records data. The timing and structure of the interview process should always be properly planned, and the interview advisor can help detectives do just that.

"The interview setting when questioning suspect interviewees has to be thought through, too," says Gregg:

> not only things such as the room layout itself and recording facilities – have they been tested and are they working properly? – but also, in my view, the interviewers themselves. Standards of appearance, deportment, and all-round professionalism are important, helping to ensure that the interviewer is taken seriously in every respect by the person being questioned.

THE ROLE OF THE SENIOR INVESTIGATING OFFICER

*The buck stops with the SIOs, who are required to lead major crime and mur-
der investigations – 'tracing', 'interviewing', and 'evaluating' suspects is a key
part of investigators' work on such cases. Detectives generally work in pairs
on major investigations, asking questions that lead to further questions: 'Where
were you?', 'Where were you going?', 'What time did you end your journey?',
'What route did you take?' In asking questions of witnesses and suspects,
you're looking to build a solid and certain picture of who is – and who isn't –
worthy of further investigation. In the wake of Sutcliffe, no detective in the West
Yorkshire force wanted to be the cop who got it wrong or overlooked a crucial
bit of evidence. You don't want to eliminate suspects too soon from your enqui-
ries if there's a chance they may worthy of further investigation.*

For anyone facing questions from a detective, the experience is out-of-
the-ordinary and can be intensely stressful, curtailing how they might
otherwise respond. Suspects – particularly guilty suspects – can be understandably reticent and reluctant to open up. Even innocent witnesses –
who may have played no part in a crime – can clam up because they think
they have become compromised in some way by observing it.

"The worst thing as an interviewer is when you have a suspect who is
giving one-word, monotone answers," says Gregg:

*Suspects might have done the most appalling things, but there can be an
emotional barrier they need to get over in order to start giving you the information you need. They don't want their loved ones – often their mum – to
think worse of them because of what they've done. The key to getting past
that is to get them sufficiently relaxed to start talking. With skilful interviewing,
you can give a suspect the sense that what has happened, has happened,
and it has consequences. It's not possible to turn the clock back. You need
them to understand that they have responsibility for what they've done.*

BUILDING THE HOMICIDE AND MAJOR
ENQUIRY TEAM

"When we created the new Team for the West Yorkshire force," reveals
Gregg:

*we brought all the learnings from previous major investigations with us,
including the Sutcliffe case. A team of eight SIOs would lead the teams,*

each being an immensely experienced investigator in their own right. We understood from experience what motivates and demotivates a team, and how best to use a finite number of staff. One of the crucial lessons learned was never to start a line of enquiry you can't finish – it can become a monster – and that happened more than once with Sutcliffe.

There was also a significant human resources/psychology issue that Gregg had to get right in building HMET. The Team was a 300-strong unit, 240 detectives and 60 support staff, all dealing with homicide and major crimes. There was no room for egos or big shots, standards were set and had to be adhered to. The key was blending together the skills of investigators, case preparation teams, exhibit officers, crime scene specialists, family liaison, and incident room teams. The full team was assembled from all corners of the force, many of whom didn't know each other or hadn't worked together previously, so it was vital to develop an ethos of total professionalism in everything they did. Everyone needed to understand precisely what their role was, the expectations of it, and deliver on every front. In creating HMET, Gregg required that selection procedures chose detectives and staff, not just with the right skills, but with the right personalities.

There were four components that underpinned the creation of the Team, all of which Gregg insisted were delivered to the highest standards. These were: (i) investigation, (ii) crime scene capability, (iii) family liaison, and (iv) court preparation. All of this demanded the use of smarter questions and using questioning techniques in the right way. For each component, Gregg ensured that they were delivered using a standardised, systematic approach:

Setting and keeping high standards demands that you work in a quiet, unassuming, professional way. It sounds simple to deliver, but it's not. But if you hold your nerve and roll it out to high standards, it can be transformational.

THE IMPACT OF DATA AND TECHNOLOGY ON POLICE QUESTIONING

In Gregg's 34-year career in policing, the process of capturing, recording, and sharing evidence has moved from entirely manual – hand-written and typed-up witness statements and tape-recorded interviews – to digital. Content created had to be seen to be acted upon, from statements to interviews, all of which existed on separate pieces of paper. These could only be connected to each other by staff working on the specific case. Today, all statements, interviews, and information in major crime cases are stored digitally, tagged, and fully searchable:

> *Investigation processes and interviewing techniques may have changed over the years, but an investigator's role remains fundamentally the same. People commit crimes, but often don't want to admit to them, so investigations are launched to identify them. It's the investigator's job to undertake a thoroughly professional investigation, gathering evidence, and where suspects are prosecuted, to then present the evidence in a structured and well organised way. The impact of data and technology is that information comes together more quickly and can be analysed and cross-referenced far more easily, so there's much less chance of crucial information not being connected, or the dots not being joined – simply that. With Sutcliffe, the interviewing officers unfortunately didn't have all of the relevant information together.*

CHRIS GREGG'S TOP TIPS FOR ASKING SMARTER QUESTIONS

1. Be calm and relax the person you're interviewing – then listen.
2. Think through the theatre of interviewing – the room, where to sit, how you're dressed.
3. Prepare thoroughly, planning the structure and flow of your questions.
4. Use open, non-judgemental questions to get people talking.
5. Give those you're interviewing the time and space to give comprehensive answers.

QUESTIONS ABOUT QUESTIONS – INTERVIEW 11 OF 14

NAME	Tom Barker
ORGANISATION	North Yorkshire Police
ROLE	Detective Sergeant

Tom Barker is a DS in the North Yorkshire Police, supervising a team of detectives, trainee detectives, and police constables – the latter being the uniformed officers "on the beat" – who gather and assess evidence about more serious and acquisitive crimes. When we spoke, I was interested to find out more about the role of asking smarter questions in police detective work.

After crimes have been committed, it's the DS who makes decisions based on the evidence presented to them: *Should we charge the suspect? Do we have enough evidence to proceed with this case? Should we press charges or take this investigation no further?* Barker runs a team of officers who deal with prisoners coming into custody for crimes ranging from shop theft to low-level robberies. Other DSs work in a more traditional CID team, supervising detectives dealing with rapes, robberies, aggravated robberies, and attempted murder.

"There are two main aspects of asking questions in my job," observes Barker:

> *The first is asking questions of suspects, victims, and witnesses to crimes; I do that daily. We have a particular style of questions we use because we need to make sure the questions we ask are fair. We are required by law to present a fair case to the court and the jury assessing a case, and if we ask unfair questions, that could impact the trial. We do this in the interests of justice AND to maintain the confidence of the public. If we start asking closed or leading questions that aren't fair of a suspect or a witness, then the public could rightly think that the police had an agenda. The second aspect of asking questions for a sergeant is the questions we ask of ourselves and what we're doing as police: the hypotheses we develop for a particular crime, 'Did it happen like this or in a different way?', and how we can improve the job we do every day.*

For Barker, a good question must be open and not leading. Police detectives are trained to ask questions using a simple but highly effective formula: TED – Tell, Explain, Describe. It's possible to construct an entire interview using these three words. Barker gives an example:

> *For instance, you're dealing with a suspect in an assault. You know the timeframe, the where and when. The TED formula allows a suspect to give their version of events, so you might start with 'Tell me about your*

involvement with x at 10pm last Thursday night ...' *If you started with a* 'What ...', *closed question, you're automatically narrowing down the information you'll get back from the suspect. You can follow up with* 'Could you explain that in a little more detail?' *and* 'Describe what happened after you left the pub ...'. *It's remarkably effective, and you can ring the changes between the three.*

Of course, guilty suspects will try to wriggle out of the situation and be advised – by lawyers and their memory of police interviews from TV, films, and fiction – to say *No comment* or remain silent. That's their right, of course, but the role of the detective is to ask relevant questions and give the suspect a chance to give an account for their involvement in the case.

By contrast, detectives are trained not to ask oppressive questions or repeat questions to browbeat those they're interviewing into submission. If they don't want to answer, they've had the opportunity. But if they subsequently give a different answer to the same question in court – a question which generated no response or a *No comment* during an earlier investigation – that's changing their story. "At that point," explains Barker:

> we will point this out to the court, to the jury, and encourage them to draw an inference from that. The best time to give an account of your actions or whereabouts at the time of a crime is during the initial interview with a police officer.

This goes back to the caution that police always give to suspects when they're arrested: *You do not have to say anything. But, it may harm your defence if you do not mention when questioned something which you later rely on in court. Anything you do say may be given in evidence.*[6] The caution is repeated at the beginning of an interview and officers check that those they're interviewing have understood the caution. "It's quite a chess move," observes Barker. "The key phrase is 'may harm your defence.'"

Another quality of good questions for Barker is putting parameters on them to avoid getting irrelevant information. Officers need to ask questions that enable those they're interviewing to focus on specifics, not generalities: *Tell me about what you remember, between 9.45 and 10.15pm last Thursday night, in the Dog and Duck on Bloggs Street* rather than *Tell me about what you did last Thursday.* This forces the suspect to think about that particular time and location. Without going over all the details, officers make suspects focus with great specificity, a technique known as "bacon slicing" – a nickname whose irony is not lost on Barker. This allows you to get super-detailed, super-fast. *Describe the scene to me in as much detail as you can – you pushed the man first. Tell me: how did you touch them?* And as they describe the facts of the case, asking *How were you feeling at that moment?* allows the officer to bring out their emotions, which can be incredibly helpful for the police to demonstrate intent in court. "It helps to reveal things about a suspect's character and their state of mind at the time of the incident," concludes Barker.

Detectives who apply the tools and techniques of police questions – using open questions guided by the TED formula: not oppressive, closed questions – are likely to get the information they need:

> You start with a relatively blank sheet of paper and progressively add colour and detail. As an investigator, it's important not to go into questioning with an agenda. You need to be totally open. If you have an agenda – and you think the suspect's guilty from the start – then your style of questioning changes. You mould you questions to fit the agenda. This stops you listening to the answers – really hearing what they're saying. There may be golden nuggets of information you miss and that's not good for the case. The same is true of asking the same question again and again in different ways – rephrasing it until you get the answer you want. It's not a good approach, it's oppressive, and you won't get a true reflection of the truth. The suspect will just get sick of the question being asked and give an answer that stops that line of questioning.

For Barker, a detective's ability to ask smart questions is a combination of both education and experience. In police training, the Professionalising Investigative Practice (PIP) qualifications have three levels: one for basic questioning, two that all detectives are required to pass, and three for advanced suspect and witness interviewing. Above that, advisors – expert interviewers – assess that officers and detectives are using the right style of questioning. The PIP ensures high standards and consistency of questioning, using the TED formula, and avoiding oppressive questioning. During training, detectives are encouraged to develop a formal plan to structure their interviews, not so much a script as a logical flow to ensure all relevant issues are covered and asked TED-style. "The training provides the framework for asking smarter questions", says Barker. "But experience really matters. The more you interview, the better you get at it. You need suspects and witnesses in front of you. With no experience, you give a robotic performance, reading lists of questions."

Bad questions and questioning techniques – oppressive, closed, or leading questions; not listening to answers and racing ahead to prepare the next question – yield bad answers. But they can also jeopardise a case. "If you do ask a series of oppressive questions and the case goes to court," reflects Barker:

> the defence barrister can apply to court and say that the interview was oppressive and that the only reason their client gave an account in the interview was to avoid getting into trouble. For those reasons, they can apply to the court to take the evidence secured during the interview out of the trial. The jury then hears the evidence but not from the interview. That can have a big impact on the case. We might have been able to draw an inference from non-responses to questions asked in the interview, but if the judge accepts the barrister's challenge, we're no longer able to do that.

Barker's description of the reality of police questioning paints a picture of a clear, calm, and methodical approach, a picture out of kilter with the popular conception that's been mediated through films and TV drama. Quiet efficiency doesn't make the grade for a prime time, but – as Barker observes – "We really don't bang desks and shout these days." As we'll see in the next chapter on bedside manner – and the approach taken by professions as diverse as general practice and journalism – some telly detectives got it just right. Particularly Lieutenant Frank Columbo and his calm, thought-through "Just one more thing …". It's got all the hallmarks of "Tell, Explain, Describe".

TOM BARKER'S TOP TIPS FOR ASKING SMARTER QUESTIONS

1. To get people talking, use the TED formula: Tell, Explain, Describe.
2. Open and fair always trumps closed, leading, and oppressive.
3. Don't narrow down too soon, but do include parameters to avoid irrelevant answers.
4. Encourage those you're questioning to recall emotional experiences as well as facts.
5. Park your agenda and assumptions at the door or else risk biasing your questions.

SUMMING UP

In the 2021 Disney+ series *Only Murders in the Building*, Detective Williams challenges the three, true crime podcast fans at the heart of the story to work out "The Who – The How – The Why – and The Why Now" of the crime they're investigating as amateur sleuths. As we've seen from the experts we've met in this chapter, in the toughest of professional settings – from talking down a terrorist to enabling a murderer to confess to their crime – it is critical that the person asking the questions remains calm. By keeping in control, tactically deploying empathy (but never sympathy), the interviewer can demonstrate to the perpetrator or suspect that their questioning has enabled them to join the dots. It shows they've been able to develop a coherent view of events and the actors' parts in it. No slammed desks. No coffee cups hurled against the wall. No histrionics.

As bosses and employees, as clients and suppliers, as parents and children, it's exactly the same. When the other party loses control and is consumed with rage, the one being shouted at gains power while the aggressor loses control. In planning that next difficult conversation or negotiation, channel your inner hostage negotiator or police detective.

Plan, sequence your questions, and above all stay calm. Get the setting, your tone, and demeanour on point. And always remember that your meeting is very much lower stakes than the true professionals. Just imagine what an advantage that gives you when negotiating a pay rise or securing a major discount on a photocopier contract.

NOTES

1 See article on the "heartbeat" law, designed to outlaw abortion as soon as a heartbeat is detectable in a human foetus, at https://www.texastribune.org/2021/05/18/texas-heartbeat-bill-abortions-law/

2 See Al Jazeera's explainer on "The Taliban and Islamic law in Afghanistan" at https://bit.ly/3He60yi

3 Chris Voss's biography is given in full at https://www.blackswanltd.com/our-team/chris-voss

4 "Chris Voss teaches the art of negotiation" on MasterClass is at https://bit.ly/3mBhFzd, while his more recent – more clearly applied – course is titled "Win Workplace Negotiations" and is at https://bit.ly/311kBgW

5 A good friend recently read Voss's book and took his first MasterClass course. He started to use mirroring when talking to his wife. He told me that she feels genuinely listened to for the first time in their 25-year marriage. All he's changed is to use mirroring rather than summarise what she says to him in his own words. By playing her language back to her, at last she feels listened to; an apparently tiny change with a galvanic impact.

6 See https://www.gov.uk/arrested-your-rights

9

DO YOU LIKE MY BEDSIDE MANNER?

Abstract

How and when we ask questions can be just as important as what we ask. Popular, successful doctors – particularly General Practitioners as we call them in the U.K. – are famous for having what is known as good "bedside manner". It's even known to speed up and improve recovery from surgery and illness. Yet, bedside manner receives scant attention during a doctor's training, often isn't even tested with nearly the rigour of medical knowledge, and falls way down the priority list compared with technical knowledge and medical expertise.

On one level this is quite right and proper. Unlike many other professions, medicine is often a matter of life and death, and we need experts with broad or deep knowledge to keep us well and help us when we fall ill, working with us – through smart questioning – to work out what's wrong and what to do about it. On another level, it's time this changed. Given the potential that good bedside manner has, trainee and junior doctors shouldn't be expected to learn by osmosis, on the job, by observing their

(Continued)

DOI: 10.4324/9781003218470-9

seniors in action. There should be greater focus on the *how* of asking smarter questions – the use of questioning techniques and analysis of paraverbal and meta-verbal cues – to get to the right diagnosis sooner. This approach is not only rewarding in medicine. It has clear application in journalism and, indeed, all jobs that depend on the application of enquiry.

THE KINGS AND QUEENS OF COMEDY AND CHAT

Although I've endeavoured to be comprehensive and catholic in where I've looked for inspiration for *Asking Smarter Questions*, there are some obvious avenues I've not explored. In both my reading and my interviews with people from different professions in which success is predicated on its practitioners asking smarter questions, I've attempted to be both broad and eclectic, from Zen Buddhists to Nobel prize-winning scientists, from police detectives to conflict mediators, from market researchers to journalists.

I don't pretend to have spoken to every profession where asking smarter questions enables them to do their jobs better. Nor am I trying to suggest that the individuals I've spoken to are necessarily representative of their profession or the Platonic form of perfection as a lawyer, doctor, coach – whatever. Rather, my intention has been to scope and catalogue the principles of asking smarter questions that have been developed and embellished from the time of Greek philosophy onwards, building up the *how to* of asking smarter questions piecemeal, from the ground up.

The role of my expert interviews is to reinforce these principles by having expert practitioners from diverse worlds explain what they mean and how they play out in practice. Along the way, we also get a fascinating glimpse into how those involved in radically different lines of work get to use very similar techniques, while some of those who work in the same field and interact with one another daily can use radically different approaches. For example, doctors and journalists, coaches and therapists all favour the open, casual, almost throwaway Columbo Question. Meantime, while police detectives may favour open questions that come with no assumptions and encourage those they're interviewing to "Tell, Explain, Describe" their version of events, when it comes to cross-examination in court both lawyers and police can make judicious use of a logical sequence of closed questions. This approach is designed to build up very specific narratives which prevent those under cross-examination from introducing doubt or facts that could undermine the questioner's case.

One area I chose not to dwell on was that of the professional interviewer – on TV, radio, and increasingly podcasts – either light-hearted chat show hosts or hard-hitting political inquisitors. In part, this is because media interviews run in an environment so unlike those in which most of us find ourselves in our daily work; my intention with this book is to provide practical, actionable advice with real-world resonance. In part, it is because it would be easy to become obsessed with the professional media interviewer at the exclusion of other professions because the examples are so vivid and present. And in part, it is because others have already analysed what makes a great TV interviewer already. What makes a lousy one is well evidenced by satire, particularly the hapless Alan Partridge, created by the actor Steve Coogan for the BBC Radio 4 spoof comedy news series *On the Hour*. Partridge has been embodied – and some would say milked – by Coogan ever since, in endless TV series, books, and even the 2013 film *Alpha Papa*.

The skills of great broadcast media interviewers have perhaps been best analysed by the veteran journalist and academic of journalistic technique Dean Nelson in his book *Talk to Me*. His focus is very U.S.-centric, but his analysis of the best – and worst – examples of TV interviews from recent decades ranges from British journalist David Frost's deconstruction of disgraced President Nixon to an analysis of the brilliance of presenters, including David Letterman and the legendary duo from National Public Radio's (NPR's) *This American Life*, Ira Glass and David Sedaris. His examples of "when interviews go bad" include two car crashes from the NPR blooper reel: David Greene interviewing Chrissie Hynde from the Pretenders and Terry Gross talking to Gene Simmons of rock band KISS.

What's compelling about Nelson's book is that he reprints large swaths of both good and bad interviews and then picks that apart for evidence of smarter and dumber questioning styles. So there's no need to go over that ground again; you can read Dean's book for that as well as many presenters' memoirs.

Professional media interviewers are required to create both the structure and the environment – the process and the atmosphere – which makes those on the couch (or in the firing line) yield information and build a compelling narrative. With a light-hearted chat show host, this usually requires putting their interviewees at their ease, comfortable and relaxed enough to give the mortals in the audience a glimpse into their lives. The *quid pro quo* of an artist appearing on a chat show – be they a musician, author, TV or movie star – is that they usually only appear at a time when they have a new production they wish to promote. To avoid the show turning into an advertorial promotion for these new productions takes resolve and skill from the interviewer. This delicate balancing doesn't always work, of course, and when the interviewer fails to make the guest feel at ease – when their attempts to display decent bedside manner manifestly fail – it's often because their agenda is not aligned with that of the interviewee and her or his public relation (PR) team. In extremis, guests are made to feel so uncomfortable that they storm off the set.

The excellent presenter of Britain's Channel 4 News, Krishnan Guru-Murthy, has a track record of asking celebrities questions that rile them so much that they cut their interviews short. He triggered this in Robert Downey Jr. When Guru-Murthy moved from talking about *Avengers: Age of Ultron* to addressing the actor's historic drug abuse, incarceration, and his dysfunctional relationship with his father, Downey Jr looked first quizzical, then pained, asking plaintively: "Are we promoting a movie? What are we doing?" Guru-Murthy replies, "Well, I'm just asking questions ..." as Downey-Junior stands up, removes his lapel mic in disgust, and walks off.

The same interviewer generated an even more hostile reaction from the director Quentin Tarantino when interviewing him about his movie *Django: Unchained*. Having established a rapport with a little frisson,

Guru-Murthy asked Tarantino: "Why are you so sure that there's no connection between enjoying movie violence and enjoying real violence?" Despite or perhaps because of the track record of violence in Tarantino's movies, the director clearly felt wrong-footed by the question in the middle of a PR junket. "Don't ask me a question like that," he retorted:

> I'm not biting. I refuse your question. I'm not your slave and you're not my master. I'm not dancing to your tune. You can't make me answer your question. I'm not a monkey ... I'm here to sell my movie. This is a commercial for my movie ... I'm shutting your butt down.

Spontaneous, prompted lines from Tarantino's mouth that wouldn't be out of place in *Reservoir Dogs*, *Pulp Fiction*, or *Jackie Brown*. All that's missing is a fistful of expletives.

Guru-Murthy – who'd looked a little nervous before plunging in the rhetorical knife on both occasions – pleaded his innocence, claiming to Tarantino: "It's my job to explore some serious themes." But in both interviews,[1] the interviewer made himself and his approach the subject of the interchange. Although he may have resented being required to become part of the PR machine to promote the movies, he also violated the norms of the genre and caused both interviews to end in acrimony. There are plenty of other examples of car crash TV interviews in entertainment history, involving celebrities as diverse as the Bee Gees, actor Meg Ryan, and the illusionist David Blaine.[2]

What none of these interviews demonstrate is the ability to ask questions in a way that keeps them going. As the rapper-turned-radio presenter Nihal Arthanayake told Gabby Logan in an October 2021 episode of her podcast *The Midpoint*:

> As an interviewer, I have the freedom to explore the world and ask questions about the world, ask questions about the human experience. I, like you Gabby, am curious. Don't strive to be interesting; strive to be interested. I'm a facilitator of storytellers – that's what I am.[3]

This humility – not being the story but helping others to tell their stories – is surely the primary role of the broadcast media interviewer.

In addition to curiosity and a dash of Socratic maieutics – midwifery – another critical facet that defines a successful practitioner of this art is bedside manner.

GREAT BEDSIDE MANNER

Nice doctors make better doctors and a good bedside manner can make a difference between the rate of a patient's recovery and – indeed – whether they recover at all.[4] Bedside manner in medicine is defined as how a doctor deals with her patients. It's predicated on the work medical professionals are prepared to invest in terms of empathy, listening, and seeing the world from the patient's point of view. For many, going to the doctor is stressful, unpleasant, and embarrassing. They are reluctant to volunteer information in the rapid-fire, clinical setting of a doctor's surgery or hospital consulting room and for very understandable reasons. Here are seven factors that can disrupt the flow of relevant information from physician to patient:

- First, it's unusual and not something we're trained for as patients. It just happens when it happens.
- Second, it concerns our personal health and well-being, and everyone knows (or knows of) someone who had apparently innocent symptoms that turned out to be an incurable disease.
- Third, there's a sense that physical infirmity may be a manifestation of moral weakness – *If only I hadn't had a kebab every Friday and washed it down with two litres of cola, I'd never have gained so much weight and got Type 2 Diabetes.*
- Fourth, and related to the previous factor, there's a possibility that symptoms could reveal a self-inflicted disease – *If only I'd quit smoking, I'd never have got lung cancer.*
- Fifth, it's not a daily – weekly, monthly, even annual – occurrence for us to take off our clothes in front of a stranger and have them prod us, outside and sometimes in.
- Sixth, if it is something serious, this could mean a radical change to or even an early end of life.

- And seventh, the environment in which medical professionals seek information from patients is often the very antithesis of calming and relaxing, somewhere we might feel happy to open up.

In reflecting on the role of place in how good questions come across in journalistic enquiry – and comparing that with medical consultations – Dean Nelson observes:

> *Doctors and nurses [often] interview their patients in tiny rooms with examination tables, bright overhead lights, and cabinets full of gloves, needles, and sutures … Sitting on an examination table in a flimsy gown surrounded by instruments of pain isn't going to put anyone at ease on its own. But if you ask good, thoughtful questions, you can help your patient ignore the surroundings. (*Talk to Me, p.159)

This presents a significant challenge for doctors – particularly general practitioners (GPs) who are the first port-of-call for potentially any condition, but also for specialists and consultants. If there are so many potential obstacles to patients volunteering relevant information, the role of bedside manner takes on an even greater significance. The ability to be empathetic and gently cajoling, interested and focused but not inquisitorial or accusatory – and all of this on demand, every ten minutes, with a new patient with a completely different condition – is not trivial. Actors involved in training and assessing medical professionals often find it challenging to adopt the persona of a patient.[5] For doctors and nurses, this is not just a persona. It's an integral part of their professional toolkit that can't appear for a second to be insincere or perfunctory.

Despite the critical importance of bedside manner, it receives laughably little time and attention in medical schools around the world. There's a similar lacuna in legal training. As legal eagle Tim Bishop told us in Chapter 3: "just like bedside manner for doctors – remarkably little time is set aside in a barrister's education to cover how to ask decent questions". This is understandable. Doctors' primary expertise is in medicine not interpersonal skills, and in terms of hierarchy, it's more important that healthcare professionals can ask the smart questions that get to the root of a condition or disease than they do so in a friendly, happy-clappy kind of way. But because of the unusual nature of a patient-doctor interaction detailed above, because it truly can be a matter of life and death, and because of the compelling evidence that the *how* of bedside manner can have positive outcomes over and above the *what* of medical questioning, it should certainly receive more time and consideration in doctors' training than it does in most countries today.

Evidence of this is reported by Will Wise and Chad Littlefield in their book *Asking Powerful Questions*, where they report a study that showed "Physicians, on average, interrupt 70 per cent of patient interviews within eleven seconds of the patient beginning to speak" (p.149). Interrupting, being brisk and brusque to churn through an overscheduled appointment calendar, talking down from a position of haughty authority,[6] these all reflect poor bedside manner and actually make it less likely that accurate symptoms will be reported by patients or spotted by physicians.

Good practice in bedside manner includes:

1. **Making a good first impression** – smiling, welcoming, getting the name right, including pronunciation, focusing attention on the patient, looking at them while talking to them, encouraging responses with nods.
2. **Clear communication** throughout, with as little jargon as possible – lose the acronyms and initialisms, unpronounceable drug names, metaphorical language, and Latin- or Greek-derived abstract nouns. Many don't know what "prognosis" means the first time they hear the word, for instance.
3. **Sitting down** so that there isn't a physical gulf as well as knowledge gap. The Curse of Knowledge is troublesome enough for the doctor-patient dynamic. It doesn't need any more help from physical distancing, with a patrician GP looming over his (always his) patient.
4. **Resisting the temptation to interrupt**, allowing patients to talk and describe their symptoms and concerns before plunging, leaping, or butting in.
5. **Adopting an adult-adult** approach to questioning and dialogue, to borrow from Transactional Analysis,[7] not Parent to Child which was

the way many decades ago. Some (often older) doctors and some (often older) patients still believe in how a medical conversation should go, to the detriment of both parties.

6. **Active listening** and observation of body language cues and tics, as we've already explored in Chapter 7.

At the peak of the COVID-19 pandemic, the proportion of GP consultations conducted by phone or over video conferencing software was as high as 70% in the U.K., and this figure was similar in many other countries too. Although in-person consultations have become more common since the peak, at the time of writing, online consultations are still much more common, typically around 60/40 in Britain compared with 20/80 pre-COVID. Routine appointments are generally not remotely problematic when conducted online, provided patients have experience, confidence, privacy, technology, and a sufficiently robust WiFi connection to run a call. There are understandable concerns about both the less affluent and older patients less familiar with Zoom and Teams than many of those working in the knowledge economy, for whom a video call is now second nature. For many and in many circumstances, online GP appointments are here to stay.

That said, there are also profound challenges for GP consultations run remotely. Despite the ubiquity of video conference calls (2020–2022) – from work and school to family get-togethers, from virtual Pilates to Zoom pub quizzes – as everyone who's ever had one will know, it's incredibly easy online to miss out on nuances, body language, eye movements. Zoom doesn't just allow participants to wear a jacket and tie from the waist up and pyjamas and slippers from the waist down. In two dimensions, we are very much harder to read.

It is harder for GPs to deploy or benefit from a well-developed bedside manner online, particularly – but not exclusively – when patients choose to pause or stop video and put themselves on mute when they're not talking. These decisions may be for perfectly rational reasons – sharing living space with family or flatmates, background noise from children, pets, or others working in or on the home. But they rob doctors of quite literally vital signs. The more cues we remove, the harder it is for

GPs to get a sense from the metaverbals and paraverbals – Mehrabian's frequently misquoted and misunderstood 93% of communication that's non-verbal.[8]

In 2021, researchers at the University of Cambridge interviewed more than 1,500 primary and secondary care doctors – GPs and expert clinicians – as well as a cohort of patients. Although the study found that all parties thought virtual consultations were more convenient than real-life appointments, they were also less accurate. The *i* newspaper reported: "Some 86 per cent of patients and 93 per cent of clinicians thought that web or phone medical appointments were worse than face-to-face consultations for accuracy of assessment, while some reported misdiagnoses."[9]

Some of what was gained in terms of minimising COVID transmission in surgery or hospital has been lost because doctors are unable to exude and patients unable to benefit from bedside manner online. As early as May 2021, the U.K.'s Royal College of General Practitioners concluded its analysis of the impact of the pandemic with a paper titled "GP consultations post-COVID should be a combination of remote and face to face, depending on patient need".[10] Quite so.

QUESTIONS ABOUT QUESTIONS
INTERVIEW 12 OF 14

NAME	Dr James Lewis (*nom de médecin*)
ORGANISATION	National Health Service
ROLE	Locum GP

James Lewis is a GP with more than 20 years' experience. For most of the last ten years, he has chosen to work as a locum, taking short-term roles in a variety of different practices – some urban, some rural; some in relatively affluent districts, but more in areas of deprivation. "They're just more interesting than dealing with the 'worried well' all the time, and you feel like you can have more impact." With engagements lasting several months and rarely more than a year, he's less able than many GPs to build long-lasting relationships with patients over many years – decades even – because he's always moving on. Accordingly, his doctor's antennae, his bedside manner, and his ability to ask revealing questions have to be even more attuned than a single-practice career GP.

"Asking questions is a fundamental part of my job – of course it is," says Lewis:

> But I also rely a lot on non-verbal communications. I start by assessing patients before we even meet, going out into the waiting room to greet them, seeing how they get up, how they walk, what clothes they're wearing, who they've come with. I don't bring assumptions or prejudices with me, but experience has taught me to look out for clues that would mean nothing to non-doctors but can give me an early-warning.

STARTING OPEN

Lewis starts with a smile and a friendly introduction. If he's not met the patient before, he'll introduce himself and start with an open question: "Hello, I'm Dr Lewis. Sorry I'm running a bit late. What can I do for you today?" In the U.K., GP appointments typically last a sparse ten minutes, including the full consultation, checking the patient understands what's next (prescription, letter of referral to a specialist), prescribing any relevant drugs or therapies, and writing up notes on the online record-keeping system.

> That doesn't allow much time for small talk or many questions, and patients often want to talk about multiple issues; they save them up. They'll present with one minor, routine ailment, but there's often something else new that's nagging quietly away. They're worried about it and don't know how to talk about it or even if they should 'bother' you with it.

Nevertheless, the role of the GP is to use open and very gently directive questions to encourage the patient to go through their story and lay out their symptoms. The more precise they can be, the better, and phrases like *came on rapidly* or *three hours ago* can really help. "The temptation is to cut in if they reveal what sounds like a crucial bit of information," observes Lewis:

> but you have to let them talk or they'll lose their train of thought. This can be frustrating when they start off with: 'I was on a coach last Tuesday – off the garden centre, I always go there on a Tuesday. With my brother, you know him – you saw him last week for his ulcer. Anyway …' But however strong the temptation, I let them talk for 60 seconds. Then I start using questions to add weight to their answers to rule things in or out. For example, if they're complaining of abdominal pain and I ask where and they indicate lower left, then we can start to rule out appendicitis.

The appendix – almost always – is lower right.

This process allows a GP to narrow down and start to consider conditions related to certain organs and bodily systems, though experience has taught Lewis not to narrow down too soon. "A condition can be blindingly obvious and sometimes you get lucky and have a run of quick wins – typically with urinary tract infections (though not necessarily what's causing them) and ear infections."

Often, however, people present with much vaguer symptoms. *I'm feeling a bit headachy* could be anything. Dehydration, inflamed sinuses, raised blood pressure, a brain tumour:

> That's what's so interesting about having so little time to get to understand what's going on. There's been lots of work on the use of AI to work on algorithmic diagnosis, but I think we're a long way off that. People don't provide accurate, textbook answers because they're facing symptoms they can't easily or fully describe. There's a lot of nuance, fuzzy logic, and random jitter, and no AI I've seen can handle that.

DR GOOGLE AND MR ZOOM

For many healthcare professionals, the advent of Dr Google is a mixed blessing. It can be a blessing when patients start experiencing unusual symptoms and look up what they might mean. This allows them to present with *It feels a bit like ... something's happening in my guts ... I read something on the internet.* It's more of a curse when they stumble into conspiracy theories in Facebook groups and elsewhere, much in evidence with the anti-vaxxer movement under COVID. And, of course, if the patient's personality type means they catastrophise and assume that a pulled muscle in the back immediately means terminal lung cancer – that can be problematic, too.

"On balance, though, Dr Google is helpful," says Lewis:

People come with interesting ideas and I welcome that. It shows they're interested in what's happening and they've done some pre-work for me. But you need to beware of conditions that become 'fashionable' – among patients, in the media, and so with doctors – and the medications associated with them. This has happened during my career with ME, adult-onset ADHD, and postural hypertension. It's even happened with bipolar disorder, as this condition can appear in creative artists who talk about it in public. There is a cohort of people whose lives don't work out and they externalise this and look for a medical diagnosis to validate it. In the face of some of the half-baked theories about conditions and treatments that can appear in the popular media, we have to work hard to use smart questions to get to the truth, not the dumbed-down, off-pat solutions presented in the papers.

During the pandemic, the ratio of GP consultations flipped from 80/20 in-person/online or on the phone to 30/70 the other way. Like many GPs, Lewis found this made him much more productive and time-efficient while reducing his ability to spot and act on nuances. But even in person, it pays to be cautious – not leading patients down a closed line of questioning too soon, not making assumptions, resisting the impact of time constraints on rigour, preventing the tiredness that comes with the job from making you miss something or cut corners.

Lewis believes that the biggest change brought about by the move online or to telephone consultations is that patients are less likely to volunteer the real reason why they've booked an appointment. Because it's easier to bring a call to an end, he's found he's less likely to ask the Columbo Question – *Is there anything else?*, and see below – he usually would when the patient gets up from the chair and moves towards the door:

> *So often, this is where you get patients saying:* 'I'm sure it's nothing really, but last night I had a real feeling of tightness across my chest ...' *Because it's easier and quicker to end a call than a face-to-face consultation, I've found I have to consciously force myself to ask them that. Because you're not in person, you don't have the chance to spot a melanoma on the skin of a patient presenting with a chest infection. Zoom removes that critical element of serendipity.*

BEDSIDE MANNER TRAINING, FOR GOOD OR ILL

Like many in the medical profession I've spoken to in the course of research-ing this book, Lewis is amazed at how little time is dedicated in medical training to asking smarter questions. "We had tutorials about taking a history from a patient, and there's a pro forma set of open questions you should use to determine the presenting complaint, past medical history, social history, medications taken, allergies and so on – that's all pretty standard."

"The more experience you have in general practice, the more you learn to start to apply the 'surgical sieve' – and that can help you filter down and determine whether the condition is medical, psychological, meta-bolic, biochemical." As with training in cross-examination for lawyers, so in training for GPs in using questions to find out what – if anything – is wrong in a scant ten minutes. The bare bones are taught, but skill comes with experience and application.

The qualities of a substandard questioning style are, for Lewis, all about starting with closed questions and progressively closing off too soon. This leads you down a predictable path, the path that many patrician "doctor knows best" GPs followed for much of the twentieth century:

> *Some older patients still like to be told what's wrong, but there's a sea change happening in medicine right now. Compliance-based medicine is out and we now talk a lot more about concordance. That's based on an open discussion and open questions between doctors and patients. It's the doctor's responsibility to ensure that their patient agrees that your hypothesis – based on the evidence, on their answers to your questions – is reasonable. This is a very welcome advance.*

Lewis ends our conversation by saying that he believes empathy is over-rated in a GP:

> Of course you feel for people who have a serious condition that affects them profoundly, that limits their lives or means they die young. But empathy doesn't make any difference in how you manage them. It's important to appear empathic while trying to remain as objective as possible. Spending too much time putting yourself in your patients' shoes can cloud your judgment and mean you take their problems home with you. That's to no one's benefit – not yours or your family's, but more importantly, not the patient's either.

Neither cynical nor manipulative, Lewis's prescription of how to use empathy sounds very much like the application of the hostage negotiator's toolkit from Chris Voss that we considered in Chapter 7, particularly Voss's prescription of tactical empathy. Tools include the slight tilt of the head when listening, resisting the urge to interrupt, and mirroring the language patients use to describe their symptoms. Talking down an armed robber may not be so different from gently encouraging a patient to reveal hidden symptoms after all.

DR JAMES LEWIS' TOP TIPS FOR ASKING SMARTER QUESTIONS

1. Engage all of your senses when trying to make sense of a situation – the answers people give you in words, of course, but also the tone of voice they use, and all the paraverbal cues of body language and motivated behaviour.
2. Be open, friendly, and disarming, but don't get sucked into small talk.
3. Give other people the time and space to actually answer your questions. Don't butt in too soon and avoid talking over their answers.
4. Be wary of the time efficiency yielded by video conferencing software. It is the enemy of nuance and subtlety.
5. Don't underestimate the power of the Columbo Question – *Is there anything else?* – at the end of a consultation.

THE FOURTH ESTATE

One of the very real pleasures I've experienced in researching and writing this book – particularly in the expert interviews I've done – has been identifying where the planets align and where they diverge. This has helped me understand how different types of profession use the same type of questioning style to achieve similar or different goals. The same is true when it becomes evident that different situations presented by the same job or work environment demand a 180-degree switch in questioning style.

For instance, as we've just seen in the interview with James Lewis, general practitioners are encouraged to use open questions to determine what's happening in their patients' lives that compel them to make an appointment with a doctor. Lewis explicitly advises against using closed questions and closing down too soon. And yet Lewis is the first to admit that closed questions do have their place in emergency situations, either when GPs are talking to family or caregivers in person or on the phone when patients are unable to talk; if they've had an accident, a heart attack or stroke, and cannot speak for themselves. As they wait for an ambulance, paramedics, or a doctor to arrive, careful, directive scripting using tree diagrams of tiered, closed questions can help keep patients alive until emergency medical staff can attend to a patient. This is how emergency call operators work, for instance.

In a separate conversation with *Daily Mail* feature writer Jane Fryer,[11] I had a similar revelation and alignment of the planets – what the Greeks (and lucky Scrabble players) call syzygy – between general practice and journalism. Just as the most revealing question a GP can ask and the most relevant answer a patient can give can come right at the end of a medical consultation when the doctor asks, *Anything else?*, so the juiciest story or killer anecdote can come as the journalist is bringing the interview to a close. Timing is everything.

Asking the toughest questions first, plunging in with what might appear to be a full-frontal assault, is most likely to be counterproductive. In the memorable analogies at the heart of Julia Dhar's TED talk, this is tantamount to using the tactics of a cage fighter and not a wall climber.

As a result, the person being interviewed will feel hunted and likely clam up and provide no meaningful answers. Journalist Dean Nelson, author of *Talk to Me*, advises:

> … if you have a tough question to ask, don't start your interview there. You have to ease into it. I generally place a tough question about two-thirds of the way into the interview. You must develop enough rapport or the person to trust you. Timing is everything. (p.243)

My conversation with Jane Fryer reveals much more about the importance of timing and demeanour in questioning – and several other smarter questioning techniques besides that go to make up the journalist-interviewers' craft.

QUESTIONS ABOUT QUESTIONS
INTERVIEW 13 OF 14

NAME	Jane Fryer
ORGANISATION	*Daily Mail*
ROLE	Feature Writer

When *Daily Mail* feature writer Jane Fryer is preparing to conduct an interview, she never writes a list of the questions she plans to ask. Some subjects – particularly prickly celebrities with chequered pasts or their overprotective PR people – ask to see and vet a list of questions before agreeing to an interview, but Jane prefers to steer them towards a set of topics she intends to cover. This doesn't mean she's not prepared for the interview; far from it. She trained and practiced as a solicitor before realising early that law was very definitely not for her: "I was rubbish lawyer." But she brings a good dose of the rigour and discipline characteristic of the legal profession to her journalism.

"Conversation and dialogue just doesn't work like that," she observes:

> You wouldn't – I hope – prepare a checklist of questions for a date or a party and go through them one by one. That stifles natural conversation. As a feature writer – with time to cover people and what they've done in depth – I'm looking to have as natural and human a conversation as possible.

Fryer typically spends an hour or so with those she's interviewing, and she sets out the topics she wants to cover on a single page she can refer to – a set of bubbles or circles, connected thematically with arrows. A bit like the mind mapping technique for the *What lights you up?* exercise in Chapter 4:

> *I never start at the beginning of their life, their career, or their business and work through chronologically. That's not interesting or any way to tell an interesting story. To get them comfortable with talking to me – and talking to a journalist can be intimidating and even threatening to people who aren't used to it and think I'm there to trip them up or catch them out – I get them talking about what they want to talk about first, not what I want to find out.*

The bubbled topic guide serves as an aide memoire to ensure the interview stays on course:

> *I'll say 'I just wanted to check / ask you about <THIS> or <THAT>'. It shows the other person you've prepared properly. Often my questions aren't questions at all, just unfinished statements or musings … which the other party tends to complete, because we humans are like that. We can't bear for thoughts to be left hanging and we like to fill the sound of silence with words.*

Asking difficult, deeply personal questions – about a personal or financial scandal and the subject's role in events – can be challenging. Experience has taught Fryer that this is certainly not the place to start and a sure-fire route to a subject clamming up or storming off and then ending the interview; an outcome that makes journalists just as unpopular with their editors as their subjects. Fryer tends to leave more challenging questions until a personal rapport has been established, perhaps until right at the end of the interview, even to the time when the photographer is taking pictures:

> *With a couple of fairly obvious exceptions, you can really ask anyone anything, so long as you do it nicely. It's more about when during an interview you ask and how you ask them, rather than what you ask. If you can show that you've really done your research on them – by*

referencing something else they said or did, particularly if it was years ago – they'll feel you're worth having a conversation with, however personal you get.

Fryer writes the kinds of articles she likes to read, about the little details of people's lives, what makes them tick, how they're defined by their daily routines. This, in turn, shapes the types of questions she asks. If the story demands asking big, personal questions, Fryer finds that's much easier to do if you've asked them little detailed questions about them and their lives – *Why do you eat the same thing for lunch every day?* – first off. "Contrary to the stereotype of a tabloid journalist, I'm not trying to trick subjects to tell me their innermost secrets. On one level, my job is really about making people comfortable enough to chat – and then writing that up."

If she can see that subjects are nervous because they've been thrust into the middle of a news story or cycle they never expected to be part of, Fryer often fumbles in her bag – "looking like a bit of a gumby" – which helps subjects relax and open up. But she doesn't avoid difficult questions:

> *The best way is to be really direct. Ask the question directly. If they stonewall, ask it again. And if they still refuse, try either, 'I don't understand why you don't want to answer this. Could you explain?' or else 'Why would it make you upset to answer this question?'.*

Both these questions – meta-questions: questions about the questions rather than the questions themselves – can make it easier for subjects to answer what you want to know. This approach is very similar to the depersonalising approach coaches and conflict mediators use to encourage their coachees or charges to open up – as the coaches Rob Varcoe and Tim Johns and the mediator Pip Brown explained in their interviews in Chapter 5. Fryer's meta-questions are like a coach asking *What would your best friend advise you to do?* or *If you knew someone who was in your situation, what would your advice be to them?*

Being casual – not formal – also helps subjects open up. Fryer much prefers to do interviews with subjects in their own space, where they feel at home, in command, and comfortable. The pandemic made this more challenging, and interviews on Zoom mean you lose too much in translation. Having been welcomed into the subject's personal space, home or office, she folds herself up into an informal, relaxed body shape and lolls about a bit. This is the very antithesis to being poised and ready to strike, postures that make subjects tense and less likely to respond – with interesting, relevant content, if at all:

> So much of being a good feature interviewer is about putting people at their ease, being charming, being courteous, taking your cup into the kitchen, showing you're human, asking if you can use the loo when your arrive. Being relaxed makes others relaxed.

When interviews go wrong – and the story of the interview gone wrong replaces the interview itself – that's a sign that the interviewer has messed up and hasn't worked on making the subject feel relaxed. Just like Guru-Murthy with Downey Jr. and Tarantino above. Fryer notes:

> With nothing useful to report, some try to salvage their interview by writing about how uncooperative or elusive a subject has been, but for me that's evidence of a bad day at work. The subject and their people are upset. You're upset. And your editor will be upset. The more often this happens, the less you'll be trusted by future subjects. The truth is that most people enjoy being interviewed and talking about themselves. If they agree to talk and don't feel in any sense coerced to do it, they'll welcome you into their space, enjoy the conversation and the company, and relish talking about themselves. Giving their side of the story.

Jane ends our discussion by reflecting on the responsibility she has to protect those she interviews for the *Daily Mail*. Despite its popularity and sales figures, the *Mail* is a publication which – for many, including some of those she interviews – is very definitely not their favourite publication: ideologically, in terms of the subjects it covers and the campaigns it runs:

> If people become too relaxed, they'll say too much and can get interviewees' remorse once it's over. If, during or after an interview, they ask for comments to be cut because they've given away a confidence about someone else, I'm always happy to do that.

JANE FRYER'S TOP TIPS FOR ASKING SMARTER QUESTIONS

1. Don't write a list of questions. Create a mind map of topics, linked thematically.
2. Work hard to put the other person at ease. Be casual, informal, but respectful.
3. Don't start with the hardest question first. Build rapport and work up to it.
4. *When* and *how* you ask matters more than *what* you ask. You can ask anyone anything.
5. Use meta-questions: *What would your advice be to someone in your situation?*

THE COLUMBO QUESTION

Turning bedside manner on its head, the Beat Generation writer William Burroughs said, "You need a good bedside manner with doctors or you will get nowhere." Before we leave this chapter on bedside manner and this exploration of what some kinds of quacks and hacks do to put others at their ease so that they provide useful answers, it would be remiss of us if we didn't spend a little time with the fictitious Lieutenant Frank Columbo of the Los Angeles Police Department (LAPD).

Peter Falk dominated TV screens either side of the Atlantic and in many more countries during the 1970s. Dressed in his trademark rumpled, Cortefiel raincoat – a Spanish brand, whose name means "good tailoring" – Falk's Lieutenant Columbo of the LAPD bumbled his way through apparently naïve and vain attempts to solve crimes. But solve them he almost always did, and for the sake of dramatic tension and satisfying the demands of the three-act story structure, never before the third and final act.

Towards the end of every episode, when hints and clues – often last minute red herrings – had viewers screaming at the screen, Columbo would utter the immortal four words: "Just one more thing ...". He'd then present facts about the case that appear to conflict, giving his suspect the benefit of the doubt, and ask one final question by way of clarification. In essence, the Columbo Question asks: *Is there anything else that I haven't asked you that I should have asked you?* And this truly is a smarter question.

As we've seen from my conversations with Dr James Lewis and Jane Fryer, when patients or interview subjects believe that a period of intense questioning is over, they're more likely to let their guard down. In the case of a visit to the GP, after six or seven minutes of gentle, open questions, which become progressively more focused and closed, it is perfectly possible that the proximate cause that led the patient to set up the appointment in the first place has still received no air time. To an experienced GP, Lewis believes, this can be obvious. The text of the appointment has been all about a repeat prescription or an established, ongoing complaint, and that could probably have been dealt with online or by consulting a practice nurse. As they gather their things – their bag, their coat, the "scrip" for more of the same types of drugs – Lewis always asks: "Anything else troubling you?" Text is replaced by subtext.

More often than not, the Columbo Question yields a negative response the first time it's asked. In the moment, Lewis often offers: "Are you sure?" at which they may well still demur. The next time they have an appointment, however, the real cause of the previous visit may be elevated to the top of the agenda. It may come towards the end of the consultation. Or it might need another Columbo Question to get it out of a truly reluctant patient. When new, unexpected, unfamiliar symptoms arise – symptoms that could simply be part of ageing and have no life-threatening or life-limiting consequences – some people are understandably reluctant to volunteer details. But by asking a Columbo Question – by showing awareness that there might be something else on their minds – patients can feel acknowledged and heard even before they start to talk about the fact that their urine sometimes looks like Coca-Cola (likely not good long term; possible kidney trouble) or they've got a grumbling in the lower right of the abdomen (acute but easily dealt with if caught in time; appendicitis).

I well remember receiving a call from my dear mother, Bay, in late January 2017. Her mother, Theodosia, had a basso profundo voice – trained (though never deployed) alongside Hollywood royalty Charles Laughton at the Royal Academy for Dramatic Arts in London in the mid-1920s. Bay took the plummy depths of her mother's voice and notched them down an octave.

That January morning, however, there was no basso profundissimo. In place of her usual fruity tones was a croak. A survivor of breast cancer surgery and radiotherapy a few years before and apparently in remission, she was no stranger to the GP's surgery. Like many in their late 70s, she was constantly being screened for this and that and the other. Her GP suspected the croak was simply laryngitis, but she was unconvinced, as she had no other symptoms that might suggest that. When visiting the following week for something else – probably low platelets or some other minor but irritating, time-consuming complaint – she saw the same GP. "Just one more thing: any change in the laryngitis?" and Bay croaked that it didn't seem to be changing very much. On a hunch and aware of her previous brushes with cancer, the GP referred Bay for a thorough chest scan, just to determine if there was anything more sinister going on.

This "Just one more thing" opened up the last chapter of my mother's life. Three weeks later, I sat with her as her rapporteur in a consultant oncologist's office when he – with great bedside manner – gave her a terminal diagnosis. Her cancer had returned (he mercifully didn't say metastasised) to her lungs and liver, and one of the things it had knocked out early was the vagus nerve which controls – powers – the voice box. Hence the croak. It was clear to us all that there wasn't much time left, and that "things" had moved beyond radiotherapy or chemotherapy, hope or prayer. With her trademark good humour, Bay wondered whether this might have been the result of "smoking Gauloises Disque Bleu on the Rive Gauche when I was eighteen with a very naughty French boyfriend". The consultant had the bedside manner to let her reminisce beyond our allotted time but also confirm that no, this was not likely. For the next three months, she dazzled all about her with her active acceptance of her fate, being driven to see family and friends just one more time. And rather than having to undergo all sorts of other tests and probes and scans, the Columbo Question from Bay's GP had shortcut that indignity.

In the use case deployed by Jane Fryer, the interview subject will have given their version of events and revealed as much of the story as they feel comfortable to tell. There's a shift of pace and intensity in the interview as interviewer and subject move from question and answer (Q&A) to gathering belongings and photos being taken. This relaxation and change of tempo is what enables *Is there anything else?* to have its effect, to encourage the subject to go further than they did in the "formal" questioning. Both are Columbo Questions, both reveal more than those being asked thought they might reveal, and both give clues as to how you might use this format in your own work – in sales or in counselling, in research or in building rapport with commercial partners. With the Columbo Question, timing is everything. By working the *how*, it gets to the *what*. Try it. I think you'll like it.

Great insights – profound and useful understandings of a person, an issue, a topic, or a thing – can appear when those we're quizzing think that our interaction is over. If you're the one asking the questions, increase your vigilance as you come towards the end of an interaction or an interview and don't let your alertness slide.

SUMMING UP

Whatever we're seeking to understand or learn from the questions we ask, we should remind ourselves that questions have an asker and an answerer. The circumstances of a medical interview and being quizzed by a journalist are abnormal and can be among the most emotionally extreme we face. By looking at the strategies that both medical and media professionals deploy to put their patients and subjects at ease – to make them sufficiently relaxed, comfortable, and motivated to respond – we can extrapolate general principles that are applicable in many other circumstances.

If you take nothing else away from this book, I'd recommend you hone your skills in the timing and deployment of the Columbo Question. It might have been an innocent little tic or trope created by actor Peter Falk or the show's scriptwriters, but I'll guarantee you'll find it one of most useful additions to your armoury as you look to ascend to ninja levels of asking smarter questions.

NOTES

1 The Guru-Murthy/Downey Jr. interview is available to watch on YouTube at https://bit.ly/3oKvrzT, while the Guru-Murthy/Tarantino interview is over at https://bit.ly/3kWrDtY

2 See "The six most excruciating interviews of all time" in this *Guardian* summary at https://bit.ly/3FEYbRt

3 This episode of the podcast is available to stream at https://apple.co/30PBwCX

4 For more on the transformational impact of good bedside manner on patient recovery and prognosis, see Elizabeth Renter's 2015 article "Why nice doctors are better doctors" at https://bit.ly/3DKPEvB

5 I know this from working several times with a company called Interact, Europe's leading provider of actors and theatre directors to corporate training and development. In conversation with Interact's founder Ian Jessup – himself an actor, director, and playwright before starting the firm – it became clear to me that using actors as patients is the only way to fairly train and examine doctors – and others who interact with others, that is, everyone. This is because of actors' unique ability to develop, sustain, and repeatedly recreate the same character in the face of potentially radically different responses from doctors under examination.

6 In his book *A Sense of Style*, Harvard psychologist Steven Pinker identifies medical professionals as among those most prone to the Curse of Knowledge, a phenomenon that Pinker defines as: "The difficulty in imagining what it's like for someone else not to know something that you know". This happens all the time in medical consultations, with doctors using medical terminology and unpronounceable drug names with scant concern for patients' pre-existing knowledge or understanding. Indeed, some old school "Doctor knows best" medics appear to embrace the Curse of Knowledge as a means of keeping patients in the dark. For more on the Curse of Knowledge and its disruptive influence on clear communication, see *Narrative by Numbers*, particularly Chapter 5 (which bears the name of the phenomenon), pp.81–102.

7 Transactional Analysis (TA) was developed during the 1950s by the psychiatrist Eric Berne. There's a 101 on TA on the Good Therapy community website; see https://bit.ly/3cNPVSP

8 Albert Mehrabian's pioneering studies in the late 1960s, written during the 1970s, established the 7-38-55 rule which has been misused and abused ever since. He opens the preface to his 1971 book, *Silent Messages*, by saying:

> Our speech-oriented culture is just beginning to take note of the profound and overlooked contribution of nonverbal behavior to the processes of communication. The contributions of our actions rather than our speech is especially important, since it is inseparable from the feelings that we knowingly or inadvertently project in our everyday social interaction ...

*our facial expressions, postures, movements, and gestures are so import-
ant that when our words contradict the silent messages contained within
them, others mistrust what we say – they rely almost completely on what
we do.*

The 7-38-55 rule states that we deduce 7% of meaning (liking, emotion conveyed about words) from the words themselves, 38% from intonation, and
55% from facial expressions. More information is conveyed by non-verbal
(metaverbal and paraverbal) than by the spoken word itself. This article from
the British Library archive is instructive here: https://www.bl.uk/people/
albert-mehrabian#

9   Poppy Wood, "Virtual medical appointments 'more convenient' but 'disas-
    trous' for some patients who warn of misdiagnoses", *i news*, 02.11.21, https://
    bit.ly/3ORUR6G

10 For the full Royal College report, see https://bit.ly/3CJeESF

11 For Jane's recent articles, see https://bit.ly/3FLo55S

10

JUST HOW SENSITIVE SHOULD A QUESTION BE?

Abstract

"It ain't what you do, it's the way that you do it – that's what gets results". So sang Fun Boy Three and Bananarama on the soundtrack to my youth in the early 1980s. In the case of asking smarter questions, both content and form – words and intentions – are equally important. What we ask and the mood we create by asking questions really matter.

Implicit and explicit prejudices and assumptions can blow well-intentioned questions and questionnaires off course even before they're asked, with the implicit deeper-rooted and harder to eradicate. Questions that don't consider or ride roughshod over ethnicity and race, gender, and sexuality can generate meaningless results. Worse still, they can skew strategies adopted in response to answers given, reinforcing stereotypes. Often, this is because questioners are blind to their positions of privilege and authority. This chapter focuses on the specifics of sexism in marketing and market research to underline the general principle of how important it is to be assumption- and prejudice-free in the questions we ask.

DOI: 10.4324/9781003218470-10

THE TWO BIGGEST LIES YOU'LL EVER HEAR IN TRAINING

One of the very real benefits of the remote working revolution enforced by the pandemic is that more diverse teams who live in multiple locations and different time zones are now working together regularly in ways never previously believed to be possible. It's a classic case of making a virtue out of necessity. As many of the world's knowledge economy work-ers have become increasingly skilled and got to grips with the full and growing functionality of different video conferencing software packages – principally Zoom and Teams – we're getting more used to more dynamic, efficient, and effective ways of working, as we explored in Chapter 7.

One aspect of interrogation that is often better in an online meeting or webinar is the poll or survey, whether run by functionality from within the platform itself (such as Zoom polls) or by using a stand-alone service such as Slido, Menti, or SurveyPlanet. Teams can debate a topic and then put options to a vote – a secret ballot mediated behind the scenes where oth-ers can't see which option each team member takes until or unless they want to make it public. This is excellent practice. It prevents the loudest or most senior voice – still too often a white, male voice – carrying the day, ensuring more democratic, diverse, and inclusive decision-making. Many more voices matter, for sure, but too many pay lip service to this mantra. The online poll gets all voices heard fairly and efficiently.

Lie #1: "That poll result is so interesting"

Despite the online meeting poll minimising audience and participant effects – making it more likely that those following the first or early votes will stick to their own opinions on the question at hand and less likely that they'll be unfairly influenced – there is one aspect of them that represents one of the biggest lies in meetings, training, and team development ses-sions. After the host launches a poll and as the votes are being cast, once the poll is closed and the answer revealed, I have never heard anyone who's asked for delegates' input say anything other than: "Well, that's a really interesting result." It could be a totally bland response; an online

"Meh!" from a disinterested team. It could be 100% predictable – the way the company has always thought and behaved. Or it could be 180 degrees from what the host was anticipating. Whatever the outcome, they'll always say it's "interesting". Not "interesting" in the passive-aggressive British meaning of "completely disruptive" or "really boring because we're going to have to scrap what we were planning". Just plain, innocent, regular "interesting", when in fact it's usually nothing of the sort. Often, the problem is that the question itself is not a smarter question, and despite the obvious psychological and behavioural benefits of removing audience effects, the answers have advanced us no further.

Lie #2: "I learn more from those I train than they learn from me ..."

The second biggest lie in training – online or offline – comes when trainers say: "I think I learn more from my delegates than they do from me." It's a self-effacing, modest, and inclusive thing to say, but too often those running training don't give their trainees the time, scope, or space to share anything of value with their peers and course leader. This is often because training is run like too much of a formal education and the questions asked and tasks required by the trainer are too narrow and closed. They simply can't accommodate clear, open-minded, mind-opening responses. Trainers have a checklist of tasks for trainees to get done, and if something genuinely interesting or novel comes up, it'll be parked on a "parking lot" flipchart or PowerPoint slide, never to be consulted again.

This is unfortunate because it stifles the asking – and answering – of smarter questions. Perhaps I'm lucky, because one of the areas where I train people is in insightful thinking and how to be insightful. As a very light touch, pre-workshop homework exercise, I ask all delegates to spend about 15 minutes thinking up a very short list of individuals, brands, or companies they believe to be insightful and why, entities that collectively have a great understanding of the drags and drivers of their customers' attitudes, behaviours, and beliefs. Often, the results are predictable – and good examples of insightful businesses – such as Always, Amazon, Apple, Disney, Dove, IKEA, LEGO, Netflix, Nike, Spotify, Telsa, or Uber. All great case studies. All great users of insight – generated by asking smarter questions of their available data – which they then go on to use to drive strategy. All easy to anticipate and probably the result of five minutes' thought rather than the full 15 minutes.

But sometimes – in greater numbers since COVID and in much greater numbers among younger, less experienced but more curious individuals – delegates bring forward challenger brands such as Etsy, Glossier, or Oatly. Sometimes, they give hyperlocal examples of new start-ups that have disrupted a market in delegates' own countries only, but that clearly have the potential to be as globally disruptive as an Amazon or a Netflix. And sometimes – again in greater numbers in the pandemic years – they suggest authors of books. As an insatiably curious individual, for me these are the responses I like best. During a virtual coffee break, I'll have ordered a book on a topic or by an author I'd never come across before. When I get and devour the books soon after, my perspective changes. I become more inclusive and I wonder whether – after all – "I learn more from those I train than they learn from me" isn't such a lie after all. At least for me.

DIVERSITY AS THE ANTIDOTE TO NARROW-MINDEDNESS

The pandemic and successive lockdowns have made some people do more of something than they did before (from sourdough starters to ultra-long-distance running). It's made some do a lot less (from meeting others to travelling to Jakarta for 15 minutes at the end of a week-long "workshop" of reading PowerPoint presentations). But one area that sales of books and e-books demonstrate a lot of us are doing a lot more of is reading and reading of non-fiction in particular. The more stimulus we are exposed to – the more "stuff" we put, open-mindedly, into the hopper of our subconscious mind – the more likely we are to be open-minded and accommodating of multiple perspectives.

Three examples of authors and books I've been prescribed during insightful thinking training sessions I ran in 2020–2021 are: Renni Eddo-Lodge and her book *Why I'm No Longer Talking to White People About Race*; Florence Given and *Women Don't Owe You Pretty*; and Ashley "Dotty"

Charles and *Outraged: Why Everyone is Shouting and No-one is Talking.* I started to reframe my thinking about the preconceptions we bring to the questions that we ask in a fundamental and uncomfortable way with the first. I started to formulate a principle of questioning with the second. And by the time I reached the third, I was changed for all time. Perhaps not top of a fiftysomething, privileged white man's reading list, I hear you say? Cast those prejudices aside right now!

Throughout this book, I've talked about the importance of leaving your prejudices at the door, of steering clear of allowing assumptions, prior knowledge, and attitudes to shape the questions that you ask. Socrates's starting position of ignorance – if taken literally and adhered to religiously – should mean that prejudices and assumptions don't influence questioning style. But in a world of work, whose rules are being rewritten with genuine equal rights for all front and centre, it's more important than ever to do this self-consciously and explicitly than assume it's being done. In moving from unconscious incompetence (where assumptions and prejudices skew questions, answers, and strategies) to unconscious competence (where assumptions and prejudices don't exist and so can't have their wrecking ball impact), we need to pass through conscious incompetence (where we get it wrong but correct ourselves) and conscious competence (where we get it right, but not on autopilot).

The market research industry is perhaps the industry above all others that depends on asking smarter questions to satisfy clients and be commissioned to do more work. Its very role and raison d'être is to ask smarter questions, even as the data-tech explosion means it's morphing into the research, insights, and analytics industry. But like all other white-collar professions that it serves and serve it, market research was created by privileged, white, middle-class, middle-aged, straight men whose services were commissioned, used, or otherwise ignored by other privileged, white, middle-class, middle-aged, straight men.

Fortunately, the world is growing up and the world of work better reflects the glorious diversity of ethnicity, race, gender, sexuality, sexual orientation, age, disability, neurological status, religion, and marital status. In many countries around the world, companies are required by law not to discriminate against anyone on any of these dimensions.

The discomfort that many feel as society comes to terms with what an enshrined policy of anti-discrimination means in practice – well, this says more about them and the assumptions and prejudices they've been brought up alongside than whether or not this is the right direction of travel.

There are some inevitable speed bumps along the road from a position of casual tolerance of intolerance to intolerant outlawing of all forms of discrimination, and the "political correctness gone mad" wing of the rabid right find this particularly hard to accept, regularly railing against it. Progress towards anti-discrimination has spawned Black Lives Matter, #metoo, #seeher, the removal of statues of slave traders, cancel culture, and intolerance to those espousing opinions about whether gender identity outweighs biological sex. I live not four miles from where Sussex academic Professor Kathleen Stock had worked, but ultimately felt compelled to resign in 2021 because of opposition from trans and non-binary students, who themselves said they had been depicted as "powerful political operators".[1]

The crucible of fighting discrimination is febrile. I don't believe I have any legitimacy to voice an opinion on that particular debate – nor others like it – from my privileged, male, white, middle-class, middle-aged, straight worldview. I can't add anything and I can't think why anyone would want to listen to my opinions on it. It's not because I fear being criticised or even cancelled myself because of antediluvian views. Actually, I think what I've learned recently – thanks in no small part to recent insight trainees' book recommendations – combined with an open and curious nature makes me relatively unprejudiced. But only relatively. As I'm learning, privilege can't see the barriers that privilege removes because, for the privileged, those barriers simply don't exist. I am still what I am, despite attempts to combat it. I'm not being unnecessarily hair-shirted, coy, or self-critical. I just don't think I've got anything useful to contribute here. In Rebecca Solnit's brilliant neologism that arose as a result of her seminal 2014 publication *Men Explain Things to Me*, I have no doubt I'd be guilty of "mansplaining".

What I can do is observe how vital it is in developing questions to use in any line of enquiry – from Boolean strings in social media analytics to journalism, from medical trials to market research – to frame questions that don't reinforce any kind of prejudices or stereotypes. Not only this, but how questions are framed should – wherever possible – serve to pulverise prejudice, demonise discrimination, and smash stereotypes by their very even-handedness and inability to offend. Just because we don't intend to cause offence is no guarantee that we'll succeed in doing precisely that.

This doesn't mean making every question so vanilla that it doesn't stand a chance of finding out anything interesting. Far from it. What it does mean is considering the impact of a question's intention, its liability to offend or prejudice. Thinking in this way is about both what a question asks and how it asks it. It's also about appreciating how a series or sequence of questions can engender an atmosphere or set of expectations because of what follows what. Hell, even the U.K. Cabinet Office has some very helpful guidance on "Inclusive language: words to use and avoid when writing about disability".[2]

As Terry Fadem says in his book *The Art of Asking*, there are a number of different (types of) questions that should really be avoided at all cost.

> *Avoid questions that intentionally mistreat anyone. Others are subtle, such as prejudicial questions – questions that offer a judgment as part of the question, and that judgment is unnecessary. Try [also] to avoid … questions that belittle, demean, humiliate, or otherwise cause harm to another person. (p.47)*

Micro-aggressions of all sorts are most definitely out.

To demonstrate what this means in practice, let's spend a little time with Jane Cunningham and Philippa Roberts, founders of PLH Research and authors of 2021's smash hit *Brandsplaining: Why Marketing is (Still) Sexist and How to Fix It.*

QUESTIONS ABOUT QUESTIONS 14 OF 14

NAME	Jane Cunningham and Philippa Roberts
ORGANISATION	PLH Research – *Brandsplaining*
ROLE	Co-founders – Authors

In the mid-2000s, Jane Cunningham and Philippa Roberts swapped planning and client services roles at ad agency Ogilvy & Mather to co-found PLH Research, a company that describes itself as "the U.K.'s leading market research agency specialising in female audiences". As a statement of intent for their distinctively inclusive, human, and gender-sensitive approach to research, in 2007 they published an excellent book called *Inside Her Pretty Little Head*.

The way the title of this book satirises generations of patronising, assumptive, sexist research is delicious, and for me it's also always had echoes – but very much more progressive, evidence-based echoes – of David Ogilvy's line: "The customer is not a moron. She's your wife".[3] Ogilvy was one of Madison Avenue's founding "mad men". As Andrew Cracknell observed in a 2012 article for *The Huffington Post:* "though today sounding a tad gender insensitive [Ogilvy's observation] was nevertheless a timely rebuke for the moronic way the business went about creating its product".[4] There is also something satisfyingly Gestalt about the fact that *Inside Her Pretty Little Head*'s authors both worked for the agency that bears Ogilvy's name immediately before founding their own business and writing their book. The book summarises an 18-month study into female motivation and how brands connect most powerfully with female audiences, embedding themselves reliably in women's minds and lives using one of four codes: the Altruism Code, the Connecting Code, the Ordering Code, and the Aesthetic Code.

The pioneering duo spent the following 15 years working with major national and global brands, always focused on helping them to better understand and motivate female consumers. It is true that during that period, there had been some encouraging changes of approach and tone, including Dove's Campaign for Real Beauty, Always' "Like a Girl", and Sport England's "This Girl Can", not to mention the creation of the cross-industry Unstereotype Alliance at the initiative of consumer goods giants Unilever and P&G.[5] But these were twinkling stars in an otherwise dark night sky of misogyny and mansplaining, sexism and stereotypes. Advertising may talk a good game about its ability to effect meaningful societal change on issues as important as racial and gender diversity, but in the U.K. at least, action lags many years behind intention. Progress towards inclusion and equality in advertising are – if anything – slower than in the society that commercial communication reflects and seeks to influence.

Brandsplaining

In part to help accelerate change and hasten the demise of sexism in the sector, Cunningham and Roberts published a new book in early 2021 titled *Brandsplaining: Why Marketing Is Still Sexist & How to Fix It*. In the preface of the book, they observe: "the majority of brands still speak to women from a male perspective, explaining to them what they are telling them and what they can be" (p. xi). Inspired by both the title and central message of Rebecca Solnit's *Men Explain Things to Me*, Cunningham and Roberts's latest book charts how we got to where we are now. Most excitingly, they map out where we go next in a drive to fix marketing's sexist words and deeds, identifying "ten principles for the new conversation", from "accept that women now please themselves" to "prepare for the primacy of female-made brands". And because the authors are such experienced, expert researchers, this new manifesto for change is predicated on marketing's ability to ask (and answer) smarter, non-prejudiced questions.

We spoke in spring 2021, as *Brandsplaining* was making waves and noise well beyond the confines of marketing trade publications, with profiles and interviews appearing in *The New York Times* and *The Guardian*, *The Daily Telegraph*, and *The Daily Mail*, not to mention scores of broadcast and podcast interviews. Although very definitely aligned in their thinking, the authors are also deft in taking turns to answer questions, tackling the issues closest to each of their hearts.

For Jane, good questions are both full of assumptions but also assumption-free, particularly when talking to women:

> *Women have been 'on receive' for years, and we want them to be 'on transmit'. When we ask women open questions, we bring an understanding of this bigger picture and we are keen to discover what women are both thinking AND feeling. Women aren't asked research questions often, and hardly ever **as** women.*

Philippa adds:

> *Asking about feelings is hugely important. In recent years, it seems as if the act of asking questions has become increasingly disconnected from trying to really understand what people feel and need. Asking women to choose between two or three options and forcing a rational response doesn't give an opportunity to reject them all and ask for something else, completely different. The male lens has dictated these options and seeks to ask women to choose between options that men might want. This has to change.*

Philippa believes a person who asks good questions is open and a good listener, someone who doesn't inhibit answers by being overly directional or prescriptive. The central thesis of *Brandsplaining* is that brands tell women how to behave and what they should become. Through rigorous and detailed case studies, the book pulls into the light how brands do that. In so doing, it provides a constructive framework to help brands listen to women better, to their genuine wants and desires and how their feelings influence choice. Smart questions empower respondents to be ruminative and consider the shades and nuances of response. Jane expands:

> *Being empathetic definitely helps you to ask better questions. When we're doing research, a lot of what we're doing is constantly trying to put ourselves into the shoes of those we're interviewing, connecting their answers back to the network of beliefs that's making those words come out of their mouths. Unless there's empathy in the conversation, then that process can't happen. You can collect information but not reveal or feel what's being felt.*

DATA TOO BIG FOR ITS (MASCULINE) BOOTS?

For Jane, the fetishisation of bigger and bigger data over recent years has got out of hand, driven by a desire to push down cost – and it's very definitely a masculine fetishisation. While data has made it easier to get a more granular understanding on consumer behaviour, the focus on what we do has been at the expense of understanding why – the underlying motivations that drive behaviour in the first place. This has widened the gap between the female audience on the one hand and brands and products on the other. "Close-in, intimate conversations really matter, especially if you want to change things and keep up-to-date with an ever-changing, increasingly diverse audience."

Philippa agrees, and emphasises that this is particularly true of some groups of women more than others:

> *Women with lower disposable income, women of colour, and older women are missed out of research samples as a matter of course. If they're included at all, it's only as a footnote, but usually they're neither seen nor heard at all. Sexism is all of our problem and still impacts all of us all of the time. Unless you have a specialist lens like ours to help you understand how it impacts and where, it's just too easy for sexist stuff to get through because in our society and culture, almost no-one ever notices.*

PLH encourages research respondents to prepare before they come to discussions. It's a masculine assumption that women who don't know each other will be prepared to come up with confident answers to questions they've not considered before in a group setting. "But we're not interested in women 'sounding off' like men," Philippa observes. "We give our respondents a chance to prepare their thoughts AND feelings before they take part in our studies. This makes them much more likely to engage in a truthful conversation."

PLH's approach is founded in the psychology of gender and the ways in which men and women converse as well as gender differences on certainty. The company also deploys a framework of three selves: the actual self (what women do every day), the hopeful self (how they are at their best and how they want others to see them), and the feared self (how they're afraid others might think of them). It's between these different selves that Jane and Philippa are able to identify genuine needs by examining deeply how women feel about themselves and so what they need – to keep on being the actual self, to move towards the hopeful self, and to see off the feared self.

Jane says: "Brands that can understand women and the hidden aspects of their lives in this level of granularity are brands that resonate with women. This is where the frustrations and details of life – especially family life – reside." Importantly, brands that navigate these spaces effectively don't arrive with pockets full of assumptions. Rather, they use questioning strategies that really see and hear women as they are. They're looking for – they're finding and making sense of – subtext.

WHAT NOT TO ASK

For Philippa, questions that are driven by outdated assumptions are bad questions. So, too, are prosecutorial questions – questions that make people feel they're being judged, questions that make people feel they can get the answer wrong – that they're being rushed into giving an answer rather than being open to being understood. She expands:

> *If there's anything in the language of your questions that suggests you're going to make some kind of judgement – that's really unhelpful. And if it's not the words, then it can easily be the look that accompanies the question or the disposition of the questioner, the mood they create in the room. It's really important that those asking the questions disarm themselves, do nothing loaded or directional, and show that they're not there to be the judge or the teacher. Questioners are secondary to respondents and should start with that attitude. There's a reason why Oprah is where she is and behaves as she does, and part of that is down to how she asks questions.*

JANE CUNNINGHAM AND PHILIPPA ROBERTS' TOP TIPS FOR ASKING SMARTER QUESTIONS

1. Probe feelings every bit as much as facts.
2. Avoid a prosecutorial approach – in tone and language, content, and context.
3. Use questions that give respondents the space to be ruminative.
4. Be aware of and eliminate prejudices and a partial worldview from your questions.
5. Give those you're questioning time to prepare their answers.

GENERALISING FROM THE PARTICULAR

In our evermore digital world, market research has broadened its terms of reference and now likes to think of and project itself as the research, analytics, and insight industry, attracting and encompassing more individuals, disciplines, and job functions. This means that more people than ever working in the modern knowledge economy have their success predicated on their ability to ask smarter questions that yield more useful – more powerful, purposeful, and directive – answers.

In this chapter, I've focused on the specifics of market research as an archetypal industry sector and the issues of sexism that have prevented it from doing just that. I'm inspired by James Joyce's observation to Arthur Power, art critic of *The Irish Times*: "I always write about Dublin, because if I can get to the heart of Dublin I can get to the heart of all the cities of the world. In the particular is contained the universal."[6] As with Joyce's choice of Dublin as an exemplar city, so with my choice of sexism in marketing as an exemplar for the issues we need to keep front of mind and adapt to when asking smarter questions.

In *Brandsplaining*, Cunningham and Roberts meticulously chart the development and evolution of a number of tropes and ways of working that have long dogged market research and so have prevented marketing from properly understanding women's feelings, wants, desires, and needs. They put particular emphasis on the Good Girl – "an unseen force that drives women to shape themselves to be the one who is most pleasing to men" – and how this morphs over life stages to the ideal partner, the perfect mom, perfect housewife, and the have-it-all, high-powered career girl. They show how, through society's eyes and media and marketing pressure, women are presented via the male gaze, compelled to look at herself "as men will see her, and, in pretty much every case and situation, to then adapt herself according to his ideal and perspective. The gaze is male and the lens, all too often, is critical" (p.18). As Florence Given says in *Women Don't Owe You Pretty*: "You are never going to be your best if subconsciously you're trying to be *someone else's* best" (p.85).

My purpose in this chapter has been to focus on one specific issue in one specific area of work in which asking smarter questions is so critical, and to explore this issue and this area in detail. By considering what's gone wrong and the reasons why it's gone wrong over decades – as well as what can be done to eradicate assumptions and make things better, in this case thanks to *Brandsplaining*'s pioneering principles that show where we should go next – my intention is to generalise from the particular. Questions that are dominated, shaped, or even ever-so-subtly tinged with sexist undertones yield answers that are dominated, shaped, or ever-so-subtly tinged by sexist overtones. The same is true of ethnicity, race, gender, sexuality, sexual orientation, age, disability, neurological status, religion, and marital status – and any other issue that in-groups routinely deploy to keep out-groups out. As the computer programming acronym from the 1950s put it, GIGO: Garbage In, Garbage Out.

Those inflicting their own privileged, mainstream, accepted norms don't see them. As Reni Eddo-Lodge says, "If you're white, your race will almost certainly positively impact your life's trajectory in some way. And you probably won't even notice it" (p.87). Yet bizarrely – as the "political correctness gone mad" comment streams under news articles in right-wing tabloid news sites attest with depressing predictability – it is the oppressors who claim to feel oppressed. In the social media age, this often leads to outrage and vitriolic outbursts, frequently under an anonymous veil.[7] And it's true that addressing one's own privilege and what has been considered to be normality for generations is often – usually – uncomfortable to the oppressors; of course, it is. Being required to behave in new and different ways in the interests of fair treatment that everyone should be entitled to paradoxically feels unfair. Yet, as Florence Given so eloquently puts it: "White privilege is like an invisible weightless knapsack of special provisions, maps, passports, codebooks, visas, clothes, tools, and blank checks" (p.201).

In the interests of genuine equality, it's time to take this knapsack off. If that hurts or temporarily disadvantages the privileged few who've borne it by birthright for generations, so be it. Until and unless we can fashion knapsacks for all – or perhaps do away with the need for such knapsacks altogether – the privileged few need to suck it up and for once bear their load and responsibility by levelling down to level others up. When it comes to the questions we ask in our personal and professional lives, we can use this worldview to help make things better, too.

SUMMING UP

Gender is in the spotlight as a divisive lens through which society operates, oppressing women to men's often unseen advantage. By focusing attention on how we can unpick generations of sexist assumptions in market research and how this has misshaped marketing communications, we can establish general rules about how to ask better questions – questions that prejudice no one and include everyone. It won't be easy and it's not happening fast. This is in no small part because of vested self-interest and privilege. But it's on everyone's agenda now, and in the words of Natalie Haynes, there's no closing this particular Pandora's jar.

NOTES

1 Sensitive reporting from *i news*' equalities reporter, Jasmine Andersson, in her 30 October 2021 article "Kathleen Stock resigns: Trans students accuse Sussex Uni of depicting them as 'powerful political operators'", at https://bit.ly/3GnyFQY

2 For U.K. Government guidance on what to avoid when writing about disability, see https://bit.ly/3DC9okn

3 See Ogilvy's 1963 book, *Confessions of an Advertising Man*. The 1988 reprint of this seminal (if now dated) publication included a short list of the (11) most valuable lessons Ogilvy had learned in his long career that started out "in research with the great Dr. Gallup at Princeton". The penultimate lesson reads: "(10) Don't let men write advertising for products which are bought by women" (p.23).

4 "Ads From The Real Mad Men" by Andrew Cracknell, 5 May 2012, *The Huffington Post*, https://bit.ly/33iSo69

5 Find out all about the Unstereotype Alliance at https://www.unstereotypealliance.org/en. The U.K.'s Advertising Standards Authority has recently

outlawed the use of gender stereotypes in its Code of Advertising Practice; see https://bit.ly/3J4KptG

6   Quoted in Finton O'Toole's 24 December 2014 article "Modern Ireland in 100 Artworks: 1922 – Ulysses, by James Joyce", *The Irish Times*, https://bit.ly/3J7JfOc

7   Rapper, DJ, and writer Ashley Charles – also known as Amplify Dot or Dotty – has addressed outrage culture eloquently in her 2020 book *Outraged*, an extended exploration of the themes she first reluctantly aired in her 2018 *Guardian* article, "The Currency of Outrage", https://bit.ly/3shryFS. As she identified in that article, "I represent a 'triple jeopardy' intersection: a black, gay, woman. If we were playing Outrage Monopoly I would have properties on the high-ticket streets."

11

WHAT ARE THE BEST QUESTIONS IN THE WORLD?

Abstract

Asking smarter questions can help to reset our world jumped off its axis. This is a bold claim, but one which should be manifest if you've read this far. While previous chapters have focused on different aspects of how to ask smarter questions, this final chapter sets out dozens of examples of the "what?" – questions that truly are smarter. The examples draw inspiration from sources as diverse as Marcel Proust, management consultancy Bain & Company, advertising agency J. Walter Thompson, and former U.S. Secretary of State Donald Rumsfeld. In so doing, we help to rehabilitate the latent wisdom of Rumsfeld's obsession with "unknown unknowns". The book concludes with 15 of the smartest – and simplest – questions in the world.

WHY WE NEED TO ASK SMARTER QUESTIONS

A "wicked" problem – a term I've used more than once in this book – is defined as "a problem that is difficult or impossible to solve because of incomplete, contradictory, and changing requirements that are often difficult to recognise". The cup-half-full optimist in me likes to think more of wicked problems being "difficult" rather than "impossible". As we walk the tightrope of the early to the mid-2020s, the cup-half-empty pessimist in me sees the wicked problems mounting up: climate change, gender equality, fractured political discourse, and self-interested leadership – oh, and SARS-CoV-2 and its variants and how best to tackle them.

At a time when we've never been in greater need of calm, respectful, informed debate on all these issues and many more, the evolution of social media platforms has instead pitched us headlong into a febrile atmosphere of dogma, demagoguery, shouting not listening, *I'm right and you're wrong*, flaming, trolling, ghosting, and astroturfing. The technology could be – should be – empowering and democratising, but instead the loudest voice wins out. This status quo was satirised brilliantly by Cormac Moore in a film on Twitter in late 2021 in which he boasts of gaining his PhD in Virology from the University of Facebook in just four days.[1] "Thankfully, the University broke the information down into digestible, bite-sized memes that weren't peer-reviewed at all, which was crucial." Mmhmm.

I, for one, have had enough. The collective of human ingenuity has led to the development of pencils and the computer mouse, for heaven's sake, creations so complex that no one on earth could make either one alone from a standing start. The hive mind of human intelligence doesn't obey the linear laws of an arithmetic progression. Instead, the recombinatorial power of everyone able to stand on the shoulders of those giants who came before them follows a geometric progression, leading not to incremental but exponential growth.

As Yuval Noah Harari shows in *Sapiens*, our species has had the ingenuity to move through the cognitive, agricultural, industrial, and digital revolutions to get us to where we are today. We got here by evolving to develop language, harnessing the power of Simon Baron-Cohen's *if-and-then* Systemizing module, asking *Why?*, and developing hypotheses on possible solutions to progressively more wicked problems by asking *How might we …?*. From survival to co-operation, from collaboration to statecraft, from literature to philosophy. It cannot be beyond the wit of the human hive mind to address today's evermore wicked problems – not by harking back to some mythical golden age or by going back to how things were before everything went South, but rather by striding confidently forward into a post-oil, post-sexist, post-COVID world. We have the technology – or at least the potential to develop the technology – and the ability to harness the power of the data. We have the brainpower. In pockets at least, we also have the will.

My motivation for writing this book has been to draw a line in the sand and provide an armoury of tools and techniques that can help anyone who's interested in doing things differently to help solve even one small corner of whichever wicked problem is most meaningful to them. I've magpied these tools and techniques from many different professions, which depend for their success on the ability to ask smarter questions, to listen to and act upon the answers they generate. What's clear from the topics we've covered and the experts we've met is that there are some pretty universal principles of asking smarter questions. These obtain irrespective of the domain or sector in which you operate.

1. **Curiosity** – harnessing the human instinct to understand *why?*
2. **Open-mindedness** – no prejudices or assumptions
3. **Preparation** – of questions and environment
4. **Openness** – in our questions, not closing options, encouraging storytelling
5. **Simplicity** – in intent and language, no "side"
6. **Listening** – taking the time and leaving the space for others to answer

With these principles in mind, in this final chapter we'll consider what I believe to be among the very best – the smartest – questions there are in the world. You'll find that not all of them will work for every situation in which you need to use questions. But I thought it was worth bringing them together as a summary of the most impactful tools you can deploy in finding out what you want – and need – to know. The questions are very much the *what* to the very many different elements of the *how* of the universal principles that we've considered, in the main, up to this point.

THE FAINT WAFT OF FRESHLY COOKED MADELEINES

French writer Marcel Proust has given his name to a questionnaire that some have thought are the most important questions a person can answer, though he didn't create it. The answers to the questions in the Proust Questionnaire (PQ)[2] formed the basis for a popular Victorian parlour game and were believed by the author of *À la recherche de temps perdu* to reveal the true nature and most important facets of an individual. Questions sought to determine a player's favourite virtue, qualities in a man or woman, occupation, colour, flower, bird, prose author and poet, heroes and heroines in fiction, painters, and composers. It delved a little deeper by asking what a player's chief characteristic was, what they most appreciated in a friend, their main fault, and ideas of both happiness and misery. It also asked if you couldn't be you, who would you be and where else might you live. Not a bad set of questions, if perhaps a little dated and elitist, Judaeo-Christian, and white.

The PQ spawned two hugely popular, highbrow talk shows on both sides of the Atlantic. In France, Bernard Pivot hosted more than 700 episodes of *Apostrophes*[3] on prime time Friday night TV from 1975 to 1990, applying the PQ to leading novelists, actors, and politicians, including Nabokov, Solzhenitsyn, Le Carré, Umberto Eco, the Dalai Lama, and Roman Polanski. In the U.S., the Questionnaire and *Apostrophes* inspired *Inside the Actor's Studio*,[4] hosted from 1994 to 2018 by James Lipton, Dean Emeritus of the Actors Studio Drama School at Pace University, New York. The ten questions used by Lipton included guests' favourite/least favourite word, what turned them on/off, loved/hated noises, their favourite swear word, the profession other than theirs that they'd like/dislike to try, and – as an episode closer – *If heaven exists, what would you like to hear God say when you arrive at the pearly gates?*

In the U.K., the most enduring and enduringly rigid format for an interview show is the BBC Radio 4 series *Desert Island Discs*, created in 1942 by the broadcaster Roy Plomley.[5] As with *Apostrophes* and *Inside the Actor's Studio*, a fixed set of questions is intended to have guests open up and talk about their lives from within a common framework, although of course the presenters of all three shows extemporise and weave additional questions in between to build a sense of narrative. In *Desert Island Discs*, the formal questions invite the guest – as if about to be cast away for all time onto a desert island – to select eight recordings (usually music), a book (other than the Bible and the complete works of Shakespeare which they're forced to take with them), and a luxury item. At the end of the interview, they have to select one recording to "save from the waves". The format has been enduringly popular for the ability of such a limited number of questions and choices to get beneath the skin of more than 3,000 castaways over the past 80 years.

Individually, *Apostrophes*, *Inside the Actor's Studio*, and *Desert Island Discs* may not have produced the definitive set of questions. All of the questions that they ask may not observe all of the universal principles of asking smarter questions outlined above. But it's clear from the enduring appeal of each programme that there is sustained appetite in popular culture for broadcasts that allow thoughtful questions to be asked of figures in the public eye who are then given the time, space, and silence to give considered answers.

THE NET PROMOTER SCORE

The word "Google" has long since acquired Hoover or Xerox status. The company name has become the default verb for the behaviour that it exists to facilitate, a linguistic process known as anthimeria. Nevertheless, the archives of Google do not appear to be the place to look for inspiration for smarter questions.[6] According to the search engine's parent company Alphabet, the top three questions posed in 2021 were: (i) *What to watch?* (9 million), (ii) *Where's my refund?* (7.5 million), and (iii) *How (do) you like that?*

Perhaps the best business question of all time was developed by Frederick F. Reichheld, a fellow of Bain & Company, the management consultancy. Reichheld et al. were responsible for developing the Net Promoter Score (NPS). The NPS first appeared in the December 2003 edition of the *Harvard Business Review*, in an article titled "The one number you need to grow".[7] One of the attractions of the NPS is that it is incredibly simple. The question behind it is this:

> On a scale of 0–10, how likely is it that you
> would recommend this company to a friend or colleague?

Those who record scores of 0–6 are counted as detractors, 7–8 as passives, and only 9–10 as promoters. To calculate the NPS, you simply subtract the total number of detractors from the total number of promoters; passives – those who like you quite a lot but not enough to give you a nine or ten – are ignored. Although there are cultural differences – consumers and customers in Japan and Europe tend to score companies lower than those in the U.S. or Australia, for instance – a score above zero is deemed to be positive (more promoters than detractors), 20 is favourable, 50 excellent, and 80 world class.

Because the NPS is so simple to administer, there is a huge database of normative data across multiple sectors, categories, and markets. Not only that, the NPS correlates strongly with growth and is the best single measure – and predictor – of customer loyalty. The NPS is more reliable and has stronger predictive ability than any other single or compound measure of brand health, loyalty, or affinity. This is because if you have a lot of customers who score you at nine or ten – and particularly if they outnumber your detractors – they have already become your volunteer salesforce. You're meeting – exceeding – customer expectations, and they're rewarding you by bigging you up to friends, family, and colleagues. While there are some critics of the NPS and some limitations to its use, it is surely one of the best questions ever asked in business.

The NPS has also spawned other indices that use the same format with similar impact, including the Net Purpose Score®™ from IceSight, a business run by the super-smart former Unilever duo, Sean Gogarty and Simon Thong. This other NPS assesses the extent to which customers – familiar with products, brands, and services – believe the company "makes the world a better place". IceSight has found that purpose strongly correlates with consumer preference and that companies that score highly on purpose are also much more likely to grow faster. The top two highest-scoring U.S. companies on Net Purpose Impact were Google (+64%) and Whole Foods (+42%), while the bottom two were Marlboro (–82%) and Goldman Sachs (–45%). In Chapter 1, I mentioned Crown Worldwide, which my consultancy Insight Agents helped to land a powerful purpose statement ("Making it simpler to live, work, and do business anywhere in the world"). Part of the reason that the Crown purpose programme won five industry awards in 2021 is because it created and rolled out a new Net Simpler Score using NPS principles to measure the extent to which its purpose is lived with colleagues, customers, and collaborators.

SMARTER, SIMPLER QUESTIONS; SMARTER BRIEFS

If you work in an organisation that provides products, services, or consultancy to other organisations – and that describes a remarkably large proportion of the workforce – the chances are that you'll be asked fairly regularly to tender for business. This could be from completely new clients in totally unfamiliar categories or sectors. It might also be from long-established clients with whom you have a partnership lasting several years, but who have a new product or service they are introducing and for which they need your help. On the other side of the table are the clients briefing their partners.

In order to turn what the client wants into something they can buy requires briefing – from a new supply chain for sustainably sourced chocolate nibs to a research project with single mothers, from a secure video conferencing solution for government departments to an advertising campaign designed to tackle teenage obesity. This will likely include a first briefing meeting; ideally a written brief in a standard template that both parties sign off; a period of research, reflection, and creativity on behalf of the service provider; their formal tender; perhaps a second meeting for clarification, negotiation, and demonstration of the offer in action; and so on. In all sorts of organisations, this is the point at which questions matter most. Even if you or your clients do have an established briefing template – and this can be problematic, because it can become a straitjacket that advances in technology or market dynamics can quickly render redundant – what you definitely need is a set of smarter questions that can act as guardrails for a smarter briefing process.

Stephen King (no, not the horror novelist) is generally agreed to be one of the founding fathers of the discipline of strategic planning in advertising. He created and codified the discipline in the London offices of the ad agency J. Walter Thompson (JWT) in the late 1960s. In 1974 – still at JWT – he wrote and published a planning guide, which includes a simple and straightforward framework for planning.[8] This framework asks five simple questions. There have been many embellishments and additions to the framework by many hands in many agencies since then, but as a tool that asks the most important questions for anyone taking a brief from any type of client, it stands the test of time. It is also much more broadly applicable than simply being a representation of the planning cycle in advertising, asking as it does: (i) Where are we?, (ii) Why are we here?, (iii) Where could we be?, (iv) How could we get there?, and (v) Are we getting there?

King's template handily asks a number of follow-up questions under each of his five principal buckets, making it a tool that can help those taking a brief leave no stone unturned. These are:

1. **Where are we?**
   - Where does our brand stand now (compared with competitors) in the market and in people's minds?
   - If a new brand, where do the competitors or substitutes stand?
   - Where have we come from?
   - In what direction do we seem to be going?
2. **Why are we there?**
   - What factors have contributed to our brand's strengths and weaknesses?
3. **Where could we be?**
   - What realistically could be the position of our brand in the future?
   - Is it a new position or maintaining our present position?

4. **How could we get there?**
    - What changes to what elements in the marketing mix could achieve it?
    - What are the roles and objectives for advertising?
    - What campaigns could achieve the advertising objectives?
5. **Are we getting there?**
    - Is the advertising achieving its objectives and is the total effect working?
    - If an area test, which area did better?

There are two main reasons why those coming since King have sought to evolve or adapt the template. The first – easily dismissed – is Not Invented Here Syndrome. Others from other competitive agencies want to put their own non-JWT stamp on how they do briefing. The second – equally easily dismissed, this time Shiny New Object Syndrome – is that technology and market dynamics make the template outdated. Again, there's no technology – in advertising, research, analytics, processing power, logistics, anything – that King's template can't accommodate. As commentators from AdContrarian Bob Hoffman to the creative guru Dave Trott repeatedly observe, despite all the shiny new objects in marketing, the principles of motivating behaviour change in consumers remain unchanged – not just from 1974 but for tens of thousands of years. All that's changed is the wrapping and means of delivery, as the political slogans preserved in volcanic ash at Pompeii show.

To King's core questions I might add *(vi) What's standing in our way?* and, as a subsidiary to the first question, add *(vii) What's changed recently that means we need to take action?* That should accommodate any and all potential advances in technology that Zuckerberg and others may seek to usher in with the Metaverse and so on. With those seven questions addressed in the course of a 90-minute briefing, any service provider worth its salt and capable of responding to the brief should be able to develop a robust and buyable proposal. Provided they listen to the answers, of course.

THE WIT AND WISDOM OF DONALD RUMSFELD

At a briefing on the role that Iraq may (or may not) have played in providing weapons of mass destruction to Islamist terrorist groups, George W Bush's then Secretary of State for Defense for George W Bush, Donald Rumsfeld, said:

> *Reports that say that something hasn't happened are always interesting to me, because as we know, there are known knowns: there are things we know we know. We also know there are known unknowns: that is to say we know there are some things we do not know. But there are also unknown unknowns – the ones we don't know we don't know. And if one looks throughout the history of our country and other free countries, it is the latter category that tends to be the difficult ones.*

At the time, Rumsfeld was ridiculed for his apparent bungling and mangling of both English and logic as well as his application of this way of looking at the world to the West's insistence that Saddam Hussein was hiding chemical and biological weapons – which were never discovered – as the basis for war. Yet, despite the fact that the aftershocks of this unjust, unsubstantiated war are still being felt in the Middle East and right around the world almost 20 years on, the ridicule was not deserved. The known/unknown paradigm – and the 2×2 matrix it spawns – is a framework for problem-solving that has been used for many years by security and defence strategists as well as National Aeronautics and Space Administration (NASA). It has its roots in psychology and the Johari Window[9] created by Joseph Luft and Harrington Ingham (hence the name – Jo + Hari), developed to better understand interpersonal relationships.

The veteran advertising planner and trainer, John Griffiths, wrote an excellent blog about this rare moment of Rumsfeldian genius in July 2021, just after Rumsfeld's death was announced.[10] Griffiths uses the known/unknown dimension to establish the nature and location of knowledge within a client business, with known/knowns representing "explicit knowledge", unknown/knowns "tacit knowledge", known/unknowns "known gaps", and unknown/unknowns "unknown gaps". He commented:

> *By far the most interesting and valuable aspects of research is the ability to find out what you didn't know you already knew because your customers*

or others in your organisation already knew it – and you asked them to tell you using an open or unstructured answer.

So many times working with global multinationals – particularly Unilever, over the years – I have heard the refrain "If only Unilever knew what Unilever knew". Technology and the spread of relational databases are improving institutional knowledge and access to that knowledge. So, too, does the Rumsfeld matrix.

Consider the wicked problem of the future habitability of planet Earth through this lens:

- **Known/knowns** = the clear and present dangers of greenhouse gases and global warming
- **Known/unknowns** = risks you are aware of but that haven't happened yet
- **Unknown/knowns** = risks you are aware of that could happen but are on no one's radar
- **Unknown/unknowns** – risks that arise from situations that are so unexpected that you wouldn't think to predict them, such as the moon – or a big asteroid – hitting the Earth

So, as well as looking to populate all dimensions of a Rumsfeld Matrix when you're looking to the future, be sure you invest your time and attention in unknown/unknowns, what some might call blue sky thinking. *What are our unknown/unknowns?* is most definitely a smarter question.

SMARTER QUESTIONS GALORE

So, to round out this chapter and the book, here are 15 more questions that I believe are properly smart questions for you to ask. I've given a little justification or rationale as to why I think they're smarter. They won't all necessarily be relevant for your next call or meeting or casual encounter. Taken together, I think they're a pretty impressive bunch. I trust you find that, even if one or some or all aren't what you need, the universal principles they embody and what they can lead to mean that you can use the implicit template underpinning them all to make your own smarter questions.

> How do you spend your time?

We know so little about what our nearest and dearest do – to steal the title of Richard Scarry's memorable book title *What do people do all day?* – but asking them *What do you do?* leads to an automatic default to explain the minutiae of their job. Too, too dull. *How do you spend your time?* – as an ice breaker at a party, when gathering for a workshop, at work or at play – gets people to focus on what makes them *them* – what truly defines them – rather than how much they resent having to complete timesheets. It is Derren Brown's favourite question. In *Confessions of a Conjuror*, he says:

> How often does knowing what sort of office people go to every day really help us to get to know them .... Leil Lowndes' How To Talk to Anyone ... tackle[s] this very problem. Her answer is to change the question: she suggests ridding one's mind of the useless 'What do you do?' and replacing it with 'How do you spend your time?'. (2010, p.173)

> What lights you up?

Our passions – at work or at play, on the sports field or in the ashram – can tell others a lot about us. Whether we're solitary or a "team player", whether we're ascetic or sybaritic – all sorts. Asking *What lights you up?* is so much more engaging, poetic, and all-encompassing than *What are your hobbies?* or *What do you do in your spare time?*, both of which come loaded with assumptions. Sales trainer Stuart Lotherington told me after we'd finished our interview (Chapter 6) that his wife has a variant on this smarter question, which is *What do you do for fun?*

> What would Jesus / Kanye / Klopp / Beyoncé / Oprah / Yoda do?

Who's the person, from history or contemporary society, literature or mythology, you most admire? Who does the person that you want to influence most admire? Flex your empathy (but not sympathy) muscles and put yourself into the mind, mindset, and shoes of that individual and think through your wicked problem from their perspective. This is a sister question to coach Tim Johns' magic questions, *Who's the brightest person you know? What would they advise you to do? So, does that work for you?* By depersonalising the challenge from yourself and subcontracting it to the object of your admiration, you make it easier to answer yourself, for yourself.

How are you? <BEAT> How are you really?

Asking how another person is – particularly if you haven't seen them for some time – has become just social grooming. English people will knee-jerk either *Fine* or *Good, thanks.* I know I've talked a lot in this book about the importance of not interrupting and allowing your smarter questions to have their impact. In this case, timing is everything. Ask *How are you?* and even as your interlocutor starts to open their mouth, follow-up with *How are you really?*. This will pull them up short and get them to see you're interested in more than just social grooming, the verbal equivalent of primates picking fleas from one another's fur. *How have you been since I saw you last/since last we met?* can have a similar impact, because it encourages access to short-term autobiographical memory, using as it does a continuous past tense *How have you been ...?* But the formulation of *How are you? <BEAT> How are you really?* is even more impactful.

What's it like being you?

Another smarter question focused on the individual, and the "emergency" question that comedian Richard Herring asked of polymath Stephen Fry, leading him to feel comfortable enough to reveal a recent suicide attempt (see Chapter 4). In our First XV of smarter questions, this is perhaps as close as we get to those posed in the opening stanza of the title track of Monty Python's *Meaning of Life*:

What is life? What is our fate?
Is there heaven and hell? Do we reincarnate?
Is mankind evolving or is it too late?
Well tonight, here's the Meaning of Life.

Who am I talking to?

This isn't so much a question to ask out loud, more a question to ask of yourself as you prepare to make a pitch, give a talk, or presentation. If you really know your audience, you will tailor what you know and what you say about what you know to make sense for them, not just show off your expertise. An exercise in empathy, this question to self allows you to get into the mind, the mindset, the shoes of those you're addressing, enabling you to assess the likely tolerance of the audience for data, jargon, and specialist knowledge (ideally, all low, whatever the audience). When you ask that question of yourself, spend 15–20 minutes writing a 150-word pen portrait of your audience. For data storytelling in particular, *Know Your Audience* is one of the six golden rules.

What can I control?

A second question to ask of yourself. The Stoic approach to dealing with life requires practitioners to accept they cannot control events or circumstances – a pandemic or a recession, a new marketing director at a long-established client who has their own favourite agencies which don't include yours. A Stoic realises that all they can control is how they react to events or circumstances. Difficult to do, transformational if you pull it off. *To catastrophise or not to catastrophise: that is the question.*

> *What three things am I grateful for today/this week?*

A third question just for you. By instituting a gratitude practice – putting a time in your diary to think about and write down three things you're grateful for, and perhaps share them with family, partners, or colleagues – is a stepping stone on the route to happiness. Gratitudes don't need to be big or life-changing, but the cumulative impact of acknowledging and vocalising them can be. The motivational speaker Tony Robbins – not to everyone's taste, for sure – hosted an excellent blog on his website written by his colleague Tori Kunz.[11] Titled "The three questions that will completely reframe your daily life experiences", Tori's first question is a variation on the theme of a gratitude practice, asking *What is something I can do for someone else today?*. Do try it.

> *Is this statement true and how might we corroborate it?*

The fact-checking website PolitiFact and the hundreds of other sites and organisations dedicated to eradicating genuinely fake news – not Trumpian, Johnsonian "fake news" which basically means "stuff I don't like/ agree with" – plays an important role in setting the record straight. But we need to apply these principles to what colleagues, clients, agencies, politicians say in daily life. We don't want constantly to be querying and quibbling with what others say, but nor should we accept baldly stated facts as true without critical faculty. The spirit of the Massive Open Online Course (MOOC) Calling Bullshit can help us individually as communities and as a global village to put pervasive factoids out of their misery.

> *Why?*

The world's simplest and most powerful question – within reason, so long as it's not used incessantly as in an interrogation. Forty thousand *Whys?* by the time we're five, but first school and then the workplace attempt to squish the epistemophilic instinct out of us by favouring "correct" answers only. It might be simple, but as a manifestation of Simon Baron-Cohen's Systemizing module, *Why?* can determine cause and effect and separate both from coincidence. Works especially well when a series of five, fully articulated *whys?* form part of a root cause analysis.

> *I never really thought about it that way before. What can you share with me that would help me see what you see?*

This is the question that TED Salon talker Julia Dhar's father used in to get a clearer understanding of why people had supported Trump in the 2016 election. This is also an exercise in empathy, and it turns a conversation between opposites – ideological, cultural, religious – from antipathy to accommodation, from a cage fight into a climbing wall of footholds and handholds.

> *How might we ...?*

The three magic words from questions set in the Design Thinking process that can be so liberating and open up potential. No assumptions or answers as the question is asked, endless possibilities and potential through "might" and genuine collaboration and co-creation from "we".

> *How many pairs of scissors are there in the world?*

OK, you don't have to ask this precise thought experiment that my brother Jeremy posed to me and my family 40 years ago. But the spirit of this question – with no research allowed until you've considered it from all angles and spawned a whole series of other questions in response – is a brilliant way to start tackling a problem, micro or macro, benevolent or wicked.

> *Tell, Explain, Describe*

This open formula deployed by the police is tremendously powerful. We first met it in Chapter 8 in my interview with Detective Sergeant Tom Barker. Its variation and the three verbs used to encourage suspects, witnesses, and victims to tell the story of an incident in which they were involved (or saw taking place) is calm, gentle, and encouraging. But it can be used in any setting. The trainer Chris Merrington – author of an excellent book on sales and negotiation called *Why do Smart People Make Such Stupid Mistakes?* – has a variation on this formula as being the best networking event icebreaker. He recommends asking: *Tell me a bit about your business and how you're doing in the current market*. By setting the person and the business in the context of the current market, you won't get pigeonholed by a widget salesperson boring you about their widgets. And the encouragement to tell is much more likely to result in a story.

> *Just one more thing … is there anything that I haven't asked you that I should have asked you?*

The Columbo Question. The most open of questions, favoured by doctors and journalists, and so helpful in those getting the reluctant to express the real reason they've come to see you. Chapter 10 will still be so fresh in your memory that there's no need to say more. Remember the ringing endorsement of general practitioner Dr James Lewis and journalist Jane Fryer.

SUMMING UP

Well, that's all folks.

Do come and have a look at www.AskSmarterQs.com, where I'm creating a community and establishing a growing library of resources, designed to help anyone ask smarter questions. Do follow @AskSmarterQs on Twitter and do feel free to share your killer questions with me there. I trust you've enjoyed the ride and that you now have the tools, permission, and confidence to ask smarter questions – questions that will give you the data and information you need to surface and articulate genuine insights into those whose lives you can impact. Armed with these data-driven insights, you'll be able to tell more powerful and persuasive stories, stories that can effect genuine change, in your personal or business life. This is true whether you work in a company, a charity, a government department, or in academia. Amazing what you can achieve by creating and asking smarter questions, shaped by our six universal principles (Figure 11.1).

Thank you for listening.

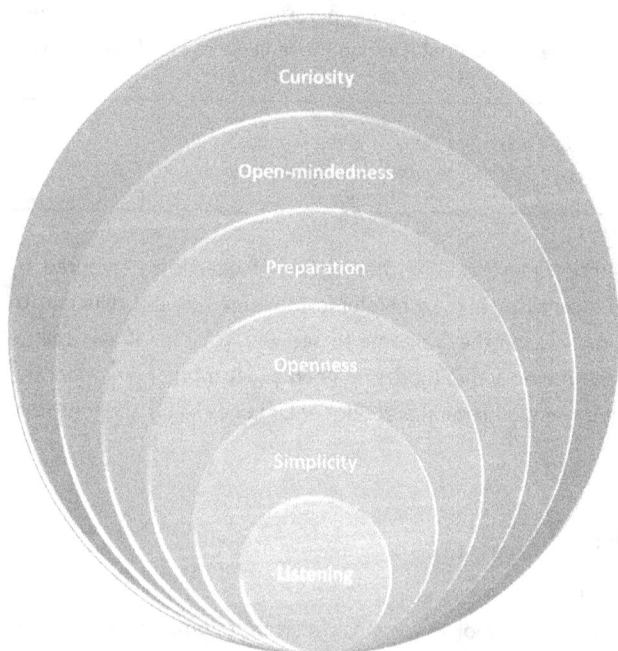

Figure 11.1 The six universal principles for asking smarter questions.

NOTES

1   Cormac Moore's 90-second testimonial for the University of Facebook – strap line "It's crazy what you'll learn" – is at https://bit.ly/3mMSda0

2   The full set of questions in the PQ are summarised in this *Vanity Fair* article at https://bit.ly/3pPT8bS

3   For details on *Apostrophes*, see https://www.thetvdb.com/series/apostrophes

4   There's more on *Inside the Actor's Studio* at https://www.imdb.com/title/tt0169455/

5   *Desert Island Discs* was voted "the greatest radio programme of all time" (albeit in a BBC poll). The archive, dating back to 1942, can be accessed at https://www.bbc.co.uk/programmes/b006qnmr

6   For Google's own analysis of what we Googled in 2021, see https://about.google/stories/year-in-search/, together with an analysis by type of question conducted by Keyword Tool https://keywordtool.io/blog/most-asked-questions/

7   Frederick F. Reichheld (2003). "The one number you need to grow", *Harvard Business Review*, https://hbr.org/2003/12/the-one-number-you-need-to-grow

8   Stephen King (1974). *Planning Guide.* JWT, http://plannersphere.pbworks.com/f/JWTPlanningGuide.pdf – many thanks to Richard Shotton for sharing it on Twitter (@rshotton) in September 2020 at https://bit.ly/3sQ0ayV

9   For more on the Johari Window, see https://bit.ly/3qHiVSA

10 See John Griffiths "Farewell to Donald Rumsfeld but not his quadrant – because it is SO useful" blog on LinkedIn dated 01.07.21, https://bit.ly/3mQbLu6

11 Tori Kunz, "Ask better questions" blog on www.tonyrobbins.com at https://bit.ly/3sUAktM

WHERE CAN I FIND OUT MORE?

Here's a selection of the books and authors who've inspired me – directly, obliquely, and often quite laterally – in my personal quest to understand how to ask smarter questions. As usual in my '*Where can I find out more?*', end of book sections, there are some TED Talks and other stuff too, in a few pages, but mostly this is a bibliography. The book is dead? Pah! Long live books!

BOOKS AND ARTICLES

Aristotle (~330BCE). *The Art of Rhetoric*. In (1991). *The Art of Rhetoric*. Translated by Hugh Lawson-Tancred. Penguin Classics

Aristotle (~330BCE). *The Metaphysics*. In 1989 Loeb classical library simultaneous translation, Harvard University Press

Aristotle (~330BCE). *The Poetics*. In (1996). *The Poetics*. Translated by Malcolm Health. Penguin Classics

Baron-Cohen, Simon (2003). *The Essential Difference: Men, Women, and the Extreme Male Brain*. Allen Lane

Baron-Cohen, Simon (2020). *The Pattern Seekers: A New Theory of Human Invention*. Allen Lane

Berger, Warren (2014). *A More Beautiful Question: The Power of Enquiry to Spark Breakthrough Ideas*. Bloomsbury

Brown, Derren (2010). *Confessions of a Conjuror*. Transworld Publishers

Camerer, Colin, Loewenstein, George, and Weber, Martin (1989). "The Curse of Knowledge in Economic Settings: An Experimental Analysis". *Journal of*

Political Economy, 97 (5: October 1989). https://www.journals.uchicago.edu/doi/abs/10.1086/261651

Charles, Ashley 'Dotty' (2020). *Outraged: Why Everyone is Shouting and No-one is Talking.* Bloomsbury

Covey, Steven (1989). *The 7 Habits of Highly Effective People.* Free Press

Cunningham, Jane, and Roberts, Philippa (2021). *Brandsplaining: Why Marketing is (Still) Sexist and How to Fix It.* Penguin

Csikszentmihalyi, Mihaly (1990). *Flow: The Psychology of Optimal Experience.* Harper and Row

Daley, Kevin (2005). *Socratic Selling Skills: The Discipline of Customer-Centered Sales.* Routledge

D'Angour, Armand (2011). *The Greeks and the New: Novelty in Ancient Greek Imagination and Experience.* Cambridge University Press

D'Angour, Armand (2021). *How to Innovate: An Ancient Guide to Creative Thinking.* Princeton University Press.

De Bono, Edward (1985). *Six Thinking Hats.* Little Brown and Company

Diggle, James (2021). *The Cambridge Greek Lexicon.* Cambridge University Press

Eddo-Lodge, Renni (2017). *Why I'm No Longer Talking to White People About Race.* Bloomsbury

Fadem, Terry (2009). *The Art of Asking: Ask Better Questions, Get Better Answers.* FT Press

Gallop, Angela (2019). *When the Dogs Don't Bark.* Hodder & Stoughton

Given, Florence (2020). *Women Don't Owe You Pretty.* Octopus Publishing

Guilford, J.P., Christensen, P.R., Merrifield, P.R., & Wilson, R.C. (1960). *Alternate Uses.* Sheridan Supply Company

Harari, Yuval Noah (2015). *Sapiens: A Brief History of Humankind.* Vintage

Haynes, Natalie (2019). *A Thousand Ships. This is the Women's War.* Mantle

Haynes, Natalie (2021). *Pandora's Jar: Women in Greek Myths.* Picador

Heath, Chip, and Heath, Dan (2007). *Made to Stick: Why Some Ideas Survive and Others Die.* Random House. A summary of Elizabeth Newton's 'tappers and listeners' experiment is in the Heaths' 2006 *Harvard Business Review* article at https://hbr.org/2006/12/the-curse-of-knowledge

Henson, David (2017). *Your Slides Suck!* mPower Ltd

Herring, Richard (2018). *Emergency Questions: 1001 Conversation Savers for Every Occasion.* Sphere

Holiday, Ryan (2016). *Ego Is The Enemy.* Penguin

Holiday, Ryan (2016). *The Daily Stoic.* Profile Books

Hollweg, Lucas (2011). *Good Things to Eat.* Collins. The book led Lucas to win the 2012 Guild of Food Writers Cookery Journalist of the Year.

Homer (C8th BCE). *The Iliad.* Edited by Jones, Peter; translated by Rieu, Emile Victor (2003). Penguin Classics

Johns, Tim (2020). *Leading from Home.* Amazon

Kahneman, Daniel (2011). *Thinking, Fast and Slow.* Penguin

Kirkbride, John (1978). *That'll Teach You.* Wildwood House Ltd

Knapp, Jake (2016). *Sprint: How to Solve Big Problems and Test New Ideas in Just Five Days.* Simon & Schuster

Knowles, Kenneth (1952). *Strikes: A Study in Industrial Conflict.* Basil Blackwell, Oxford

Knowles, Sam (2004). You were perfectly fine: The effects of alcohol on memory for emotionally significant events. Doctoral thesis, University of Sussex. https://ethos.bl.uk/OrderDetails.do?uin=uk.bl.ethos.407733

Knowles, Sam (2018). *Narrative by Numbers: How to Tell Powerful and Purposeful Stories with Data.* Routledge

Knowles, Sam (2020). *How To Be Insightful: Unlocking the Superpower that Drives Innovation.* Routledge

Lewis, Michael (2021). *The Premonition: A Pandemic Story.* Allen Lane

Liddell, Henry George, and Scott, Robert (1843). *A Greek-English Lexicon.* Oxford University Press

Mehrabian, Albert (1971). *Silent Messages.* Wadsworth Publishing Company, Inc.

Merrington, Chris (2011). *Why do Smart People Makes Such Stupid Mistakes.* Ecademy Press

McKee, Robert (1999). *Story: Substance, Structure, Style and the Principles of Screenwriting.* Methuen Publishing

Mlodinow, Leonard (2018). *Elastic: Flexible Thinking in a Constantly Changing World.* Allen Lane

Nelson, Dean (2019). *Talk to Me: How to Ask Better Questions, Get Better Answers, and Interview Anyone Like a Pro.* Harper Perennial

Newton, Elizabeth (1990). *The rocky road from actions to intentions,* Stanford University. Her full thesis can be read at https://bit.ly/3jz5Jwm

Ogilvy, David (1963; 1988). *Confessions of an Advertising Man.* Southbank Publishing

Pink, Dan (2014). *To Sell is Human.* Canongate Books

Pinker, Steven (2014). *The Sense of Style: The Thinking Person's Guide to Writing in the 21st Century.* Allen Lane

Plato (~399 BCE). *Apology.* In (2010) *The Last Days of Socrates: Euthyphro, Apology, Crito, Phaedo.* Penguin Classics

Randolph, Marc (2019). *That Will Never Work: The Birth of Netflix and the Amazing Life of an Idea.* Endeavour

Scarry, Richard (1967). *What Do People Do All Day?* Random House Books for Young Readers

Shotton, Richard (2018). *The Choice Factory.* Harriman House

Silver, Nate (2012). *The Signal and the Noise: Why So Many Predictions Fail — But Some Don't.* Penguin

Smithers, Alan (2014). *A-levels 1951–2014.* University of Buckingham

Solnit, Rebecca (2014). *Men Explain Things to Me.* Haymarket Books

Sullivan, Wendy, and Rees, Judy (2008; 2019). *Clean Language: Revealing Metaphors and Opening Mind.* Crown House Publishing

Suzuki, Shunryu (1970). *Zen Mind, Beginner's Mind*. Weatherhill

Trott, Dave (2021). *The Power of Ignorance*. Harriman House

Voss, Chris (2016). *Never Split the Difference*. Random House Business

Winstanley, George (2000). *Under Two Flags in Africa: Recollections of a British Administrator in the Bechuanaland Protectorate and Botswana in 1954 to 1972*. Blackwater Books. The book is out of print, and if you're interested but can't get a copy, there's a summary here https://bit.ly/3CzO0LT

Wise, Will, and Littlefield, Chad (2017). *Ask Powerful Questions – Create Conversations that Matter*. We and Me Inc.

Wiss, Elke (2021). *How to Know Everything: Ask better questions, get better answers*. Arrow Books

TED TALKS, VIDEOS, PODCASTS, AND OTHER WEBSITES WORTH THE DETOUR

Daily Stoic podcast – https://dailystoic.com/podcast/

D'Angour, Armand (2012). *Getting in the flow*. TEDxOxbridge. https://bit.ly/3GB2caG

Dhar, Julia (2021). *How to have constructive conversations*. TED Salon: DWEN. https://bit.ly/2ZI5PQP

PolitiFact – https://www.politifact.com

Ridley, Matt (2010). *When ideas have sex*. TEDGlobal 2010. https://bit.ly/3D5YV0g

Robinson, Ken (2006). *Do schools kill creativity*. TED 2006. https://bit.ly/3nFmMOq

Sinek, Simon (2009). *How great leaders inspire action*. TEDxPuget Sound. http://bit.ly/38DkR4z

Sinha, Ruchi (2021). *3 steps to getting what you want in a negotiation*. The Way We Work. https://bit.ly/3wO6184

Small Data Forum podcast – https://www.smalldataforum.com

Tortoise Media – https://www.tortoisemedia.com

INDEX

For Product Safety Concerns and Information please contact our EU
representative GPSR@taylorandfrancis.com
Taylor & Francis Verlag GmbH, Kaufingerstraße 24, 80331 München, Germany

www.ingramcontent.com/pod-product-compliance
Lightning Source LLC
Chambersburg PA
CBHW051953270326
41929CB00015B/2636